THE SOCIAL ORGANISATION IN NORTH-EAST INDIA

IN BUDDHA'S TIME

THE SOCIAL ORGANISATION
IN NORTH-EAST INDIA

IN BUDDHA'S TIME

BY

RICHARD FICK

TRANSLATED BY

SHISHIRKUMAR MAITRA,

M.A., Ph.D.

LATE DIRECTOR, INDIAN INSTITUTE OF PHILOSOPHY,
AMALNER.

GYAN

Published by

Gyan Publishing House
5, Ansari Road
Daryaganj, New Delhi-110002
Phone: 011-47034999, 9811692060
E-mail: books@gyanbooks.com

Distribution Network
gyanbooks.com
India, USA, Canada, UK, Australia, France

ISBN : 978-81-212-2722-3 (HB)
First Published, 1920

2nd Impression 2021

Printed at: Gyan Press, Delhi.

The Social Organisation in North-East India
Author: Richard Fick

THE SOCIAL ORGANISATION IN NORTH-EAST INDIA IN BUDDHA'S TIME

BY

RICHARD FICK

TRANSLATED BY

SHISHIRKUMAR MAITRA, M.A., Ph.D.
LATE DIRECTOR, INDIAN INSTITUTE OF PHILOSOPHY, AMALNER.

PUBLISHED BY THE
UNIVERSITY OF CALCUTTA
1920

TRANSLATOR'S DEDICATION

To the Memory of

My dear departed brother

Prof. NIKHILNATH MAITRA,

to whose encouragement I owe the impulse

to translate German works into English,

This translation is

humbly dedicated by his unworthy brother

AUTHOR'S PREFACE

The title requires some explanation and justification. The sources upon which the inquiry that follows is based are the so-called Jâtakas or legends of previous births contained in the Pâli Canon of Southern Buddhism, that is, they are the stories which relate to the five hundred and fifty existences which Buddha in his various forms, ranging from that of an animal to that of a god, must have gone through before his final existence. The true and most ancient germ of the Jâtaka collection is contained in the verses (gâthâs) which exhibit *in nuce* the essential events of the legends and whose number determines the arrangement of the Jâtakas. These verses constitute, with the prose-commentary which gives the legend a more explicit form, the so-called *atītavatthu*, the "story of the past" which has for its subject-matter the experiences of Buddha in one of his former existences. Each of these stories is preceded as an introduction by a *paccuppannavatthu* or "history of the present times," which tells us of the event in Buddha's life which impelled him to narrate the history of the past for illustrating the events of the present day. Then follows the *samodhâna*, or "connexion" by which Buddha, who remembers not only his own previous existence but that of people around him, identifies the persons of the *atîtavatthu* with those of the *paccuppannavatthu*.

The Jâtakas are most varied in their subject-matter: they consist, in part, of stories, parables or fables of animals, partly, of scenes from Indian folk-life of a cheering or edifying character. Consequently, our source is not only competent to arouse interest in the domain of the history of literature; the collection of legends is of more importance as a reservoir for materials for culture-history. Every account of the life in ancient India which will ever be written in future must take account of the Jâtaka which has justly been called a thesaurus of Indian antiquities, State and private.

That I have placed the culture which the Jâtakas exhibit in North-Eastern India, will, I hope, not provoke any opposition. For although most of the stories contained in our sources are, so far as their contents are concerned, the common property of the Indian people and were known all over India, yet in the form in which they appear in the Jâtakas, they belong to a particular part of India, namely, the north-east, the home of Buddhism.

Here, in the kingdom of the Kâsi-Kosala and Magadha, in the States where Buddha, according to tradition, lived and taught, the somewhat ancient stories took the garb of Buddhistic birth-legends; here the acts of by far the largest majority of the Jâtakas were performed, and if some particular incidents among them occurred elsewhere, even in the most distant west, still the whole mass of detail, in which all the Jâtakas agree, points to the fact that what we find here is only an external transference of the scene.

It may seem to be a very bold thing to take an entirely determinate period, namely, the age of Buddha, for the age of the legends and the state of civilization depicted in them. Taken as a whole, the collection of Jâtakas in their present form surely does not represent any single culture period. Many of the Jâtakas are undoubtedly very old and belong, so far as their origin is concerned, to the pre-Buddhistic period. That they were known in the third century B. C. and that too in the form of legends of previous births of Buddha designed for the education of laymen—for this we have irrefutable evidence in the sculptures in the third century B. C. which are found in the tombstones of Sanchi, Amaravati and Bharhut; these reliefs represent scenes from the Jâtakas and the superscriptions which are added to the individual representations agree with the titles contained in our texts. If these sculptures give us, as the lower limit of the age of the Jâtakas, the third century B.C., there are reasons—as has been shown clearly by Bühler (*Indian Studies*, No. 3, p. 17 sq. in the "Sitzungsberichten der Wiener Akademie, Philos-hist. Classe" Vol. 132)—for placing it in a still earlier age.

On the original bed much clay was deposited in the course of centuries, till the Jâtakas came to acquire the form which they at present have. The introductory narratives are, although they relate to the time of Buddha and go back to the older portions of the Pali canon, manifestly composed after the beginning of the Christian era; the conditions described in the *paccuppannavatthu*, the life of the cloister which is portrayed with the minutest detail and regulated by precise rules, the relation between the laymen and the confederation and many other matters show a departure from the culture-period of the *atîtavatthu* and point to a time when Buddhism had already become a power and ruled over everything. If the view of culture to be sketched by me appears somewhat uniform, it is because the later components of the Jâtaka collection are left out of account; where they have been considered, I have brought out always very prominently their character as *paccuppannavatthu.* Now, even in the oldest form, there was some portion which was specifically Buddhistic and there was a good deal of subsidiary matter that was introduced later to continue the thread of the narrative. In general, we can suppose that our legends have changed very little from their original form, as the oral transmission of such stories is generally true to the letter of the original and has preserved the form in which they obtained currency among the disciples of Buddha and spread from mouth to mouth.

Out of the rich historical material which the Jâtakas contain, I have put together in the present work first that which refers to the social organisation and specially to the caste-relationship; from this, the inquiry has no doubt at times drifted to other matters. A thorough-going account of the political and economical relations, as they ruled in Buddha's time in North-East India, I hope to be able to give at a later time on a broader basis by drawing upon the whole Pali canon, but I do not think of dealing with this problem before I have made myself clear on a question without a solution of which a complete understanding of the life of ancient India is unthinkable.

The responsibility for this work is entirely mine but I feel it my duty to thank Prof.

Oldenberg for various suggestions and kind help. I have also to give my thanks to Prof. Jacobi, who was kind enough to go through the proofs, as well as to my friend and former colleague, Dr. Wischmann, who has also helped me in reading the proofs.

The quotations from the Jâtakas refer to Fausböll's editions, of which up to now five volumes have appeared. The sixth volume which is being published I have not been able to make use of.

Regarding the transliteration of Pali and Sanskrit words it is to be remarked that *c* (च) sounds like the German "tsch" and *j* has the same sound as in the English word 'journey'; *ś* and *sh* are pronounced like the German* 'sch,' *s* is as sharp as "ss" and *e* and *o* are always long.

---

* That is, like *sh* in the English word *shame*—Translator.

PREFACE TO THE ENGLISH EDITION.

Thanks to the original conception and adroit execution of Sir Asutosh Mookerjee, Sarasvati, President of the Post-Graduate Department, a special Degree in M.A. in Ancient Indian History and Culture was instituted by the Calcutta University in 1918. And as the course in its entirety was too vast for the comprehension of any student within the time at his disposal, the subject was divided into four Groups. One of these Groups is Social and Constitutional History dealing with social life, manners, customs and ceremonies, as well as economic life, principles and methods of administration and ethnology. It is impossible to exaggerate the special difficulty with which the University lecturers had to struggle, because there were very few manuals or text-books which could be prescribed for the use of the student. Of the few books again that were available, most were either in German or in French. Such, *e.g.*, was Dr. Richard Fick's *Die Sociale Gliederung im Nordöstlichen Indien zu Buddhas Zeit*. The importance of this book for the social and administrative history of ancient India cannot possibly be denied, based as it is on the Jātakas of the Pāli Buddhist canon. One has only to look to the contents of this book to be convinced of it. The different subjects handled in the different chapters throw a flood of light on the social life of northern India in and before Buddha's time which is believed to have been portrayed by the Jātakas. Unfortunately for the students of India, Dr. Fick's work is in German and could in no way be useful to them, most of them not being acquainted with German. In these circumstances the Board of History recommended that it should be translated into English and that this translation should be published by the University. It was no easy matter, however, to find out a scholar capable of undertaking this translation. Just at that time Dr. S. K. Maitra, Director, Indian Institute of Philosophy, Amalner, came to Calcutta from the Bombay Presidency on some business. He had already undertaken the translation of Dr. Ludwig Stein's *Die Philosophischen Strömungen der Gegenwart* for the Calcutta University and done it satisfactorily. The History Board was thus in a way induced to approach him with their request, and he with his inherited zeal for the cause of education allowed this new task to be imposed on him, in spite of the multifarious duties that pressed on him heavily at that time. For the present publication, therefore, the

University is highly indebted to him. How beautifully Dr. Maitra has performed his task will be seen from the fact that none who goes through the book ever feels or even suspects that it is a translation.

D. R. BHANDARKAR,
Carmichael Professor of Ancient
Indian History and Culture,
Calcutta University.

CALCUTTA:
The 8th August, 1920.

CONTENTS

Chapter XII

CHAPTER I

Introduction

......ce n'est pas la théorie qui peut rendre compte des faits; ce sont les faits qui aident à voir la théorie sous son vrai jour, à la ramener dans ses justes limites.

Senart, Les Castes dans l'Inde.

The time is past when people used to think that so far as ancient India was concerned, it was enough to consider only Brahmanical literature. The view that for ancient Indian culture and ancient Indian life, we require only to consider Brahmanical sources, is necessarily one-sided, because these sources were written from a one-sided point of view. For their authors immersed in the priestly views, the world which surrounded them, material as well as spiritual, existed only so far as it related to the sacrifices with their litany and their ritual which filled all their thoughts and aspirations, and where, as in the text-books of law, there was a departure from this special view-point and the entire domain of law and morals for private as well as public life was taken into account, this was still done from the standpoint of theorising

Brahmanism[1]; nay, even in epic literature, where one could expect most a view of the real state of things, this was prevented or, at any rate, rendered

[p. 2.]* difficult by the all-eclipsing underwood of theories and systems. No wonder that this world which the Brâhmaṇas interpreted in their own way appears so foreign and so strange to us; no wonder that in many points it agrees so little with what we know of ancient India from other sides. Now-a-days, however, we no more consider a non-Brahmanical source, such as the accounts of the Greek messenger Megasthenes, unreliable simply because it cannot be brought into harmony with the Brahmanical theory[2]; we try, on the other hand, to collect all available material, whether it is of Buddhistic, Jaina or Greek origin, which exhibits the priestly theories in their true light—nay, we do not even hesitate to make use of the conditions of modern India which on account of the

---

* The figures on the margin [2], [3], etc., relate to the page numbers of the original German.—*Translator.*

[1] Oldenberg, *Religion des Veda*, p. 25.

[2] So writes Max Duncker, *Geschichte des Alterthums*, 4th Edition, Vol. III, p. 319. "When the Greeks give seven instead of four castes, when the officials, the spies and the artisans, and lastly, the hunters and the shepherds are designated as separate classes by them, this error arises from the reason that they look upon these as caste-divisions." Cf. further Lassen, *Indische Alterthumskunde*, 2nd edition, Vol. II, p.715, "Why he (Megasthenes) took seven instead of four is not clear."

stability of most Oriental cultures have preserved so much of the past, for comparison with, and for the explanation of earlier periods.

Nowhere does the one-sidedness of Brahmanical explanation seem so manifest as in the manner in which the Indian society is shaped in priestly literature. Heedless of all reference to facts, the Brâhmaṇas built up a theory which appeared to them to establish for ever, through eternal and Divine reasons, their rule. As the foundation for their caste-theory, they made use of certain class-distinctions which, as everywhere, existed in a wholly analogous manner among the Iranians and which existed in India even in the oldest Vedic age and were trans- [p. 3.] mitted to the Vedas. Here they found as a line of demarcation which was authoritative for them and which was not too circumscribed, that suggested by the opposition between the ruling classes, the priestly classes and the common people and the still sharper separation of the entire Aryan population from the peoples who were inimical to them, namely, the *dasyus*, who by their dark skins were distinguished from the fair conquerors, and, so far as they were subjugated, were employed in the capacity of slaves. With these distinctions of profession and race, the authors of the lawbooks made certain rules concerning religious rites and regulating marriage and food which probably had been current from ancient times in many tribes of the people and specially, in their class, and thus developed the concept 'caste,' whose chief characteristic they took to be that which was the most obvious mark of the four castes, namely colour (varṇa).[1]

The Brahmanical theory divides Indian society into four castes and prescribes for each of these wholly fixed professions and activities. At the head stand the Brâhmanas; they represent the priest and teacher class. They have [p. 4.] for their work the teaching and study of the Veda, the offering of sacrifices for themselves and for others and the receiving and giving of alms. The

---

[1] It is beyond the scope of my problem which is only concerned with the condition of a particular period, to examine in detail the question of the origin of the castes and especially, of the influence which the institution of family has upon the building up of caste. I refer the reader to the article of Senart, *Les Castes dans l'Inde* in the "Revue des deux mondes" (Vols. 121, 122, 125), which I consider the most sensible and acute thing that has ever been written about the Indian castes. In particular points the statements no doubt stand in need of proof before they can be regarded as scientific facts. Especially, the proposition which is to be looked upon as the cardinal point of his theory, namely, that "caste is the normal development of the ancient Aryan family conception" seems hardly to meet adequately the objection that no traces of this development of the family into the caste are to be found in the Vedas, with the help of the following statement: "The development might have taken place too slowly, it rests upon too instinctive, too primitive elements to give us much evidence of this element in a literature such as that of the hymns."

Kshatriyas or "warriors" have for their duty the protection of the people, the giving of alms, the offering of sacrifices and the study of the Vedas; to the Vaiśyas, breeding of cattle, trade and agriculture were assigned as their work, but along with these, giving alms, offering sacrifices and study are made their duties; the Śûdras, finally, have only one work and that is to serve the other three castes (Mânavadharmaśâstra I. 87-91). The authors of the lawbooks could not possibly conceal the inconsistency of this their theory with the surrounding facts. Most early probably, the two highest castes, the priests and the warriors, were brought into relation with the real facts, but the great mass of the people who in the course of a progressive civilization were assigned the various professions could only be held fast by doing violence to facts. But how to explain the existence of innumerable facts contradicting the theory? It would not do to introduce new castes without destroying the sacred old tradition. "The Brâhmaṇa, the Kshatriya, the Vaiśya, these three castes have two births, the fourth has only one birth; and there is no fifth (caste)"—so it is said in Manu (X. 4).

People joined with the already current theory another, and that was the theory of mixed castes.

Acting upon this, people began to look upon only the children by properly wedded women of the same caste as belonging to the caste of their father and the children resulting from the union of different castes as mixed castes, and this in the following way: the higher the caste of the mother and the lower the caste of the father, the lower became the caste of the issue. Thus, the child born of the union of a Brâhmaṇa with a Vaiśya girl was called an Ambashṭha, so it was called a Nishâda when the union was with a Śûdra's daughter; the issue of the marriage of a Kshatriya with the daughter of a Śûdra was called [p. 5.] Ugra; the children resulting from the opposite kind of union, namely, when the mother belonged to a higher and the father to a lower caste, were called in the descending order of their social rank, Sûta, Mâgadha, Vaideha, Âyogava, Kshattri and Caṇḍâla. All these mixed castes were characterised as of low birth (apasada), the lowest and most contemptible was, according to the theory, the Caṇḍâla, because resulting from the union of a Brâhmaṇa's daughter with a Śûdra. Through further combinations, through further alliances between the four recognised castes and the mixed castes and through marriages among the latter, there arose a further number of mixed castes. Among others—I only mention the names which occur to me in this connexion—the issue of the union of a Nishâda with a Śûdra wife was called Pukkasa and the Veṇa was the issue of the alliance between a Vaidehaka and an Ambashṭha woman. This, however, in no way exhausts the number of mixed castes; here come first the so-called Vrâtyas, who are the issue of legitimate unions of the three higher castes but who through neglect of religious obligation, that is, neglect of taking admission into their caste (upanayana) at the right time, lost the right to belong to that caste. Their descendants fall again into different groups of castes, according as they were orginally of Brâhmaṇa, Kshatriya or Vaiśya origin We shall in course of our enquiry come across them as Mallas, Licchavis and Naṭas who were all descended from the Vrâtyas of the Kshatriya caste. Innumerable despised mixed castes, again, are the offspring of those who through some fault—adultery, consanguineous marriage, abandonment of the prescribed profession—are excommunicated from the Aryan Society; thus we have the origin of the Kaivarta out of the union of a Nishâda with an Âyogava woman. To these mixed castes professions were assigned with as much strictness as in the case of the four official castes; for instance, to the Sûta was assigned the work of a cart-driver, to the Ambashṭha, the medical profession, to the Mâgadha, trade, to the Nishâda, the killing of fish, to the Pukkasa, the capturing and killing of [p. 6.] the cave-dwelling animals, to the Caṇḍâlas, the carrying of corpses and the execution of criminals.

So much for the theory of the Brâhmaṇas (according to Manu, X. 5 sq). It is *prima facie* evident that we cannot possibly have in it a true picture of the real state of things; and it is not difficult to see how there has been developed such a system. The names of the particular mixed castes show very plainly the material out of which the system is built; throughout it is either geographical or ethnical relations, names of lands or peoples, which give them their distinctive names, as, for example, Mâgadha, Nishâda, Vaideha, Ambashṭha, Malla, Licchavi and Caṇḍâla. Along with these and to a much smaller extent, professional categories determine the names, as, Sûta, cart-driver, Veṇa, maker of reeds, Naṭa, dancer, Kaivarta, fisherman. The self-contained existence of these and similar groups separated from the Aryan Society, through contempt shown towards their race or their callings, was too evident to make it possible to ignore them quietly or to bring them under one or other of the four castes. The theory was widened and the mixed castes were annexed to the four original and recognised castes by giving their families or professional groups a wholly arbitrary genesis.

That the inadequacy of the orthodox theory and the necessity for making certain concessions to truth was felt is shown by numerous exceptions to the general rule recognised for particular cases. The law, according to which every caste was assigned a wholly fixed calling, could not be maintained in this its exclusive form; people permitted at first the higher castes to follow the mode of life of the caste next in order in the system, but people could not stop there and allowed, evidently, under pressure of circumstances, the higher castes to adopt the professions which were originally considered proper for the lower ones. Thus, a Brâhmaṇa may, if he cannot earn his living by the work proper to his own caste or by that of the warrior caste, adopt the life of a Vaiśya and earn his livelihood by agriculture and rearing cattle. (Manu X. 82). In practice people went further and we may suppose that even among the Brâh-
[p. 7.] maṇas of ancient times the ways of earning a livelihood were no less manifold than they are to-day.[1]

[1] From the list of Brâhmaṇas who according to law cannot be invited to take part in the offering to one's departed ancestors (Manu

If we thus have in the Brahmanical theory anything but a picture of the real social conditions, we should not also lose sight of the fact that this theory after it was promulgated without much reference to facts, reacted powerfully upon the facts (actual conditions). The more Brahmanical culture spread in the course of centuries, the more did the priestly classes succeed in stamping their desired physiognomy upon the Indian society. through their religious and social influence. The superiority of the Brâhmaṇa caste which came gradually into recognition and at first, surely, not without opposition, influenced to a great extent the further

III. 151 sq), we can get an idea of the multifariousness of the professions followed by them in spite of the prohibition. We thus meet with players (kitava), medical men (cikitsaka), butchers (mâṃsavikrayin), shopkeepers (vipaṇena jîvan) paid professions (preshyo grâmasya râjñaśca), usurers (vârddhushi), herdsmen (paśupâla) actors (kuśîlava) singers (bandin), oilmillers (tailika), dealers in spices (rasavikrayin), makers of bows and arrows (dhanuḥśarâṇâṃ kartâ) restrainers of elephant, cattle, horses and camels (hastigośvoshṭradamaka), astrologers, tamers of birds, instructors in the use of the weapons (yuddhâcârya), architects, tamers of dogs (Śvakṛîḍin), falconers (śyenajîvin), agriculturists (kṛishijîvin) and even carriers of corpses (pretaniryâtaka)—Now-a-days one can find, as stated in Nesfield's *Brief View of the caste system of the North-Western Provinces and Oudh*, Allahabad, 1885, Brâhmaṇas following any paid profession, with the exception of such as bring on religious defilement and eventually, loss of caste, such as, for example, that of a sweeper or a washerman. We find them following the occupation of a water-carrier, cook, cart-driver, watchman, field-watch, postman, policeman, professional singer, dancer, etc., etc.

development of the social condition; it was essentially the prime cause of the various groups [p. 8] of the Indian society which had been formed on the lines of professions or of races, modelling themselves upon the Brahmanical castes and so becoming what the theory had already made them.

This superiority of the Brâhmaṇa caste, however, extended in no way over the whole province of ancient India conquered by Aryan culture. The proper centres of Brahmanism, the provinces which in Manu were styled the land of Brahmarshi, comprise the countries of the Kurus, Matsyas, Pañcâlas and Śûrasenas. The land bordering this, the portion of Northern India which was called Madhyadeśa or middle land, forms, starting eastward, a region indicated by a line drawn from the Himâlaya through Prayâga, called Allahabad to-day, towards the high land of Amarakaṇtaka[1]. The provinces to the east of this line, the countries known to-day as Oudh and Behar, where in Buddha's time we find the people of Kâśi, Kośala, Videha and Magadha, are excluded from Brahmarshideśa. According to the evidence of the Brâhmaṇa texts and the lawbooks, there can be no doubt that these people, especially, those of Magadha

---

[1] Cf. Lassen, *Indische Alterthumskunde*, 2nd Ed., Vol. I. p. 152.

and Videha came late in contact with Vedic culture and were never influenced so much by it as the western people. We should not forget that the Aryan immigration in India took place by stages and was not uniform throughout; the Aryan races, who proceeding farthest east, subjugated first the Gangetic people, may have separated themselves from the great body of the Aryans for a time, when there was still no culture which we are accustomed to designate by the term "Vedic." Also it is doubtful whether these advanced guards of Aryan civilization ever succeeded in fully absorbing the aboriginal races who, however inferior they might have been to the Aryans in point of culture, were numerically much stronger than their invaders. So also the circumstance that in Manu the names of some of these eastern races, namely, those of Magadha and Videha, are applied

[p. 9]

to the mixed castes not belonging to the Aryan family, points to the conclusion that they were not regarded as of the same rank by people who considered themselves true representatives of Aryan culture[1]. The possibility, therefore, is in no way excluded

---

[1] Cf. The excursus "Über das geographische Verhältniss der vedischen und der buddhistischen Kultur" in Oldenberg's *Buddha*, Berlin, 1881, p. 390 sq.

that we have to see in the individual races of princes repeatedly mentioned in the Pali texts, such as, the Licchavis of Vesâlî and the Mallas, the lords of Kusinârâ and Pâvâ, who were both looked upon by Manu as the descendants of a *Vrâtya* of the Kshatriya caste, the non-Aryan aboriginal rulers.

If this supposition of an ethnical and cultural opposition between the specifically Brahmanic west and the less Brahmanised east, the home of Buddhism, is correct, then we can presume that even the social conditions, as we find them here, are different from those of the west; for the social organisation of a people is essentially dependent upon the above-named factors and is probably more so in India than elsewhere; ethnical differences and religious views have principally determined the social physiognomy of the Indian people. To this we have to add a circumstance which even for India cannot be left out of consideration and has to be brought in here for the explanation of the opposition mentioned above, namely, the influence of climate and the soil; climâtical and geographical differences have even in India, which is so often called "a world in itself," sometimes even a world which unites the greatest contradictories, played a part in the shaping of the social conditions.

Now let us leave the province of *a priori* suppositions and take our stand upon firm ground which will form the basis of the inquiry that follows. From the Pali texts and especially, the Jâtakas, we will take the material for the reconstruction of such a picture as the Indian society in Buddha's age and the [p. 10] field of his work may have presented. Here, however, we must consider that when this picture differs from that which is presented by the Brâhmanical sources, this difference arises not necessarily from local variations but in part from the nature of the texts. Just as the Brâhmaṇa texts, the lawbooks and even the Brahmanical epics reflect very little the real state of Indian culture and just as in reality they represent the state of culture as it occurs in the imagination of their Brâhmaṇa authors, so also in the case of the Buddhist texts, one should not lose sight of the subjective element. The authors of the Pali canon were Buddhist monks, and as such, kept aloof from, if they were not hostile to, Brahmanical culture. The sacrificial ceremony, the study of the Vedas, the Brahmanical caste, in short, everything which gave the Brâhmaṇas their special position, was looked upon as worthless by these and challenged. Many of the disciples of Buddha belonged, before their acceptance of the homeless life (pabbajjâ), like Buddha himself, to the Kshatriya caste and showed a preference for their former caste even when they entered the monk's state; many were rich, influential citizens, before they renounced the world, and in consequence of this, looked at their own former condition with more favourable eyes than the Brâhmaṇas; and whoever, among these classes even accepted Buddhism was very likely to view Brahmanism with great and even unjust severity. But the Buddhist monks among whom the tradition spread and to whom we owe its fixation, showed a more objective attitude towards the worldly life which they had renounced and in exchange for which they had adopted the homeless life, than the Brâhmaṇas who were always conscious of their Brahmanism which they spread over the society in which they lived.

Besides, Buddhistic narratives which are in other respects altogether different, exhibit the same tendency in the region of morals; the great mass of concrete data regarding the life of the people which are found in the realistic pictures of the Jâtakas is for them a matter of indifference; it is purely casual, and this casual manner, this parenthetic way in which these things are described, has preserved it from distortions.

For these reasons—so it seems to me at
[p. 11] least—the picture of Indian society, as we obtain it from the Pali texts and principally, from the Jâtakas, is more life-like and true than that which the Brâhmaṇas through their one-sided exaltation of their own caste have given us and so we may hope to get some material from our sources which can throw light upon the caste-relations in eastern India.

CHAPTER II

General View of the Castes

If we first seek, on the basis of quotations which relate to castes in general, a conception of their meaning, and of their relation to one another, we are confronted at first sight with a circumstance which seems to give the lie direct to the introductory words—the circumstance, namely, that even in the Pali canon we find the Brâhmanical caste-theory. The division of Indian society into four castes is in no way unknown to Buddhist literature.

"Just so, you monks"—with these words Buddha teaches his disciples in the Cullavagga of the Vinaya-Piṭaka (IX, 1, 4) about the relation of the castes to the Order—"just as the great rivers, such as, the Gaṅgā, the Yamunā, the Aciravatī, the Sarabhū and the Mahī, when they pour their waters into the great ocean, lose their names and origins and become the great ocean, precisely so, you monks, do these four castes, the Khattiya (=Skr. Kshatriya), the Brâhmaṇa, the Vessa (=Skr. Vaiśya) and Sudda (=Skr. Sûdra) when they pass, according to the doctrines and prescriptions of those who have attained perfection, from home to homelessness, lose their names and origins and take from here onward the name *samaṇa* attaching to the son of Sakya."

In Kaṇṇakathâla Sutta (No. 90 of the Majjhima Nikâya) the following words were put into the mouth of Buddha: "These are the four
[p. 12]
castes, O great king: Khattiya, Brâhmaṇa, Vessa and Sudda. Of these four castes, O great king, two stand in the front rank, namely, the Khattiya and the Brâhmaṇa, so far as relates to the salute, the seat to be offered, the extension of the folded hands and the service to be rendered."

The Assalâyana Sutta,[1] which tries to prove the worthlessness of the castes, likewise speaks of four castes: "Once stopped"—so it begins—"the Holy at Sâvatthi, in Jetavana, the park of Anâthapiṇḍika. At that time there lived in Sâvatthi five hundred Brâhmaṇas hailing from different places for some religious purpose; among them there was a rumour that this hermit (samaṇa) Gotama proclaimed the purity of the four castes. Who is in a position to challenge the *samana* Gotama with regard to this question?" As the Sutta proceeds, this division is surely not always observed: the author is occasionally—as if unconsciously and perhaps against his will

---

[1] Ed. and transl. by Richard Pischel, Chemnitz, 1880.

—forced by reality to mention, by the side of the Khattiyas and the Brâhmaṇas, the Râjannas[1] and as lower castes, the Caṇḍâla, Nesâda, Veṇa, Rathakâra and Pukkusa; but the existence of the four castes is still the tacit assumption which is in no way given up even in the admission which Gotama at the end of his dispute forces the Brâhmaṇa Assalâyana to make, namely, that caste is worthless and that the claim of the Brâhmaṇas to be the best caste is untenable.

The same subject is also handled in the Madhura Sutta[2] (No. 84 of the Majjhima Nikâya) and to some extent the same words are used. The king Madhura Avantiputta betakes himself to Samaṇa Kaccâna and puts to him the question: "The Brâhmaṇas, Kaccâna, maintain that the Brâhmaṇa is the best caste and every other caste is low, that the Brâhmaṇa is the white caste and every other caste is black, that the Brâhmaṇas are pure and not the non-Brâhmaṇas, that the Brāhmaṇas are the favourite sons of Brahma, that
[p. 13.] they are born out of his mouth, born of Brahma, successors of Brahma. What do you say to this, Kaccâna?" And Kaccâna replies that caste neither assures material success in life nor makes any difference

---

[1] Cf. with this the remark in the sixth chapter.

[2] Ed. and transl. by Robert Chalmers in the "Journal of the Royal Asiatic Society" 1894, p. 394 sq.

with regard to the punishment or happiness that awaits after death, that it does not protect wrong-doers from the punishment prescribed by law and that above all, for the homeless ascetics it is a matter of indifference. But here, too, the argument rests upon the four castes and the result is, not that these four castes do not exist but only that they are all the same.

The thought that a Brâhmaṇa does not occupy a special place by reason of his birth but that virtue alone constitutes a true Brâhmaṇa, recurs also in the Jâtakas; in many ways the theme of the worthlessness of the castes is varied and an opportunity given to the narrator for lengthy discussions on the caste. Especially, the Uddâlaka Jâtaka deals in a most penetrating way with the caste question. "A long time ago, when Brahmadatta ruled in Benares, the Bodhisatta[1] was appointed his house priest, on account of his scholarship and intelligence. The latter saw one day in a pleasant spot in the park an extremely beautiful courtesan and fell in love with her. She became pregnant (with his child) and when she recognised her condition, she said to him, "O Lord, I have received a live fruit; when it is born I will give the child the name of its grandfather." He reflected,

[1] Skr. Bodhisattwa, *i.e.*, Buddha in one of his former existences.

"A child which is born of a low woman cannot possibly be given the family name" and said to her, "My love, this tree here is called Uddâla; because you have got your child here, you may call it Uddâlaka". Then he gave her a signet ring and continued, "If you get a daughter, bring her up with this, if you get a son, you can show him to me after he is grown [p. 14.] up". She gave birth some time later to a son and named him Uddâlaka. When this son grew up, he asked his mother, "Dear mother, who is my father?" "The *purohita*, my son." "If that is the case, I will study the Vedas". With this resolution, he took the ring and the honorarium for his teacher from his mother and went to Takkasilâ and read there with a world-renowned teacher. At the sight of a crowd of ascetics, the thought occurred to him, "These must be in possession of the highest knowledge, I must learn it from them"; full of desire for knowledge, he adopted the homeless state, rendered all manner of service to the ascetics and prayed that they might teach him their wisdom. They taught him according to the measure of their wisdom, but among the five hundred ascetics there was not a single one who excelled him in intelligence; he was the wisest among them all. Therefore they agreed and made him their chief.

He said, however, to them, "Brothers, you live permanently in the woods and eat the roots and fruits of the forest; why don't you tread the soil of men?" "Brother, men want, as soon as they have given us alms, to hear in return the doctrine (*dhamma*) from us; they put questions to us and for fear of this we don't go there". "Brothers, even if a world-conqueror should come, as you have me, let the answer be my care and do not fear". With these words, he betook himself with them to the route followed by them in begging and gradually reached Benares; here he stopped in the park of the king and went next day a-begging in the company of all to a village provided with a door. The people gave them copious alms; next day, the ascetics came to the city where, too, abundant alms fell to their lot. The ascetic Uddâlaka gave the thanks, pronounced the benedictions and answered the questions. The people were greatly edified, gave the ascetics liberally, as much as they wanted. Throughout the town the rumour spread that a wise teacher and pious ascetic had come; people narrated this even to the king. The latter asked where he was staying and when he heard that he was staying with the rest of the ascetics in the park, he said, "Good, I will go and see him to-day". Somebody announced to Uddâlaka that the king was coming to see him. He called together the host of wise men and said [p. 15.] to them, "Dear brothers, if one wins a prince even for a single day, this is enough for his whole life". "What, however, shall we do, O teacher?" He gave them the following advice: Some of you should behave like a bat [1]; some of you should sit with folded legs and practise penance, some should lie on a bed of thorns, some should practise the penance relating to the five fires [2], others should plunge into the water, still others should recite verses in different places". They did accordingly. He himself, however, sat with eight or ten learned men, sourrounded by disciples upon a space specially prepared for this and placed a book upon a beautiful desk. In a moment the king came to the park with the *purohita*, surrounded by a large number of men, and as he saw the false ascetics practising penance, he reflected, "They are all free from all fear of misery," went to Uddâlaka, seated himself by his side after accosting him with reverence, and

---

[1] *vaggulivataṃ carantu.* What is to be understood by this expression, I connot state exactly; it seems to indicate a special kind of posture, by which the holy man in question performs a vow, just as is the case with the 'cock-holies' mentioned by Oldenberg (*Buddha* p. 69) who pick out their food like cocks and behave always like cocks.

[2] *pañcatapaṃ*, "the five tapas". These are the four fires directed towards the four directions and the sun which shines above,

began the following conversation with the *purohita* in a happy spirit:

"These here, who wear coarse skins, have long tufts of hair and recite verses with unclean teeth and dirty face, are they really, as they recognise this (that is, penances) as the duty of men, free from misery ?"

When the *purohita* heard this, he said to himself, "This king is favourably disposed towards wrong persons; I must not remain silent" and so he recited the second verse:

"When, O king, a learned man does an evil act, does not live virtuously, he cannot, even if he knows a thousand Vedas, be free from misery without finding the right path."

[p. 16.] When Uddâlaka heard these words, he reflected: "The king is in every way pleased with this host of holy persons; this Brâhmaṇa, however, strikes the running ox in the mouth; filth is thrown upon the prepared meal. I will speak to him". He recited the third verse directed towards the *purohita*:

"If when a man knew a thousand Vedas and yet could not be free from misery, so long as he did not know the right path, my opinion is, that the Vedas are useless, the path of self-restraint is the truth".

To this the *purohita* replied:

"The Vedas are not in any way useless, nor is the path of self-restraint undoubtedly the truth: for he who studies the Vedas attains fame, whereas he attains only peace who restrains himself in his life".

When Uddâlaka heard this, he meditated, "Towards this man here I cannot in any way adopt an attitude of hostility; if I tell him that I am his son, he cannot but show love to me; I will make myself known to him". He recited the fifth verse:

"Parents and other kinsmen one should support; he to whom one owes one's origin is identical with oneself; I am Uddâlaka, sprung from thy Brâhmaṇa family".

The former asked, "Are you really Uddâlaka", and as the latter answered in the affirmative, he said "I have given thy mother a mark of identity, where is it?" With the words, "Here is it, O Brâhmaṇa," Uddālaka reached him the ring. The Brâhmaṇa recognised the ring and said "Surely, you are a Brâhmaṇa[1], do you know however, the duty of a Brâhmaṇa?" In asking

---

[1] Cf. what is said below at p. 35. Another reading omits *brâhmaṇa*; probably, to the writer the express recognition of a bastard as a Brâhmaṇa was repugnant; this omission makes no difference with regard to the fact that the *purohita* looks upon his illegitimate son as belonging to his caste.

him about the duty of a Brâhmaṇa, he uttered the sixth verse :

"Tell me who a Brâhmaṇa is, how he becomes perfect, how extinction[1] takes place and what is to be understood by the righteous."

[p. 17] Upon this, Uddâlaka explained in the seventh verse :

"Rejecting (all worldly thoughts), taking the fire with him, sprinkling water, offering sacrifices, the Brâhmaṇa sets up the sacrificial post. Acting in this way he attains peace of mind, and for this reason he is called virtuous."

The *purohita* replied to him, finding fault with his conception of the duties of a Brâhmaṇa :

"The Brâhmaṇa is not pure through the sprinkling of water, nor is he perfect through it, nor does there arise peace or virtuousness, nor does he thereby attain Nirvâṇa"

Wishing to know how anybody could be a Brâhmaṇa if not in the way shown by him, Uddâlaka asked, reciting the ninth verse :

"How is he a Brāhmaṇa, how does he become perfect, how does he attain Nirvâṇa, what is understood by the righteous ?"

The *purohita* taught him in these words :—

"Without land, without kinsmen, indifferent to the sensuous world, free from desire, immune

---

[1] *parinibbâna*, Skr. *parinirvâṇa*, the attainment of Nirvâṇa, the extinction, abnegation of self.

from lust, careless of existence, acting in this way, the Brâhmaṇa attains peace of the soul, and so is called virtuous."

On this, Uddâlaka recited the verse :

"Khattiya, Brâhmaṇa, Vessa, Sudda, Caṇḍâla and Pukkusa can all be virtuous, self-restrained and can attain nirvâṇa ; is there any among them, when they have all attained peace of the soul, who is better or who is worse ?"

To him replied the *purohita*, in order to show him that the moment Arhatship[1] is attained, inferiority and superiority cease to exist :

"Khattiya, Brâhmaṇa, Vessa, Sudda, Caṇḍâla and Pukkusa can all be virtuous and self-restrained and attain nirvâṇa ; among them, when they have attained peace of the soul, there is no one who is better and no one who is worse"

[p. 18] Uddâlaka, however, found fault with him and said :

"Khattiya, Brâhmaṇā, Vessa, Sudda, Caṇḍāla and Pukkusa can all be virtuous and self-restrained and attain nirvâṇa ; among them, there is no one who is better or worse, when they have attained peace of the soul. If this

---

[1] *arahatta*, position of an arhat, a holy man, the highest of the four stages in the path of emancipation, complete holiness. Cf. Oldenberg, *Buddha*, p. 326 Note.

is so, then Brahmanism which you hold and your belonging to a family noted for its knowledge of the Vedas, are of no value."

The *purohita*, however, taught him through a parable and recited two verses :

"A tent is covered with fabrics of various colours, but the colour does not follow the shades of the fabrics. So it is also with men ; always men attain purity ; the virtuous don't ask a person about his birth, when they have recognised his piety."

As Uddâlaka could not regain his ground, he sat down, without answering. The Brâhmaṇa however, said to the king : All these, O great king, are cheats, they will ruin the whole of India with their hypocrisy. Make Uddâlaka give up his asceticism and make him my disciple ; make the rest return to their former condition, give them arms and make them your servants." The king was pleased with this advice of his teacher and so they were all enlisted in the service of the king.

The fundamental thought appears in a somewhat different way in Sîlavîmaṃsa Jâtaka (III. 194 sq). The *purohita* of the king of Benares wants to examine him with a view to knowing whether he esteems him on account of his virtuousness or on account of his learning. He commits theft, is shown to the king and learns that the latter only esteems him for his virtue. With this knowledge he resolves to renounce the worldly life and with these words takes leave of the king :

"Whether virtue is better than learning—about this I had doubts ; that virtue is better than learning, of this I doubt no more.

Birth and caste cause conceit ; verily, is virtue the highest ; he who does not possess virtue, for him learning also has no value.

A Khattiya who has aimed at vice and a
[p. 19.] Vessa who acts viciously, both come to grief after they have passed away from the world.

Khattiya, Brâhmaṇa, Vessa, Sudda, Caṇḍâla and Pukkusa will be all equal in the world of the gods, if they have acted virtuously here.

Of no value are the Vedas, of no value is birth or kinsmen for the future world, only one's own pure virtue brings him happiness in the next world."

The same account of castes and the same conception of their equality, as viewed from the ethical standpoint, meets us in Amba Jâtaka (IV. 205), where it is said :

"As a man who seeks juice in the forest considers that tree the best in which he finds it, whether it is the *eraṇḍa*[1] tree, the *pucimanda*[2] tree or the *pâlibhadda*[3] tree,

So also among the Khattiyas, Brâhmaṇas, Vessas, Suddas, Caṇḍālas and Pukkusas, he is the best from whom one can learn what is right."

Thus we meet everywhere in the Pali canon and even in the Jâtakas[4], although the worthlessness of the castes is emphasised, with the Brahmanical caste theory and the division of society into four castes, the Khattiya, Brâhmaṇa, Vessa and Sudda, as something self-evident, and nowhere is any doubt expressed. Still let us look a little more minutely at these passages. These are, so to speak, academical discussions regarding the value of castes which all only serve—not to give us a picture of Indian society—but to oppose the claim of the Brâhmaṇas to be through their caste in sole possession of truth, of the knowledge of the path of
[p. 20.] emancipation. In my opinion,

[1] Ricinus shrub.

[2] Skr. picumanda, Azadirachta Indica.

[3] Skr. pàlibhadra, Butea Frondosa.

[4] That in the passages quoted from the Jātakas, not four but six castes, that is, in addition to the official castes of the Brahmanical theory, the two castes, Caṇḍāla and] Pukkusa, reckoned among the mixed castes, are enumerated, has for its reason this, that people felt in the circles from which the verses came, the non-reality of the Vessa and Sudda castes and thereby the two hated classes, whose real existence people could perceive everyday, were added. Our position that the Brahmanical caste theory is present even in the Jâtakas is thereby not modified.

there is no more reality in these theoretical speculations than in the theory of the Brâhmaṇas; they are nothing else than a reflex of the priestly literature and show us that the Brahmanical theory was not only well known to the Buddhist monks but was so strongly inbedded in their consciousness, that they could not free themselves from it, although in all probability, they were quite convinced of its incongruence with the real world as well as of the worthlessness of the caste. Moreover, the Buddhist writers never cared in the least to contradict the caste-theory as such and thereby introduce a better organisation of society; what they tried to do was simply to show that caste is of no value for the striving for emancipation.

Only this much appears to me to emerge clearly out of these theoretical discussions, that the castes in Buddha's time and in the eastern lands were an important factor in the social life. The question, in my opinion, can never be of any influence which Buddha's doctrine of the worthlessness of the castes may have had upon the existing condition of society, of any weakening of the class-oppositions through Buddhism. The conception of the non-existence of caste-distinctions which we notice everywhere in Buddhistic writings, may (at first sight) seem to suggest the thought that we are to see in this peculiarity of the Buddhistic doctrine, a reformatory act of Buddha and have to look upon Buddha as the destroyer of rigid limits fixed by orthodox practice. This view, however, is not at all correct.[1] The castes continued after the spread [p. 21] of the Buddhistic doctrine quite as well as before; the social organisation in India was not in the least altered by Buddha's appearance. We see that there is constant reference to the institution of castes and that not simply in the older portions of the Pali canon. Even the later portions, the commentaries on the Jâtikas bear witness to this, that in the caste-distinctions one has to see a real force, even long after Buddhism had acquired a firm footing and Buddha's doctrine of the worthlessness of castes had found universal acceptance as a means of acquiring emancipation.

Even among Buddhist monks we find this conception of the distinction of castes, of the value of high birth, in no way extinguished. As

---

[1] cf. Koeppen (*Die Religion des Buddha*, Berlin Vol. I. p. 127 sq) against whom the unjustified polemic has been thrust by Hopkins (*The Religions of India*, Boston and London, 1895 p. 586 note) that he saw in Buddha an emancipator, a political reformer. Cf. further Oldenberg's *Buddha* p. 155 sq—When even in the second edition of Ratzel's Völkerkunde (Leipzig and Vienna 1895 p. 599), it is said of Buddhism that it "abolished the castes" and not "that it was in a position to check its further growth," it is hoped that it will not be considered beating the air if I polemise against this conception.

evidence of this, we have the introduction to the Tittira Jâtaka (I. 217 sq.), where it is said that the disciples of the six[1] (chabbaggikâ) requisitioned all places for themselves and their teachers, so that the wisest men who came later got no quarters. When Buddha became aware of this, he called an assembly of monks and put the question, Who deserves to have the best quarters, the best water, the best food ? He received from some the reply, "He who was a Khattiya before he became initiated" (khattiya kulâ pabbajito) ; from others, "He who was a Brâhmaṇa or a gahapati (brâhmaṇakulâ gahapatikulâ pabbajito). Here the three classes looked upon by the Indians are narrated in their order of succession and even though Buddha himself in summing up the debate recognises no privilege grounded on birth, the narrative still shows that in the consciousness of the great majority of the monks the caste distinctions had value. The action of Devadatta[2] and Kokila mentioned in the introduction to Jambukhâdaka Jâtaka (II. 438) is also evidence of the respect which people had for the higher
[p. 22] castes—the action, namely, of their trying to revive their lost reputation.

---

[1] The six monks who in the Vinaya Piṭaka play the rôle of the scoundrel and who try to go aganist Buddha's prescriptions in every possible way. *Cf.* Oldenberg, *Buddha* p. 342 sq.

[2] Buddha's cousin and rival. See Oldenberg, *Buddha* p. 162 sq.

The two, that is to say, visit the householders, moving from house to house, sing praises of each other and speak with pride of each other, one stating that Devadatta is descended from Mahâsammata[1] and can point to an unbroken succession of princes in the royal house of Okkâka,[2] the other that Kokila had belonged to a north-western Brâhmaṇa family before he was initiated (udiccabrâhmaṇakula nikkhamitvâ pabbajito).

But the question whether or not Buddhism has changed the caste-relationships is not of great value for us, as we, starting from the assumption[3] that the Jâtakas in their older forms exhibit the social condition of India, as it existed in Buddha's time, have only made this the subject of our study. In any case, one thing appears very clearly from the passages of a theoretical character quoted above, and that is, that the concept of caste, of *jâti*,[4] was widely prevalent in Buddha's

[1] The traditional name of the first king.

[2] Skr. Ikshvaku, name of a mythical king.

[3] Cf. the Preface.

[4] The word jâti, i.e., "birth" is also in Sanskr. the term for the concept "Caste." By the side of *jâti*, there occurs in the Pali texts in the sense of "caste," though much more rarely, the word vaṇṇa (=Skr. varṇa) and *kula*. Cf. Vinaya Piṭaka, ed. by Oldenberg Vol. 2 p. 239, cattâro' me vaṇṇâ khattiyâ brâhmaṇâ vessâ suddâ· Vol. 3. p. 184 *sq.* cattâri kulâni, khattiyakulaṃ brâhmanakulaṃ, vessakulaṃ suddakulaṃ. The use of *kula* which as a rule denotes family in the sense of "caste" shows how much the two concepts overlap each other in the consciousness of the Indians and how closely allied they are.

time. Consequently, our purpose is not much achieved if we consider how far the views relating to the essence of the caste are divergent, how much the views of the different authors vary here and there, when the question is to determine the concept of caste for a special period of Indian culture-history. Our problem will be to determine what is to be understood by caste in this period and
[p. 23.] to answer the question: "How far is the concept of caste, as it has come to us from the Brahmanical theory, or as we are accustomed to use it, when we speak of the modern conditions of India, applicable to the *jâti* of the Pali texts?"

We must distinguish between the two concepts, between the modern caste and that which the Brahmanical law-books understand by caste; they do not coincide with each other in any way and it would be a great mistake to make them identical. We cannot also hope to arrive at a universally valid definition by a combination of the two; a definition like this which is true of all stages of evolution of Indian culture, cannot at all be given; we can only try, through a comparison of the different stages which the caste has gone through in the course of centuries, to find persisting, and consequently, probably essential moments, in order, with the help of these, to get an approximate idea of the general meaning of caste in the earlier Buddhistic age. On the other hand, we must not ignore the development of the modern castes and confine ourselves wholly to literary tradition, for it is precisely the modern castes which give us many valuable parallels where the Brahmanical theory leaves us in the lurch, and many conditions of the social life of ancient times are only intelligible to us in the light of the present day.

By a caste of modern India, we understand, if I am to adhere in all essentials to the definition given by Senart,[1] a self-contained body which with a certain traditional and independent organisation, has a chief as well as a council, the membership of which is hereditary and which is thus determined not by chance or free selection but by birth, which gathers more or less fully on certain occasions, for instance, in certain festivals, and which is generally held together by a common hereditary [p. 24.] calling, which observes the same customs, especially, with regard to marriage, eating and various acts of purification, which, finally, is provided with a judiciary that makes the authority of the corporate body felt

[1] Revue des deux mondes, Tome 121, p. 605.

principally through the punishment of excommunication. The essential element by which the castes are even now characterised as an order *sui generis* and are distinguished from other similar social groups, is to be sought in the customs relating to the *connubium*, interdining and contact of impure persons; it is precisely these rules which set up absolute barriers between the innumerable modern castes and thereby give the Indian society its own proper physiognomy.

We must at once eliminate, if we wish to determine the concept of caste as it agitated the minds of the authors of the lawbooks, some of the attributes which have only reference to the castes of the present day; they are obviously of modern origin, for neither in the lawbooks nor anywhere else are found any traces which point to their existence in a former age. The caste in the Brahmanical theory is, although no less strictly isolated and self-contained, still externally not so well organised as the modern caste. A chief, a council, we notice as little as common festivals or assemblies for other purposes; what unites the castes of ancient times and isolates them from one another—be it well-understood, according to the theory—is, along with the confinement of every class within a wholly fixed profession, those customs which rule the modern caste. Precise rules with regard to marriage, food and even touch govern the mutual relationship of the castes in its minutest detail and try to prevent their fusion. Thus a Brâhmaṇa, although he is allowed wives of other castes, should have for his first wife one belonging to his own caste; for only such a one can attend to his bodily needs and can stand by his side in the performance of religious rites [1]; she alone

[p. 25.] assures for the son his belonging to the caste of the father. The Brāhmaṇa is forbidden[2] to take food from a man belonging to a lower caste, and as especially impure, the leavings of a Sudra's table[3] are regarded. Even the sight of a despised human being, especially, of a *Caṇḍâla,* whose touch itself causes impurity [4], is sufficient to spoil a Brâhmaṇa's meal.[5] All these prescriptions have the force of laws, a transgression of which involves

---

[1] Manu IX. 86:

Bhartuḥ śarîraśuśrûshâṃ dharmakâryaṁ ca naityakam svâ caiva kuryât sarveshâm nâsvajâtiḥ kathaṃcana.

[2] Manu IX. 210 sq; Vasishṭha XIV. 1 sq; Âpastamba I·16·22; Gautama XVII 17; Vishṇu LI. 7 sq.

[3] Manu XI, 153; Vasishṭha XIV, 33; Vishṇu LI. 50, 54, 56.

[4] Manu V 85; "If he (a Brâhmaṇa) sees a Caṇḍâla, a menstruating woman, a man excommunicated from the caste, a woman in childbed, a corpse, or a person rendered impure by the touch of a corpse, he will purify himself with a bath.

[5] Manu III, 239: "A Caṇḍâla, a hog, a cock, a dog, a menstruating woman and a eunuch should not be seen by a Brahman while eating.

special expiatory ceremonies and as the severest expiation, excommunication from the caste.

If we can thus see in the practices mentioned here, an essential and permanent characteristic of the caste, we shall—in order now to pass to the caste-relations, as they are described in the Jâtakas—look here for their presence. The scrupulous care with which the proximity of a person belonging to a despised or even a very low caste is avoided is evident in numerous instances contained in the Jâtakas.

In Kâliṅgabodhi Jâtaka (IV. 231), there occurs the following conversation
[p. 26.] between a king's son living as an ascetic in the forest and a princess likewise seeking shelter with her kinsmen in the forest, whom he sees sitting on a mango tree: "Well, who are you?", he says to her. "I am a human being, gentleman", "Then descend" "That is not possible, my dear sir, I am a Khattiyâ. "Well, I am also a Khattiya, so descend" "That means nothing, my dear sir, nobody is a Khattiya by his word merely; if you are a Khattiya, say the Khattiya formula."[1]

[1] *Cf.* Dhammapadam, *ed.* Fausböll p. 155. For the explanation of the expression "Khattiya-formula "(Khattiyamâyâ) a practice prevailing among modern castes may be cited, which Jacobi mentions in the "Zeitschrift d. Deutsch. Morgen. Gesellschaft" Vol. 48. p. 417 According to an oral communication from Mr. Grierson, caste in Behar has got its own epic song, romance or ballad, of which everybody knows something and very few know everything.

They recited together the Khattiya formula and then it was that the king's daughter descended.

The first question which the Brâhmaṇa youth Satadhamma asks a *Candâla* who happens to travel the same way with him is about the caste. "To what caste do you belong" (*Kimjâtiko si* II. 82), asks the Brâhmaṇa his travelling companion. "I am a Caṇḍâla", answers the other and asks the Brâhmaṇa the same question. Haughtily comes the latter's reply, "I am a Brâhmaṇa from the northwest" (ahaṃ udiccabrahmaṇo)[1] and it seems to be a wonder when it is further narrated that the two continued to go by the same road. Another person, likewise a youth belonging to a Brâhmaṇa family in the northwest, of whom it is expressly stated that he is very proud of his caste (*tassa jâtiṃ nissâya mahanto mâno ahosi* III. 232) exhibits greater anxiety for "atmospheric purification". On his return to the town of Benares he meets a Caṇḍâla. "Who art thou", he asks him and as the latter replies, "I am a Caṇḍâla", he tries to run away from him, for fear lest the wind which has moved through the body of the despised creature should touch him, and cries out loudly, "Damn you, Caṇḍâla, raven
[p. 27.] of evil omen, move out of the wind."

---

[1] *Cf.* what is said in the eighth chapter on the *Udiccabrâhmaṇa*.

Of a Brâhmaṇa ascetic whose hermitage lies on the banks of a river, it is said (IV. 388) that one day as he takes water to rinse his mouth, a toothpick floating in the water which a Caṇḍâla living near by has thrown into the water, is caught in a tuft of his hair. He notices it and cries out "Damn you, wretch."[1] With the words, "I will now see whence this evil omen has come," he moves up-stream and as he notices the Caṇḍâla he asks him, "To what caste do you belong." The reply comes, "I am a Caṇḍâla." "You have then thrown the toothpick in the river?" "Indeed, I have," replied the Caṇḍâla, and the Brâhmaṇa said, "Damn you, wretched Caṇḍâla, you bird of evil omen, you shall not live here any longer, move your dwelling down the river."[2]

As even in this narrative the pride of the Brâhmaṇa in his caste (jatiṃ nissâya mahantaṃ mânam akâsi) is strongly indicated, it is possible that the scrupulous care with which in the last two cited instances, the contact of the Caṇḍâla is forbidden or the way in which pollution from

[1] *nassa vasala*. The Brâhmaṇa curses, without knowing who has thrown the piece of wood into the stream, the man who has polluted the water through the tooth-pick. That this tooth-pick was hanging from a tuft of his hair is an unfavourable omen for him and as he now learns that a Caṇḍâla has used it, his indignation knows no bounds.

[2] A narrative of a similar kind is found in Vinaya Piṭaka (ed. Oldenberg, Vol. 4, p. 203 sq.).

his proximity is feared, is a manifestation of this pride, this arrogance of caste, and that on the other hand, the proximity of a Caṇḍâla had nothing of the character of a pollution. We find instances in which a Caṇḍâla has intercourse with a high-born without the latter making any objection to this. In Chavaka Jâtaka (III p. 27 sq.) it is narrated how a Caṇḍâla in order to get a mango for his pregnant wife, ascended a tree in the park of the king. He was surprised by dawn and continued to sit on the tree, waiting for night. In the meantime, the king came with his teacher, the *purohita*, to the garden, in order to learn the Vedas; they sat under the mango-tree, the king on a higher and the teacher on a lower seat. When the Caṇḍâla saw this, he descended from the tree and explained the impropriety of their conduct (towards each other). The king was greatly edified by the instruction he received and asked him his caste. "I am a Caṇḍâla, O King." "A great pity,[1] for if you had been born of a higher caste (jâti-sampanno), I would have resigned the sovereignty in your favour; however, I will remain king during the day and you will be king at night." He gave the Caṇḍâla a cross

[1] Manu, V. 93. "The fault of impurity does not apply to king" cf. ibid, V. 94, 97.

which he himself suspended from his neck and made him the town sentinel (nagaraguttika).

Now a king was no doubt permitted intercourse with the Caṇḍâla, for as king he seemed to be placed above the danger of pollution ; but even generally, people did not seem to be much afraid of the proximity of such a person, and it is doubtful whether there was a custom or a prescription whereby the higher classes were forbidden contact with the lower or residence in their vicinity, and if such a custom existed,[1] it is doubtful whether it was universally observed and was not rather violated every day and every hour. From the Jâtakas what appears clearly is only this, that the fear of such pollution was not confined to Brâhmaṇas proud of their caste. For specially sensitive feminine natures proud of their high descent, the mere sight of a despised person sufficed for the production of the feeling of impurity in their minds. As the daughter of the *seṭṭhi*, who as the daughter of a *gahapati* belonged to a respectable but always
[p. 29.] middle class family and that of a *purohita* of Ujjayini who had gone to the city

---

[1] That the law-books contain such a prescription for the Brâhmaṇas has been already mentioned. This, however, does not prove its existence at the time and in the places with which we have to deal.

gate to play, noticed two Caṇḍâla brothers, they washed their eyes with scented water and returned to the town. The people, to whom on such occasions food and drink were provided gratis, regarded themselves as cheated of a fine meal by the maiden's going away and so gave the Caṇḍâlas such a sound beating that they were almost dead (IV. 391). A similar thing happened to another Caṇḍâla who wanted to go to the gate of Benares, but encountered the daughter of the *setthi* and attracted by her beauty, stood gazing. The maiden who was peeping through the curtain of the palanquin in which she was carried, saw him and asked, "Who is this?" and as the answer came, "A Caṇḍâla, noble one," she washed her eyes with scented water, saying, "Oh, I see something which I should not see" and went back. Her escort struck the Caṇḍâla with his hands and feet till he fell down (IV. 378).

It is clear that the impurity of a person extended to the objects touched by him; this was especially the case with everything that had reference to food. When we remember how great a religious importance the meal had at all times for the Aryans, how eating together served as an external sign of sameness of blood, it seems possible to

assume that this principle of the exclusion of all impure people from the common table came from ancient times, was carried from the family over to the caste and was here developed with great precision. It should not, however, be overlooked that traces of such an exclusion of low persons from participation in the meal, as we see it in India to-day, are only
[p. 30.] found, when they are found at all in the Jâtakas, extremely rarely. The only passage which serves as evidence of the presence of special rules and customs relating to a common table, does not occur in a Jâtaka but in a *paccuppannavatthu*, in the introductory explanation in Bhaddasâla Jâtaka (IV. 144 sq.). Here it is narrated that the messengers of the Kosala king, sent to the Sâkiyas of Kapilavatthu, in order to bring a girl of this family for their chief, express doubts about the purity of her birth ; they are afraid of being cheated by the Sâkiyas who are proud of their family and so demand that the girl should dine with them. The Sâkiyas who as a matter of fact, wanted to pass on to them an illegitimate girl, namely, a Vâsabhakhattiyâ, the daughter of Mahânâma and a slave, are embarrassed and don't know what to do. Mahânâma says that they should not give themselves any trouble about the matter, for he knew a method : when he was

eating, they should bring the Vâsabhakhattiyâ, adorned with her ornaments, and as soon as he swallowed one mouthful, show him a letter with the words: "O prince, King so and so sent a letter, hear first this message." The Sâkiyas are satisfied with the plan and when Mahânâma sits at his dinner, they adorn the maiden with ornaments. Mahânâma cries out, "Bring my daughter here, she shall eat with me." After making some delay under the pretext that she must be adorned first, they bring her. With the words, "We will dine together with my father," she held a dish. Mahânâma takes with her a lump and puts it into his mouth; when he, however, stretches out his hand for the second lump, he is brought a letter, as previously arranged. He puts his right hand into the dish, encouraging his daughter to eat and takes the letter with his left hand and reads it: the latter, however, continues to eat, whilst he explains the message. When she finishes eating, he washes his hands and rinses his mouth. In this way the messengers come to the conclusion that she is his daughter and overlooks any distinction of caste.

The father avoids not only eating with his illegitimate daughter but even eating the food brought by her. In the first place, [p. 81.] he puts his hands without any scruple into the dish simultaneously with his daughter; as soon, however, as the hands of the impure have touched the food, it becomes impure for him; he stops, therefore, taking a second mouthful and lets the daughter eat alone, apparently absorbed in reading the letter. Not eating in the same table, but only eating from the same dish out of which the table companions have already eaten, the contact with the food already touched by them, is the criterion for a common caste.

Consequently, we cannot speak of any rule relating specially to persons having a common table which excludes lower castes [1]; on the other hand, there can be no doubt that prescriptions which forbade contact with food touched by the impure and, specially, with the leavings of their table, and punished transgression, existed and too often showed themselves effective.

The eating of the leavings of a Caṇḍâla's table was looked upon, according to the Jâtakas, as such a great sin for the Brâhmaṇa that it had for its consequence exclusion from the caste.[2] In the Mâtaṅga Jâtaka it is narrated

---

[1] Senart's remarks on this point (Revue des deux mondes, vol. 125, p. 328 sq.) seem to me to go too far, as they do not apply to all stages of evolution of the Indian caste.

[2] Acc. to Manu XI. 149, a Brâhmaṇa who had drunk water which had previously been drunk by a Sûdra, must drink *kuśa* water for three days and a Brâhmaṇa who had eaten the table leavings of a Sûdra or a woman must drink barley water for seven days (XI. 153).

how sixteen thousand Brahmanas had to undergo rebirth, because water which had been mixed with rice which was the remnant left out of a Caṇḍâla's meal, dropped into their mouths. The immediate consequence of this pollution, for which they themselves were in no way to blame, was their exclusion from the caste. They ceased to be Brâhmaṇas (te brâhmaṇâ: ,imehi caṇḍâlucchiṭṭhakaṃ pîtan' ti abrâhmaṇe kariṃsu. IV 388) and left Benares in disgrace. This passage—so far as I have seen, the only one in the Jâtakas which speaks of a punishment prescribed by the caste and thus, to some extent,
[p. 32.] of a jurisdiction exercised by it—sounds extremely legendary; still the actual occurrence of an excommunication from the caste, or at least, of any other difficult expiation for the sin of eating impure food, will appear extremely probable if we consider the realistic account given in the Satadhamma Jâtaka (II. 82 sq.).

The Bodhisatta, re-born as a Caṇḍâla, undertakes a journey after providing himself with some rice as viaticum and a provision basket and comes across a youth belonging to a rich Brâhmaṇa family in the north-west who for some reason has not taken any of these things with him. After they have narrated to each other their castes—as has already been explained above—they travel together. At the time of breakfast the Bodhisatta sits down near a well, washes his hands and opens his basket while he invites the youth to eat with him. "I don't want to eat, Caṇḍâla," runs the answer. "Good" thinks the Bodhisatta and takes, that there may not remain anything in his dishes, only that much which he requires and places it on a leaf. Then he fastens his basket, places it by his side, eats and drinks. After his meal is finished, he washes his hands and feet, takes his rice and the remainder of his food and moves on with the words, "Come let us go, young man." They travel the whole day. In the evening, they come to a sheet of water and take both a bath. After finishing this, the Bodhisatta sits down at a pleasant spot, opens his basket and begins to eat without asking the young Brâhmaṇa to eat with him. The youth tired with the day's long march and feeling hungry stands by his side and looks on, reflecting, "If he gives me anything to eat, I will accept it." The other says nothing and continues to eat. The Brâhmaṇa reflects, "This Caṇḍâla eats all without saying anything to me. I will ask him for a crumb. If he gives it to me, I can throw away the outer portion which is impure and eat the rest." He carries out his intention and eats the food that remains out of the Caṇḍâla's meal. No sooner, however, did he eat this than he was seized by the thought that he had [p. 33.] eaten the table leavings of a Caṇḍâla and had thereby done a thing which was most improper for his caste, his family, his land and felt so repentant that he vomited out the food that he had swallowed mixed with blood. "For the sake of a trifling thing I have done a most improper act," so he laments, full of grief and recites the verse:

"It was a trifle that remained uneaten and he gave it to me against his will—to me, who am a Brâhmaṇa by caste! What I have eaten, I must throw out of myself" so he weeps and decides, sick of life which is worthless after such improper conduct, to die of starvation. He goes to the forest and as he does not allow himself to be seen by anybody, perishes helpless."

The instances hitherto cited, which may be looked upon in several respects as typical, give us a view which represents the society of that time as governed by strict traditional morality or caste-rules. However much in the eastern countries, where the authority of the Brahmanical theory was less strong, practice may have transcended these limits, a sharp distinction between the despised people and the rest of the population was made here also. In the eyes of the aristocratic Aryans, the lower castes, such as the Caṇḍâlas, are impure. Their very sight causes pollution; consequently, they must be excluded

from the general society and must live in a special village of their own outside of the town and earn a living by means of lower occupations. That under these circumstances, any mixture with these lower elements is sought to be prevented appears self-evident. Surely, there existed from ancient times certain usages regulating marriage among the aristocratic Aryan families which must have been built up into strict rules, as the danger of a mixture with the aboriginal tribes and the merging of themselves in these was always felt by the Aryan races, and the existence of these rules is even perceived in the Jâtakas. When it is narrated in the
[p. 34.] Mâtaṅga Jâtaka that the Caṇḍâla gets the *setthi's* daughter as wife, this is due only to his position as Bodhisatta: "For the resolve of such a man—so it is said (IV. 376)—" always realises itself" In the course of the narrative it is expressly stated that he is not guilty of a transgression of the rules relating to the distinctions of caste (jâtisambhedavîtikkamaṃ akatvâ), that is, that he abstains from sexual intercourse with the *setthi's* daughter who stands by virtue of her caste much higher than he.

In general and as a rule, we can suppose that the *jâtis* of this age were endogamous; marriage within one's own *jâti* was the rule. Everywhere in the Jâtakas, we meet with the effort to keep the family pure through marriage confined to people of one's own standing and profession and not to allow it to degenerate through mixture with lower elements. When the parents desire to marry their son, they seek a maiden of the same caste for him or give him the advice:

"Take a girl out of a family who belongs to the same family as we" (ekaṃ samajâtikakulâ kumârikaṃ gaṇha. III. 422). The Brâhmaṇa agriculturist marries his son to the daughter of a Brâhmaṇa belonging to a similar family (so [brâhmaṇo] puttassa vayappattassa samâna-kulato kumârikaṃ ânesi. III. 162. So also IV. 22); the Brahmana parents give express instructions to the people whom they send for finding a girl for their son to bring a Brâhmaṇa girl (brâhmaṇakumârikaṃ ânetha. III. 93). Among the Brâhmaṇas, it is principally the rich and aristocratic families who wished to secure riches and aristocracy through equal marriage: the son of a good family (kulaputta) is married by the parents to the daughter of one belonging to an equal family (assa mâtâpitaro samâna-jatiyaṃ kulato dârikaṃ ânayimsu. I. 199). To the inclinations of young people, very little or no weight was attached; we always read that the elders consult with each other without consulting their children—who, it is remarked, are

grown up; to the Bodhisatta who is re-born in a village not far from Benares in a gahapati family the elders send a girl of good family from Benares (kuladhitaraṃ ânesuṃ II. 121) and
[p. 35.] a *seṭṭhi* living in a small market-town in the province courts [1] for the sake of his son the daughter of a seṭṭhi in Benares. (II. 225.)

In spite of all this it seems to me to go a little too far if we are to speak of a strict rule of endogamy; there are instances in the Jâtakas in which the caste barriers are considered not insurmountable and thus the sharp lines of demarcation which we are inclined to draw by reason of the numerous instances prescribing marriage within the caste to be the rule are wiped away. If marriage within the caste was more than a universal custom, if it had been a law prescribed by the caste, then its transgression would have led to the non-recognition of children born of an illegitimate marriage. This seems, however, as a matter of fact, not always to have been the case. We have seen that the *purohita* recognises the son born of his union with a public woman, after he is satisfied about his identity, as his own son; a fact, which if universalised makes the influence of caste upon actual life very small for us. Are we, however, justified in

[1] Cf. further the introductory explanations in Asitâbhu Jâtaka (II. 229) and in Suvaṇṇamiga Jâtaka (III. 182).

making such a generalisation? It almost seems that we are, when we read the introductory explanation in Bhaddasâla Jâtaka (IV. 144 sq.), where the question whether the wife of a *khattiya* belonging to a low caste and the children born of such a wife are to be looked upon as of the same rank as the *khattiya*, is made the principal topic of discussion between Buddha and the Kosala King. The latter had—so it is narrated here—sent a messenger to Kapilavatthu for getting for him a Sâkya daughter. The Sâkya princes, very little inclined, on the one hand, to fulfil his desire,[1] and on the other hand, fearing the wrath of the king, to whom they stand in a dependent relationship, resolve,
[p. 36.] on the advice of Mahânâma, to send him his daughter, the Vâsabhakhattiyâ, who, on her mother's side is born of a slave but had a khattiya for her father. The messengers are deceived—in the manner already mentioned—by a stratagem and bring the daughter of Mahânâma to their king who makes her his principal consort (aggamahesî) and gets a son by her. This son wants, when he grows up, to see the family of his grandfather (maternal) and takes from his mother who tries in vain

---

[1] They are afraid of the traditions of the family (kulavamsa) being broken according to which, the Sâkya daughters can only be married to Sâkyas. Cf. Weber, *Indische Studien*, Vol. 5, p. 427.

to dissuade him, a letter to Kapilavatthu in which she asks her kinsmen not to notice any difference in point of birth between themselves and her son. What is feared happens, however, although things begin very well: He is taken to the audience hall and placed before his kinsmen. "This," people say to him, "my dear, is your grandfather, this your uncle." He goes round, accosting everybody with reverence, wonders why whilst he gets pain in the back through continuous bowing, he sees nobody who bows to him. But the Sâkiyas want to clear his doubts and explain to him, "The young princes, my dear, have gone to the country" and heap courtesies upon him. A few days later, he goes away in great pomp. Just at this time, however, a slave washes the place where he has eaten with milk water [1] and cries aloud, "At this place the son of the slave Vâsabhakhattiyâ has eaten." A man belonging to the retinue of the prince who has forgotten to take his weapons and returns, hears this insulting cry, asks for its cause and when he has heard the whole story, narrates it to others. Thus, the Kosala king also learns of the descent of his wife from a slave; in a fit of wrath, he divests her and her son of all honour and throws them in the company of slaves only. Some days

---

[1] Cf. above.

later Buddha comes to the place and he narrates to him the incident, complaining of the deceit practised upon him by his kinsmen. The master replies that no doubt the Sâkiyas have done wrong, they ought to have given him a girl of the same caste, but that his wife is a king's daughter and the marriage took place in the house of a khattiya king and his son also is a king's son : for—he adds—" the old wise men acted according to the principle : *the family of the mother does not matter ; the family of the father alone is important* (mâtigottaṃ nâma kim karissati, pitigottaṃ eva pamâṇaṃ) and cites as proof the Kaṭṭhahâri Jâtaka.

[p. 37.]

Have we to see in this pronouncement which is put into the mouth of Buddha, an expression of a view which was current among the people of his time, or does the prevailing conception exhibit itself in the spontaneous, unreflecting action of the king who does not look upon the son of a *dâsî* as of equal rank with him but classes him as well as his mother, as soon as he is aware of her descent from a slave, with the slaves ? The question can hardly be answered definitely ; many things seem to me to point to the prevalence of the law stated by Buddha. We meet with a tendency similar to that noticed in Buddha's pronouncement in Brahmanical law-books ;

also here the principle is expressed that—in a marriage of a higher with a lower caste—the caste of the father is the most important and seems to determine that of the son.[1] On the other hand, the view, according to which the marriage of a *dvija* with a *Śûdra* woman is considered objectionable, appears to be predominant in the law-books; it is true, a Sûdra woman is allowed even to a Brâhmaṇa, along with women of higher castes, but it is added that such marriages bring about with certainty the degradation of the family.[2] If we add to this circumstance the tendency which is manifestly noticeable in the Jâtakas, of preventing a degradation of the family [p. 38.] through mixture with lower castes and mention further the fact that even in Greek accounts[3] the prohibition of marriage between the different classes is pointed out as a characteristic feature of Indian Society, I should believe that the king followed the general rule and especially, the traditions of his class in

[1] Manu, X, 6: "Sons of the twice-born by women of the next lower caste are of equal rank (with the father, with reference to the caste) but bear the stain attached to the mother."

[2] Manu, III, 115: "The twice-born who in their foolishness marry women of a lower caste, bring their families and their descendants rapidly to the position of Śûdras." Cf. Vasishṭha I, 25-29; Apastamba I. 18-33.

[3] Cf. the quotation from Arrian which occurs below.

his views concerning the degradation of his wife and the son born of her. Exceptions—we can find these in the case of this proposition, if they are not already self-evident—occur, and here belongs the incident narrated in the Kaṭṭhahâri Jâtaka (I. 134 sq.), namely, the installation of a wood-gatherer (Kaṭṭhahârikâ) as the *aggamahesî* and the handing over of the viceregency to the illegitimate son; here belongs the story (contained in the paccuppannavatthu of Kummâsapiṇḍa Jâtaka III. 406) of the queen Mallikâ who is brought by the Kosala king from the house of her father and made the principal queen. There are again exceptions which maintain the principle of endogamy as the rule, but on the other hand, show that the boundaries of the caste organisation were not inviolable, at any rate, not for one who, like the king, stood above the prescriptions of caste and represented a power which at least at that time and in that part of India of which we are speaking, had not yet been rendered inert through priestly influence, namely, the political power, the State.

What concerned us hitherto in our investigation was to show that we find precisely the attributes which the caste of the Brāhmanical theory has in common with modern caste and in which we must look for the essence of a caste, in the *játi* of the Pali texts and that we have to recognise in them—without maintaining the existence of a strict caste order—a factor of great power which lies deeply rooted in the life of society as well as of the individual.

[p. 39.] Now the question arises, how the particular castes of that time stood, whether and how far we are justified in applying the term "caste" to all the numerous groups of Indian society which we come across.

CHAPTER III

THE HOMELESS ASCETICS

Before we attempt to analyse the structure of the social body and to look more closely to its separate parts, we must point to a circumstance which is of great importance for the whole condition of culture in the East and especially, for the position of the dominant classes and peoples with regard to the Brahmanical caste, the circumstance, namely, that the Khattiya, no less than the Brâhmaṇa, nay, even the people belonging to the middle class, renounced the world and lived as hermits in the forest. And indeed, we meet with this view not as an exception, not as a chance occurrence, of which we can speak as we do of an unusual, extraordinary thing. No, the practice seems to be as common with the king, with the householder as it is with the pious Brâhmaṇa. We have, in my opinion, to see here the key to what is often called the social reform of Buddhism, what, however, in reality, is only a further development of prevailing conditions—I mean the admission of all to the Buddhistic fold irrespective of their caste.

When later, as the followers of Buddha formed an organised body and introduced special rules, the admission of people of the Buddhist faith into the order was effected through the act of initiation and this was characterised as pabbajjâ as going out, no new thing was created; and nothing that was not known to Brahmanical law—the entrance of a Brâhmaṇa into the state of a hermit (vânaprastha) was extremely well-known—was introduced into the life of the Buddhistic order. Even before Buddha's time, the custom of escaping from the worldly state and retiring from home into the isolation of the forest, was not confined to the Brâhmaṇas. As he himself, a *Khattiya* of the proud family of Śâkya princes, exchanged the glitter and pomp of worldly life for the homeless condition of the ascetic, so other sons "of aristocratic families" followed the tendency of that time and renounced their home in order to obtain possession of " the highest perfection of a holy striving."[1] Among the disciples who followed his doctrine we find, along with young Brâhmaṇas, people belonging to his own station and sons of rich tradesmen and high officials. They are all to be looked upon by us not as members of a well-organised order of monks—such an order was created centuries later—but rather as nothing else than

[1] See Oldenberg, *Buddha*, p. 158.

Tâpasas on *Samaṇas*, whom we come across so often in the Jâtakas who group round the person of a teacher (gaṇasatthā) and listen to his word.

It will perhaps be stated against me that precisely at this point the Jâtakas do not exhibit the actual conditions of the pre-Buddhistic period but that their authors have put the later rules of the Buddhistic order back into earlier times. For this supposition, however, there is no sufficient ground, for in the first place, the possibility that all Aryan Indians in ancient times could embrace the homeless condition appears from the Brahmanical law books themselves.[1] Then again—and this in my opinion places the correctness of the accounts in the Jātakas beyond question—we find this very thing in the report of Megasthenes who was sent about the year 300 B.C., as a messenger of Seleukas to the court of Candragupta in Pâtaliputra—and thus in eastern

[p. 41.] India, the heart of Buddhism. He places at the head of the Indian society which he divides into 7 γένη as first γενος the σοφισται and says of these that they again fall into two γενη, namely, the βραχμαναι and the Σαρμαναι. Whilst he understands by

---

[1] A limitation of this to Brâhmaṇas only follows, when in a passage of Manu in which he speaks of the homeless condition of a dvija, one understands by the word only a Brâhmaṇa.

the first Brâhmaṇas in general—whom he, probably impelled by the fact that they, like the Samaṇas led the life of a hermit, puts with these in the same class—he makes the description which he gives of the Σαρμαναι applicable to the *Samaṇas* or ascetics of our text[1]; above all—and this concerns us here—he applies to them the proposition which is used wrongly in Greek reports with regard to the σοφισται in general, the proposition, namely, that whereas marriages between the separate castes are not allowed, nor is any change from one profession to another permissible, every man can adopt this condition.[2]

Also in Sanskrit literature we find instances of a non-Brâhmaṇa entering into the
[p. 42.] ascetic state and especially, of a râjarshi, king, abdicating and becoming an ascetic. The story in the Râmâyaṇa of the quarrel between Vaśishṭha and Viśvâmitra

---

[1] Strabo, Geographica, Lib XV., Cap. 1, 60.

[2] Arriani, *Indica*, Cap XII. 8. 9. Departing from this Strabo says (XV. 1, 49) that every class is assigned its special profession which cannot be exchanged for any other, that, however, the φιλοσοφοι were an exception, that is, they could adopt any profession. Whilst that which Arrian has said of the σοφισται in general is true of the *Samaṇas* and not of Brâhmaṇas, what Strabo says is true of the Brâhmaṇas and not of the ascetics. These sources supplement each other and give us the result to which the Jâtakas lead, namely, that on the one hand, ascetics were recruited from all classes and on the other, the most divergent professions were followed by the Brâhmaṇas.

is well-known. In order to obtain the cow of the holy Vasishṭha, king Viśvamitra retires into the solitude of a forest, after handing over the reins of government to his son, where by means of severe austerities he tries to acquire mastery over his opponent. He obtains through his asceticism the weapon of the gods and attacks Vaśishṭha *de novo* but the latter survives this attack by reason of his rank as Brâhmaṇa. Then the king resolves, as only a Brâhmaṇa can defeat a .Brâhmaṇa, to attain the rank of a Brahmaṇa. After a thousand years of severe austerities, he receives from Brahmâ the title of a "kingly seer (râjarshi)" ; not satisfied with this, he practises further penance till he frightens the gods and at the request of these, Brahmâ raises him to the rank of a Brâhmaṇa.

Now one cannot here properly speak of the entrance of the king into the state of an ascetic, as Viśvamitra practises austerities for the sake of a special, transitory object ; but here in the Râmâyaṇa the practice is repeatedly mentioned, by which kings when in advanced age exchanged the crown for the solitude of the forest ; thus, for examplé, we notice it when Lakshmaṇa points out to his brother Râma (II. 23, 26) that according to the custom of the old kingly seers (pûrvarâjarshivṛittyâ) residence in the forest takes place after one has left the subjects to the care of the sons, so that they protect them like children, as well as in Râma's words (II. 94.19), "This the kingly seers (râjarshayaḥ), my ancestors, named nectar, this residence in a forest for the sake of the life after death."

Very often we meet with the form *râjarshi* in the Mahâbhârata. In the celebrated Sâvitrî episode in the third book, Sâvitrî chooses as his consort Satyavâna, the son of the blind Dyumatsena who was robbed of his kingdom and practises austerities in the forest with his
[p. 43.] wife and his son.[1] In the ninth book it is narrated how Duryodhana voluntarily offered Yudhishṭhira of his own free will an uncontested kingdom, explaining that he wanted to go into the forest, clad in two animal skins (vanam eva gamishyâmi vasâno mṛigacarmaṇî IX.31.52). Yudhishṭhira declines the offer and challenges him to a duel ; but after Duryodhana is defeated and his kingdom falls to Yudhishṭhira, the latter resolves, being himself tired of sovereignty, to practise austerities in the forest. "The wrong that has happened," so he explains to his brother Arjuna (XII. 7.37 sq.) "is expiated by virtue, by open confession, repentance, begging alms or by castigation, world-renunciation,

---

[1] III. 294.9 : sa bâlavatsayâ sârddhaṃ bhâryayâ prasthito vanam mahâraṇyaṃ gataś câpi tapas tepe mahâvrataḥ.

pilgrimage to sacred places or recitation of sacred verse. He who has renounced the world cannot sin any more, so goes the revelation. When, as the revelation teaches, a man renounces the world, he has neither birth nor death, then he is merged, after he has found the right path by conscious striving, in Brahma. So will I alone, a seer in possession of knowledge, go into the forest and take leave of you all."

In the later classical Sanskrit poetry, many imitations of these old stories are found, among other places, in the Raghuvaṃśa when it is said of Raghu that "withdrawing his heart from the sensuous world he gave the young son as a token of kingly dignity the white umbrella and went with the queen to the shades of the trees of the ascetic's forest: This was what the custom of the Ikshvâku family demanded when a man's youth was over" (III. 70). "For," so it is said in another place (VIII. 11), "the descendants of Dilîpa led in their old age, after handing over the reins of government to their virtuous sons, through extreme self-discipline the life of an ascetic, clad in the bark of trees."

Consequently, the phenomenon, although in Brahmanical literature it is treated as an unusual phenomenon[1] and as the custom of a

[1] One should consider that Visvâmitra seeks to attain by his penance a special object, that Dyumatsena is robbed of his kingdom,

legendary king of ancient times, and although more frequently—as in the later [p. 44.] chapters of the Mahâbhârata—the rightness of such an act is doubted,[1] the phenomenon of a king abdicating in favour of his grown-up son and himself retiring into the solitude of the forest was not at all unknown in Brahmanical lands. What was characteristic, however, of the culture of the East, as it was reflected in the Jâtakas, was the universality which attached to the phenomenon of homeless asceticism.

Not only did world-sick old people renounce the world but even kings who were in undisputed possession of sovereignty and in the fulness of their power; young princes preferred the severe life of the ascetic to the glitter of sovereign power; rich tradesmen gave away their riches

---

that Duryodhana has before his eyes the enjoyment of sovereign power and that Yudhishṭhira is stricken with grief at the death of his brother Karṇa.

[1] *Cf.* E. W. Hopkins, *The social and military position of the ruling caste in ancient India, as represented by the Sanskrit Epic.* In the "Journal of the American Oriental Society," Vol. 13, p. 179 sq., Hopkins speaks of the entrance of a king into the ascetic state as a change of caste. A change of caste, however, this action does not itself produce, especially, when, as is related of Viśvamitra, a king tries through austerities to reach the rank of a Brâhmaṇa. The priestly compilers of the epics wanted to see in the resignation of the kingdom and acceptance of the homeless condition, as they looked upon the last as a privilege of the Brâhmaṇas, an inadmissible change of caste.

and heads of families their wives and children in order to build a hut in the forests of the Himâlaya and to live on roots and fruits or to eke out an existence by begging alms. The thought of the transitoriness of earthly goods, of the unworthiness of human existence supplies generally the impulse to renounce the world. Similar narratives to those we find in the holy texts of the Buddhists about Buddha himself and his taking leave of his home,[1] we meet with even in the Jâtakas and are to some extent like these of great poetical beauty.
[p. 45.] Thus, in Yuvañjaya Jâtaka (IV. 119 sq.) it is narrated how the heir-presumptive one day drives early in his carriage and goes with a brilliant following to a delightful spot in the park. And as he sees dew-drops sparkling like pearls in a necklace on the leaves of the trees, on blades of grass and in the webs of the spiders he asks the driver of the carriage what they are. "They are dew-drops, O King, which arise in cold weather," the latter replies. In the evening, when the heir to the throne comes again, the dew has disappeared; he asks the driver, "Friend, where are the dew-drops, I don't see them any more?" "O King, when the sun rises they vanish and disappear in the earth." When the prince hears this, he cries

[1] *Cf.* Oldenberg, Buddha, p. 106 sq.

out in grief, "Even this life,[1] this being is like the dew-drop which hangs from the top of the blade of grass; I will take leave of my parents and become an ascetic before disease, age and death overcome me." Thus, a dew-drop produces in him the thought of the non-reality of existence;[2] he goes home to his father who sits in great pomp in the Council Hall, accosts him with reverence and requests to be allowed to adopt the homeless condition:

"The lord of the chariot-driver surrounded by friends and ministers, I adore; I will go into solitude, O great king, may the Lord permit me to do this."

The king, however, wants him to desist and recites the second verse:

"If you lack pleasure, I will create this for you. I will crush him who gives you pain, don't go away, O Yuvañjaya."

To this the prince replies:

"I don't lack pleasures nor do I know anybody who hurts me; but I want to light a light which age cannot extinguish."

Repeated requests of his father do not succeed in dissuading him from his [p. 46.] resolve and even to the imploring mother he replies:

---

[1] Jîvitasaṃkhârâpi, properly, "the phemomena of life, what seems real is life."

[2] "Iti ussâvabindum eva ârammaṇaṃ katvâ âditte viya tayo bhave passanto," lit. "whilst he, starting from the dew-drops, looks upon the three states (disease, age, death) as flames."

"Like a dew-drop on the blade of grass at sunrise is the life of man (*i.e.*, as transitory as this); don't try to dissuade me, dear mother."

When finally the king gives him permission, he leaves the city with his younger brother Yudhiṭṭhila; the great mass of people who accompanies them, they send back and both go to the Himâlaya and after building a hermitage at a charming place, they lead the life of a homeless ascetic; they feed upon the roots and fruits of the forest and reach, after acquiring the highest knowledge with the help of meditation, the world of Brahma after death.

As in this narrative, a dew-drop, so in other cases (I. 138; III. 393) a grey hair, is the *ârammaṇam*, the cause which gives the king the thought of renouncing the sovereign power and going into the forest. In the Cullasutasoma Jâtaka (V. 177 sq.), the father of king Sutasoma whose barber has plucked a grey hair, tries to dissuade him from his resolve and points to his minor children. "If you, O dear Sutasoma, do not have so much love for your parents, see, you have sons and daughters of tender age who cannot live without you; when they are grown up you may go into the homeless condition." These representations, however, succeed as little in dissuading Sutasoma as the earnest prayers of his pregnant wife and his seven-year-old son who clings to his neck.

In another case, the signs of the heavens show the king the transitoriness of his worldly pomp. In the Gandhâra Jâtaka (III. 364) the minister informs the king that the moon is seized by Rahu.[1] The king looks at the moon and reflects, "This moon is soiled by accidental dirt, and rendered lustre- [p. 47.] less; my filth is this kingly pomp; it is not, however, proper that I should become lustreless like this which is seized by Râhu. Therefore I will, like the disc of the moon in a clear sky, renounce my kingdom and lead the life of a hermit. What do I care for other people's opinion? Released from my family and my followers, I will consult only myself and move about from place to place; this is proper for me." With the words, "Act according to your wishes," he gives the reins of Government to the ministers.

We should not be surprised at the fact that the prescription which among the Brâhmaṇas the law makes concerning residence in the forest as the third stage (âśrama) of life, is found also in the Jâtakas. Less obvious is the fact that even among worldly Brâhmaṇas who, as we

[1] Name of the Demon who attacks the moon and the sun, thereby causing their eclipses.

shall see, have often nothing in common with the proper representatives of their caste except the name, the adoption of the homeless condition is mentioned. So far as these Brâhmaṇas were in the service of the king, they had probably to get the permission of their lord before they could exchange their worldly state for the homeless condition; for the king did not always agree in this way to lose his servants. Kassapa, the son of the king's house priest, reflects in the Lomasakassapa Jâtaka, "My friend has become a king and will lend me powerful help. But what should I require help for? I will take leave of my parents and the king (or "ask their permission," *mâtâpitaro ca râjânañ ca âpucchitvâ*. III. 515) and adopt the homeless condition."

When a rich Brâhmaṇa on an inspection of his jewel-room reads on a gold tablet the name of his ancestor by whom the properties were acquired, the thought occurs to him, "Those by whom the riches were accumulated are no more; the treasures are still there, not a single person has taken them with him during his departure. Verily, one cannot put money into a bag and take it with him to the other world." He goes to the king, begs his permission, gives away his entire wealth and goes as an ascetic to the Himâlaya (IV. 7).

That even a whole Brâhmaṇa family, including the parents and two sons,
[p. 48.]
renounces worldly life is mentioned (V. 313). As the eldest son is not willing to lead the life of the householder and as the younger brother also wishes to adopt with him the homeless condition, the parents reflect, "These treat with contempt the enjoyment of the senses, though they are so young; how much more contemptuously should we then treat it; we will all together renounce the householder's life." They inform the king of their resolve, give away their entire wealth (eight hundred millions!) from which they keep only a legitimate portion for their kinsmen, set their slaves free and move out of the city to the Himâlaya.[1]

Often an insight into the efforts and activities of people in one's own station, the knowledge of the deceits practised by them through greediness, makes homelessness appear to a virtuous Brâhmaṇa more worthy than honour and wealth in worldly life. The young Brâhmaṇa scholar (II. 422) who receives from his teacher, in answer to the question, How can one succeed

---

[1] That women, either alone or along with their own people, retire into the solitude of the forest is very often mentioned in the Jâtakas, *e.g.*, III. 382; IV. 23, 484. According to the law books, the dvija is free when he renounces worldly life to leave his wife to the care of his sons or to take her with him into the forest. Manu VI. 3. *Cf.* Apastamba II. 9, 22, 8-9; Vishṇu LXXXXIV. 3; Yâjñavalkya III. 45.

in the world? the reply that he can do so only by intrigue and bad practices, chooses *pabbajjâ* with the words:

"Even when a man wanders homeless, dish in hand, this is better than this immorality."

Whilst we meet with instances in Sanskrit literature of Kshatriyas embracing the ascetic life, the preference among people for this practice of world-renunciation seems to be confined to eastern countries; here, however, it seems to prevail very much. Thus, we are told of members of aristocratic families who were fitted by their education to take part in the spiritual life, that even they follow this practice which owes its origin principally to spiritual causes. The rich *seṭṭhi* makes over,
[p. 49.]
as soon as his son can walk, all his possessions, along with his wife and child, to his younger brother, in the consciousness of the worthlessness of worldly enjoyments and the bliss of world-renunciation, and goes as an ascetic to the Himâlaya (III. 300). The same thing is narrated in the Veluka Jâtaka of the members of a very rich family (*mahâbhogakula* I. 245). As is natural, in these circles of householders, difficulties arise in the way of their carrying out their resolve; the relations who have to suffer in consequence of their supporter going away, try to dissuade him

in every way. Many of the Jâtakas relate the opposition between the wish of the family head to renounce the world and the claims of the family remaining at home.[1] Thus, for instance, we read in the Bandhanâgâra Jâtaka (II. 139 sq.) "Once upon a time, when Brahmadatta ruled in Benares, the Bodhisatta was re-born in the family of a poor *gahapati*. When he grew up, his father died and he supported his mother by working for a salary. His mother, however, quite against his will brought for him as his wife a girl of good family and died soon after. Now, his wife
[p. 50.] became pregnant; he, however, knew nothing of her condition and said to

---

1 Of an inner conflict between one's conviction of the worthlessness of the world and the duties towards one's dependents which in our view must arise when, on account of the bread-winner going away, the family is thrown into poverty, no trace is found; such duties don't exist for the Buddhists or are subordinate to the strong desire for emancipation. In this respect Buddhism comes in contact with the views of the older Christian Church. Hieronymus writes a letter to Heliodor, urging him to leave his family and become a monk. "Even if your little nephew throws his arms round your neck, if your mother tears her hair and cloth and beats her breast which sucked you, even if your father throws himself upon the ground before you —— move even the body of your father, flee with tearless eyes to the sign of the cross. In this case, cruelty is the only virtue." "For," says the same Hieronymus in another letter, "how many monks have lost their souls, because they had pity for their father and mother!" *Cf.* Eicken, Geschichte und System der mittelalterlichen Weltanschauung, Stuttgart, 1887, p. 125.

her one day, "My wife, you must see to it that you can maintain yourself by work, for I will renounce the world." "O Lord, I am pregnant; wait till the child is born and you have seen it, and then become an ascetic." He was pleased with this and as soon as she was confined, he said. "Now, my dear, as you are happily confined, I will go into the homeless condition." "Wait till the child is weaned." And she became pregnant for the second time.

"If I wait for her word," reflected the man, "I shall never be able to come away. I will flee and become an ascetic without saying a word to her." So he said nothing to her, got up one night and fled. The city guards arrested him. "I have to support a mother," he cried, "let me go." In this way, he got his release and went straight to the Himâlaya, when the main gate was opened. Here he lived as a hermit, became possessed of supernatural powers and enjoyed the pleasures of meditation. "The fetters of wife and child, the fetters of passion, so difficult to break, I have broken," so he shouted triumphantly and recited the verses:

"The wise have not named the fetters which are made of iron, wood or rope, but the love of precious stones and ear-rings, of wife and child.

These fetters they have called strong, rooted to the ground, broad,[1] difficult to break; when they have broken these, the wise men wander, free from passion, desire and earthly happiness."

After the Bodhisatta in this way gives vent to his feelings without disturbing his meditation, he entered the world of Brahma.

Similar domestic difficulties a potter encounters who wants to exchange his profession for the life of an ascetic (III. 381). It appears in all these stories where the question is of
[p. 51.] the retirement of people of a lower class into the ascetic life, that there is some irony which rests upon this, that in the later Buddhistic society such *pabbajitâs*, although no doubt they had the right to be initiated, were not considered to have attained full asceticism. Only rarely in the Pali texts are people of a lower caste spoken of as members of the Buddhistic order,[2] and as this represents according to its external organisation only a development of pre-Buddhistic asceticism, it is probable that even among ascetics the lower castes were only represented in exceptional cases. No doubt in the Jâtakas we come across even Caṇḍâlas who adopt the homeless condition (IV. 392);

---

[1] *Sithila*, properly, "loose"; the meaning is, the fetters sit comfortably but are difficult to loosen.

[2] See Oldenberg, *Buddha*, p. 159.

but it seems to me, judging from their isolated and low position which excludes them from all communion with the Aryan people and as a consequence of this, from all participation in spiritual life that the actual existence of such holy men is extremely doubtful.

For it is in the spiritual region that we have to seek the cause of this asceticism ; the practice of world-renunciation, the retirement into the homeless condition is only the outward expression of that striving for knowledge and for emancipation which dominated large circles of society of eastern India in Buddha's time. Neither the study of the holy scripture nor occupation with religious things in general was in that time restricted to the learned Brahmanas ; other classes and professions took part in this search for truth, in the solution of the highest questions of metaphysics ; among these we have in the front line the *Khattiyas.*

CHAPTER IV

THE RULING CLASS

It will, however, be well before we examine more closely the question of the participation of the *khattiyas* in the spiritual activities of that time, to make clear who the *khattiyas* were. We are accustomed to identify the Pali expression corresponding in Sanskrit to the word *kshatriya* with "warrior" and thus characterise the second highest caste in the Brahmanical theory as "warrior caste." If we, however, freeing ourselves from the influence of the theory consider the data relating to the *kshatriyas* contained in the epics, then we become aware that the expression "warrior" applies only in a certain sense to them, that we have rather to understand by a *kshatriya* a member of the ruling class which includes the king, his great lords and vassals, along with the higher portions of the army.[1] In a still more narrow sense is the concept of the *khattiya* of the Pali texts to be understood; it corresponds to the Vedic *rájanya* and is applied to the descendants of the victorious classes under whose leadership the Aryan people acquired their new dwelling-places in

[p. 52.]

[1] *Cf.* Hopkins, l. c., p. 73.

the Gangetic lands and to the conquerors of the aboriginal peoples who in their fight with foreign invaders maintained their independence. According to this, there belong to the *khattiya* class the kings standing at the head of the great monarchies of the east with their kinsmen—the rulers of Kośala, Magadha, Videha, etc.,—further, the ruling princely houses of the small bordering states of this kingdom, such as the family of the Sâkyas in Kapilavatthu, the Mallas of Kusinârâ and Pâvâ, the Licchavis of Vesâlî; on the other hand, the holders of high political and military offices do not belong as such to this class but only so far as they are connected with ruling houses. In the time of war, probably, there fell to the *khattiyas* who were also invested with the highest offices in the army, the chief part in the conduct of the war and so far they could be looked upon as "warriors *par excellence*"; but it would be a mistake to suppose that the *khattiyas* only held military offices or that the army was composed only of *khattiyas*.[1]

---

[1] Of passages in which *khattiya* is used as a synonym for *râjan*, I have made the following list from the Jâtakas. II. 166; III. 106; 154; V. 99 sq., 112. When the talk is of the warriors of the king, the Pali texts have other expressions, such as *balakâye* (III. 319) or *yodhâ* (Mahâvagga I. 40.2); even the esteemed military leaders (senânâyake mahâmatte) hardly belonged to the *khattiya* caste—otherwise, they would have been described as such—but rather to the *râjabhogga* or *râjañña* class of which we shall speak later.

The *khattiyas* are the representatives of political power; they symbolise the [p. 53.] idea of a community which stands above the family, above the caste, the idea, namely of the State. If, however, this is so, the question naturally arises: Are we justified in combining all *khattiyas* into a unity, to which the word "caste" can be applied? In no way, if we take the word in its modern sense. The conflicting political interests of the different ruling families would alone prevent their union into an organised body; they must render absolutely illusory the exercise of judicial rights by which offences against caste prescriptions were punished by excommunication from the caste or in other ways. But even a caste in the sense of the Brahmanical theory we cannot properly see in the *khattiya* of the Pali texts as it lacks, for reasons just mentioned, the compactness of it. Certain customs, especially, those relating to connubium and the prohibition of all impurity, may be noticed in certain ruling families which led to separation from the rest of the population; but these customs—for whose existence, moreover, only isolated evidence can be found in the Jâtakas—do not seem to have the authority of laws the observance of which was enjoined upon the *khattiyas* and whose transgression was made punishable. The king, however, according to the Brahmanical lawbooks, stands above the caste for this reason, that the prescriptions relating to impurity do not apply to him. Probably, the remaining non-ruling members of the ruling houses were more subject to rules relating to marriage and prohibition of impurity than the king himself; instances which show the actual occurrence of cases in which the transgression of caste-rules was visited with some form of punishment, especially, with excommunication from the caste, are very rare in the Jâtakas.

The *khattiyas* of ancient times formed, in my opinion, like the dynasties of princes
[p. 54.] in other lands, a class by themselves, a class with only this difference, that it acquired in India to a greater extent than elsewhere the character of a caste or rather gradually acquired in course of time this character. For to the distinct consciousness of rank, the prominent characteristic of the ruling class in other lands, there was joined in India the customs, probably handed down from ancient times, which made marriage within the jâti the rule and tried to prohibit all impurity arising from mixture with the lower classes and even contact with them, and thus led to a specially sharp, caste-like division.

We have already mentioned a significant instance to which further examples from the

Jâtakas can be joined. It is never heard that a Khattiya is addressed by his name or in the second person by any person belonging to the lower classes.[1] The mother of King Udaya whom the barber Gaṅgamâla calls by his family name (kulanamena, *i.e.*, by the name of his father Brahmadatta) cries angrily. "This filthy son of a barber, of low origin (hînajacca, III. 452), forgets himself so much that he calls my son, lord of earth, who is a *Khattiya* by caste, Brahmadatta." Even with regard to a Brâhmaṇa the *Khattiya* feels his superiority so much that king Arindama calls Sonaka, the son of a *purohita*, a man of low birth (hînajacca V. 257). Himself he calls *asambhinnakhattiyavamse jâta*, born

[p. 55.] in a family with an uninterrupted succession of princes, *i.e.*, in a family the members of which both on their father and their mother's side were recognised as *khattiyas* The *khattiyas* attached great importance to purity of blood and did not consider any person who through his mother or through his father belonged to another

[1] Even in the epics the rule holds that younger persons or persons of the same age can be addressed "thou," but that a man must address his superior (older) neither by 'thou' nor by his real name. Mhbh. XII 193·25, twaṃkâraṃ nâmadheyaṃ ca jyeshthânâm parivarjayet. Cf. Hopkins l.c.p. 25 note.

[2] For a Brâhmaṇa to be called hînajacca even by a king is rare. A similar idea is found in Kalpasûtra, Jinacarita §17 to which Prof. Jacobi has drawn my attention. Brâhmaṇa families are here placed in the same class with lower, poor, begging families.

caste, of pure blood, even if they looked upon him as of the same status as themselves. Hence also the repeatedly occurring expression used of a king (I. 177 ; IV. 42 ; V. 123) : *mahâraja mâtâ-pitusu khattiya*, "O great king, by father and mother, a khattiya."

If now even in our eyes, the *khattiyas* of the Pali texts have a caste-like character, on account of their consciousness of their high status and their attaching great value to purity of blood, we should not be surprised if they were looked upon by the authors of the Buddhistic canon as a "caste." Too much influenced by the Brahmanical theory, too much inclined by virtue of their being Indians to schematise, with the result that they made distinctions between class, caste, common status and profession, they saw in the *Khattiyas* as much a caste as in the *Brâhmaṇas*. Consequently, everywhere in the Pali texts, *khattiyas* are spoken of as a "caste"; along with the Brâhmaṇas, Vessas and Suddas, they are mentioned and mentioned as the first in the caste-series.

This circumstance that in the enumeration of the castes the *khattiyas* are mentioned first[1] (III. 19 ; IV. 205, 303) is not a matter of

[1] Digha Nikâya III 1.15, even in the mouth of a Brâhmaṇa. This no doubt fits in ill with the following words : "Of these (four castes), three, kh. v. and s., exist only to serve the Brâhmaṇas."

secondary importance. As from Brahmanical sources which place the Brâhmaṇas always at the head[1] whenever the castes are enumerated, not only the claim of the Brâhmaṇas to be the best caste but also their real position as such within the specially Brahmanical culture-sphere, can be inferred, so we have, in my opinion, in this
[p. 56.] assigning of the premier position to the Khattiyas a reaction brought about by the view which prevails in the eastern Buddhistic lands and by the balance of power which rules here. The superior position of the *khattiyas* in the eastern countries and the corresponding decline of Brahmanical influence present themselves to us with irresistible necessity when we study the Pali literature; even the Jâtakas affirm the correctness of this view.

In the introduction to the Jâtakas, in the Nidânakathâ which in a legendary form contains the history of Buddha before his last birth, as well as his life-history before the attainment of his *Buddha* condition, it is narrated that the future Buddha reflects in which caste he will be re-born. "The Buddhas," he thinks, "have never been born in the Vessa or the Sudra caste, but they have been born in one or other of the

[1] *Cf.* Weber, *Collectanea über die Kastenverhältnisse in den Brâhmaṇa und Sûtra. Indische Studien*, Vol. 10, p. 37.

two highest classes, the Khattiya caste or the Brâhmaṇa caste; and because *just now the Khattiya caste is the highest* [1] (I. 49), I will take my rebirth in this caste." One should never, however, attach much importance to this sentence as well as to the prominence given to *Khattiya* monks in other passages of the Nidânakathâ and in the explanation of the commentator mentioned above (§ 10 of Chap. 2), because the Nidânakathâ,[2] in which really we see no portion of the Jâtakas but rather a tradition independent of it and externally connected with it, as well as the

[p. 57.] commentary is of later origin and because its author probably imagines that the caste to which Buddha actually belonged is the highest. On the other hand, it must be admitted that such haughtiness as is exhibited in the words of Arindama (V. 257) already quoted, is hardly thinkable if the *Khattiya* did not as a matter

---

[1] The same view is found expressed in very similar words in the *Lalita Vistara* Ch. III : " The Bodhisattva was not born in lower families (hînakuleshu), Caṇḍâla families or in the families of flutemakers or wheelwrights (rathakara), or in Pukkasa families. Rather he has appeared only in two castes (kuladvaye), in the Brâhmaṇa caste and the Kshatriya caste. When the Brâhmaṇas are held in great esteem in the world he appears in Brâhmaṇa families; when the Kshatriyas stand in high esteem, he is born in Kshatriya families. Now-a-days, their monks hold the Kshatriyas in the highest esteem; therefore, the Bodhisattvas appear in the Kshatriya caste.

[2] I. 57 : sace pi Buddho bhavissati khattiyasamaṇeh' eva purakkhataparivârito vicarissati.

of fact feel himself as of higher rank than the Brâhmaṇas. This perfectly agrees with the description given in the Digha Nikâya of the interview between the Brâhmaṇa Pokkharasâdi and the Kosala King Pasenadi : "The latter"—so it is said (III. 26)—"never allows the Brâhmaṇa who is a dependant of his to see his face ; even when he consults him he speaks to him through a curtain." This is further in agreement with the complaint of the Brâhmaṇa Ambaṭṭha regarding the conduct of the haughty Sâkyas.[1] The complaint is as follows : He came one day to Kapilavatthu and entered the hall of the Sâkyas where they were seated upon high chairs. At his entrance he was pushed back with the finger [2] amidst a loud outburst of laughter, and indeed they made merry at his expense and nobody asked him to take his seat.

This account, borrowed from the incidents of everyday life, too circumstantial to be considered a purely fictitious example, an evidence of the haughtiness of the members of the ruling

---

[1] Even the Jâtakas narrate this haughtiness of the Sâkyas, thus (I. 88) : Sâkiyâ nâma mânajâtikâ mânatthaddhâ ; IV. 145 : ime Sakyâ nâma jâtiṃ nissâya atimânino.

[2] The "pushing with the finger" (aṅgulipatodaka) relates to the offence noted in Pâtimokkha. Patimokkha : Pâcittiya 52. Acc. to the explanation given in Suttavibhaṅga it consists in this, that every one touches the body of every one else in order to make him laugh. *Cf.* Vinaya Piṭaka ed. by H. Oldenberg, Vol. 3, p. 84 ; Vol. 4, p. 110 sq.

class in their dealings with the Brâhmaṇas, seems to me of no less weight than the later, (III. 1.24) more theoretical discussions between Buddha and Ambaṭṭha relating to the question whether a son born of the union of a Khattiya's son with a Brâhmaṇa girl was legitimate or not.

The young Brâhmaṇa must accept
[p. 58.] the answer that a son born of such a mixed marriage would get his seat and water among the Brâhmaṇas, that he would participate in the sacrifices and in the meals, that he would be instructed and that he could marry their women, but that, on the other hand, the *Khattiyas* would never take him up into their caste. For on his mother's side, he is not of equal rank with them. Similarly, should the two castes look upon a son born of the union of a Brâhmaṇa's son and a Khattiya's daughter; here also the Brâhmaṇas should look upon him as of equal rank, while the Khattiyas cannot regard him as their equal, on account of his not being of the same rank on his father's side. Even this Ambaṭṭha has to admit that the Brâhmaṇas, when they have driven one of their members for any cause out of the kingdom or town and disgraced him, cannot take him back into their society but can safely allow a Khattiya excommunicated from his caste to participate in meals, in sacrifice and in instruction, and even to marry

amongst them. "Consequently, O Ambaṭṭha," cries out Buddha at the end of the discourse, "even when a Khâttiya has fallen into the lowest depths, he is still the best and the Brâhmaṇas are (in comparison with him) low," and adds the verse which occurs repeatedly in Buddhistic Suttas: "The *Khattiya* is considered the highest by men who attach value to family" (Khattiya seṭṭho jane tasmiṃ yo gottapaṭisârino).

One cannot help noticing, while reading this paragraph, the influence of a subjective bias on the part of the Buddhistic author; it is not to be supposed that orthodox Brâhmaṇas, proud of their caste, recognised even in Buddhistic lands a Khattiya excommunicated from, and despised by his caste as a Brâhmaṇa and treated him as such; such cases may occasionally have taken place; in its general form, Ambaṭṭha's admission does not seem to me at all acceptable.

But even when we ascribe a great portion of the pre-eminence of the Khattiyas appearing in the Pali texts to the monks who were [p. 59.] ill-disposed towards Brahmanism, there remains enough ground for supposing an actual superiority of the ruling class.[1] And this

[1] Chalmers explains (*Journal of the Royal Asiatic Society*, 1894, p. 342) the pre-eminence of the Khattiya caste in the Piṭaka by saying that this confirms the old tradition which represents the original conception, according to which "the kingly classes as they arose first held the

superiority of the Khattiyas appears not only in the social domain which was assured to them through their material power itself; just in the spiritual region, the princely families of the East fought for supremacy with Brâhmaṇas engaged in the ceremonial of the sacrifice as well as with grossly worldly Brâhmaṇas. We need not confine ourselves to Buddhistic literature to prove this; it is a known fact that in the Upanishads kings appear very often as teachers of Brâhmaṇas.[1] This circumstance makes the supposition well-grounded that the deep thoughts of the Upanishad doctrine which

---

supreme position in Indian society" and that it represents the transition period in which the Brahmanical claim to pre-eminence, although advanced with great arrogance, was not universally recognised, at least not from the side of the Khattiyas. If this is true, then the Brâhmaṇa texts which assert the superiority of the priestly classes as an indisputable fact represent a later stage of evolution of Indian culture, which assumption will not, however, do. The difference between the account in the Pali texts and that in the Brahmanical ones lies partly in the real balance of power which in the east was never on the side of the priestly class and partly in the subjective bias of the Buddhistic authors, on the one hand who oppose Brahmanism and that of the Brâhmaṇas, on the other, who worship their caste inordinately.

[1] Deussen, *System des Vedanta*, Lpz. 1883, p. 18: "Numerous indications point to this, that the proper guardians of this thought were not originally so much the priestly classes who were content with ceremonials as the *Khattiyas*; over and over again, we meet in the Upanishads with the situation that the Brâhmaṇa asks for instruction from the *Kshatriya* which the latter, after all manner of reflexions on the impropriety of such a procedure, gives him." *Cf.* also the essay of Garbe, *Die Weisheit des Brahmanen order des Kriegers?* in "Nord und Süd," 1895.

culminated in the identity of the Âtman, the All-One, with one's own self did not [p. 60.] proceed from Brahmanical circles but that we have to look for the intellectual originators of this doctrine in the ranks of the *Khattiyas*. To them also fell not a small share in the further development of the ideas contained in the Upanishads, in the building up of the doctrine of the migration of souls and emancipation, and after the ground had been prepared, through a growing influence of pessimistic views, for a doctrine of salvation which showed the way out of the painful circles of the migration of souls, it was reserved for a Khattiya to show this path, namely, Gotama of the family of the Sâkyas of Kapilavatthu.

Moreover, we can strengthen the proposition that there fell to the ruling class an essential portion of the duty of solving the problems which agitated all minds before and in Buddha's time by the proof—without this it would probably have only an aerial foundation—that, according to the accounts of the Jâtakas, the Khattiya of the eastern lands enjoyed a spiritual culture similar to that of the Brahmaṇa. It is true that, in accordance with the law books even in the distinctly Brahmanical [1] lands, the

---

[1] Gautama XI. 3; Manu VII. 43.

three Vedas were prescribed for the king; as a matter of fact, however, this prescription, as the epics show, was purely theoretical; the knowledge of the Veda which is demanded of a prince, relates evidently to the *dhanurveda*, "the Veda of the bow," archery, the science of war.[1] On the other hand, there occur various passages in the Jâtakas which leave no room for doubt that the sons of princes had to devote, like the Brâhmaṇa youths, a certain time of their life to religious studies. In the Gâmaṇicaṇḍa Jâtaka the king himself gives the prince instruction for seven years in the three Vedas and in all worldly duties (*tayo vede sabbañ ca loke kàttabbam.* II. 297). Generally, the prince is sent to a Brâhmaṇa and is taught by him. The Vedas are not always mentioned distinctly as the subject of the
[p. 61.] studies to which the Brâhmaṇa introduces the young princes; what is said, on the contrary, most generally is that the prince learnt the sciences (*sippâni* II. 2) or "the science" (*sippam.* II. 278). Other passages make it appear probable that in this concept of *sippa* the three Vedas are included. Thus we read in the Dhonasâkha Jâtaka: "Princes and Brâhmaṇa youths from all parts

---

[1] *Cf.* Hopkins, l. c. p. 108 sq.

of India learnt the science from him (*khattiya-māṇavā ca brāhmaṇamāṇavā ca tass' eva santike sippam uggaṇhiṃsu.* III. 158). Even the son of the King of Benares learnt the Vedas from him." Similarly, it is said in the Thusa Jâtaka: "The Bodhisatta was a world-renowned teacher in Takkasilâ and instructed many princes and young Brâhmaṇas in the science (bahû rajakumâre ca brahmanakumâre ca sippaṃ vâcesi. III. 122). Even the son of the King of Benares went to him at the age of sixteen and learnt the three Vedas and all the sciences" (*tayo vede sabbasippâni ca*). So also in the Dummedha Jâtaka, mention is made at first of the instruction of sixteen-year-old princes in general (soḷasavassapadesiko hutvâ Takkasilâyaṃ sippaṃ ugganhitvâ. I. 259), and then there are mentioned in detail, as subjects of study, the three Vedas and eighteen branches of knowledge [1] (*tiṇṇam vedânam pâram gantvâ aṭṭhârasannam vijjaṭṭhânânam nipphattim pâpuni*). We shall have therefore to understand by *mante*,[2] which the Brâhmaṇa learnt

[1] On the *aṭṭhârasa vijjaṭṭhânâni*, see the remark on the discussion concerning the study of the Brâhmaṇas in the eighth chapter.

[2] In this sense the expressions *mante* and others are used in the Tittira Jâtaka, where it is said of the partridge that it listens, while the teacher teaches his pupils the *mante* and that in this way it learns the three Vedas (âcariyassa mânavânaṃ mante vâcentassa sutvâ tayo pi vede ugganhi. III. 537.)

in Takkasilâ and which he then, himself a world-renowned teacher, introduces to the young princes and Brâhmaṇas in Benares, very probably the Vedic hymns.

The following point also I might make good, and that is, that the young *Khattiyas* did not simply outwardly pursue the study of the

[p. 62.] Vedas, which, according to the law-books, is a duty binding upon all the "twice-born." In all places where the question is of the education of the *Khattiyas*, the age at which the youth leaves his paternal home and goes to his teacher is universally given as the sixteenth year of life (I. 259, 262, 273; II. 2, 87, 277; III. 122). If the young prince had up to then been instructed in his father's house in the elementary sciences and physical exercise, there followed, on the attainment of maturity, the higher spiritual culture, the religious study.[1] When it is explained in the Gâmaṇicaṇda Jâtaka (II. 297) that a prince who has been instructed by his father for seven years in the three Vedas, is only seven

[1] In contrast with this, the fulfilment of the duty of studying the Veda is looked upon in the epics as a purely external form. The education of the young noble seems here to end with the sixteenth year and in any case, it is inconceivable how a boy at this age not only attained perfection in the use of arms but also fortified his memory with the collection of hymns of one of the three Vedas. *Cf.* Hopkins, i, page 109 sq.

years old at the time of his father's death, we have to do with a marvellous child, a true prince of fiction,[1] whilst the remaining passages give us throughout the impression of a plain narrative.

As the place where the young princes go for their studies, Takkasilâ is invariably mentioned. The town, in Sanskrit Takshaśilâ, lies in Gandhâra land, in north-west India, and thus, far from the centres of Buddhistic culture. It seems clear that at the time to which our source refers this Takkasilâ was the centre of the spiritual life of India, a high school of Brahmanism, greater in importance than even Benares, for it is repeatedly mentioned that the kings of Kâsî send their sons to the distant Takkasilâ for study. It sounds improbable when we read of such journeys
[p. 63.] of young princes mentioned at the foot of the page[2] (II. 277), and we are

---

[1] Probably, the Maṇḍavyakumâra is to be placed in the same category, of whom it is said (IV. 379) that he was taught by Brâhmaṇas the three Vedas from his seventh or eighth year.

[2] All that the king gives his sixteen-year-old son is a pair of sandals with simple soles, a sunshade made of leaves and 1,000 kahâpaṇas, an equipment which cannot be called extravagant, when we learn that the money is not for boarding expenses but has to be handed over untouched to the teacher who asks the new-comer about the honorarium (âcariyabhâga) after he has learnt his position and family (II. 277 sq. *Cf.* V. 457).

inclined to ascribe their origin to the imagination of the narrator who knew the town probably only by name. Still one should consider that even in other Pali texts, Takkasilâ is mentioned as a great seat of learning and the destination of youths with a thirst for knowledge. Thus, we have Mahavagga VIII. 1.6, where it is explained that in Takkasilâ a world-renowned physician lived, to whom the young Jîvaka went from Râjagaha in order to learn his art. It seems to me therefore that there is no reason to compel us to mistrust the words in which the narrator praises the pedagogic wisdom of the kings of ancient times: "They sent"—so it is said in Tilamuṭṭhi Jâtaka (II. 277)—"their sons, although in their own city there lived a world-renowned teacher, to a great distance over the borders of the kingdom for learning the sciences, and they thought, in this way, their pride and haughtiness will be broken, they will learn to bear heat and cold and learn also the ways of the world."

CHAPTER V

The Head of the State

If our proposition is right, that by the *Khattiyas* of the Pali texts only the ruling families and not a nobility in possession of land and important military or political offices, are to be understood, it is clear that this class is only represented by its principal representative, the *râjan*. Apart from the mention [p. 64.] of *Khattiyas* in general, very little is said of the rest of the members of the ruling class; only, the viceroy, the *uparâjan*, appears occasionally by the side of the king, whilst this latter stands in the Jâtaka—one would like to say everywhere—in the centre of action.[1]

"The king is the head of men" (râjâ mukhaṃ manussânaṃ)—this oft-recurring expression in the Pali texts (Sutta Nipâta, p. 107; Mahâvagga VI. 35. 8), the counter-statement in relation to the Brahmanical doctrine, "The Brâhmaṇa is the head of all this" (Śatapatha Brâhmaṇa III. 9. 1, 14)—finds, as it were, an illustration

[1] That this phenomenon has its origin solely in the pre-eminent social position of the king, cannot certainly be maintained; this is partly explained by the fact that for a story "the king" is a specially favourite figure.

in the JÂtakas. The fabulous pomp with which we think the royal court of an Oriental despot to be surrounded, covers also here the king. "After his entry into the city"—so the Pañcagaru JÂtaka (I. 470) describes the royal entry of a prince—" he went to the spacious hall of the palace and took his seat in godly pomp upon a throne ornamented with precious stones, over which the white umbrella was spread ; surrounding him, there stood, adorned with all their ornaments, the ministers, the BrÂhmaṇas, the *Gahapati etc.*, and the princesses, whilst sixteen thousand dancing girls skilled in dancing, singing and music, sang and played, so that the palace resounded like an ocean with the roar of which was mixed the noise of thunder.

Corresponding to this magnificent exterior, there was not, as in the Indian courts of to-day, an inner want of power; the *râjan* of that time is not only " the magnificent, shining in royal pomp," he is, as his name signifies, in the first place,[1] " the ruling one." [p. 65.] The Brahmanical authorities, no doubt, especially, the lawbooks, see in the king in

[1] As the root from which *râjan* is to be derived, Aug. Fick (*Vergleichendes Wörterbuch* 4th Edition. Part I. p. 117) indicates *rez* with the meaning "stretch." To this root are to be traced, among others, the Sanskrit *râj*, to rule, Greek *'ορε'γω* to stretch, Lat. *rego*, to direct, Goth. *uf-rak-jan*, to stretch out, Mhd. *recken*. Sanskr. râj, râjan, consequently, denotes, exactly like the Latin *rex*, the Gallic *rix* in *Ambio-rix*,

several ways only "an appendage of the priests"; according to these the king is only there to supply the Brâhmaṇas with what they require.[1] It is different with the Jâtakas. Of a general control of the priestly caste over the administration, no traces are, in my opinion, to be found here or in other Pali literature. Where we meet with instances of a predominant influence on the part of the Brâhmaṇas, the reason is to be sought in the individual circumstances of the king and his spiritual advisers, especially, the royal house-priest, the *purohita*.

In general, the position of the king in the Jâtakas is the same as that in the older portions of ancient Indian epics, unaffected by priestly organisation. Here as there the political and military power rests with the king who is anything but a tool in the hands of the priests; for the power of the latter is here also purely personal. The Brâhmaṇas are dependent upon the king, from him they

---

the Gothic *reiks*, originally, "director, guide." The meaning "shine" from Skr. râj seems to have developed as a secondary phenomenon. At any rate, the proposition enunciated by Georg Curtis (*Kleine Schriften*, Leipzig 1886, Part I, p. 65)—Rajân denotes, "according to the derivation by the Indians, what shines, that which shows princely pomp" and this is "the most external and superficial name and one which does not touch the essence but only the appearance of royal power)"—seems to have no real basis.

[1] *Cf.* Hopkins l. c. p. 72.

receive their property in the shape of cattle and land which serves only to raise particular individuals to distinction but not the whole caste.[1]

Just as in the epic, through the varnish which the priestly authors give to
[p. 66.] the original picture and by which they soften down its colour, the picture of the old unrestrained king appears who lets himself be guided by nothing except his own, often extremely selfish desires, so also the king shows a double face in the Jâtakas which is to be traced to the Buddhistic account of the original legends. To some extent he assumes the virtues of a pious layman obeying the moral law. The ten duties of the king (dasarâjadhamme) mentioned in different ways (III. 274, 320) are nothing else than prescriptions of the general Buddhistic

---

[1] See Hopkins l. c. p. 72. The later priestly author of the epic represents naturally the relation between the king and the priest differently. According to him, their relationship is one of mutual dependence. When moreover, Hopkins (p. 152) quotes Mahâbhârata V. 37.52 sq. as a proof of this where the power of the king is represented as five-fold and his chief strength as lying in his wisdom and where it is further said: And this wisdom is the hoard of the priests: it is to be remembered that one cannot read so much in the original source. We meet with exactly the same words in the Jâtakas (V. 120), where an auxiliary meaning which might refer to the peculiar position of the priest as adviser of the king, is inadmissible. The verses are only a proverbial, everywhere current garb of the thought that the king can do nothing with physical strength and riches when he lacks intelligence.

morality applicable to all lay disciples :—

Giving alms, a moral course of life, sacrifice, truthfulness, mildness, self-denial, forgiveness, not to cause any pain to anybody, patience, a yielding disposition.

If the king follows these prescriptions as a rule of conduct, this necessarily takes much from his character as an absolute despot. As a matter of fact, with the gradual spread of Buddhism, the teachings of Buddha came to be not without influence upon the conduct of kings: Candragupta's grandson Asoka who ruled in the third century B. C., "the god-beloved king Piyadasi," as he calls himself in his stone edicts, shows himself here as a ruler who in several respects comes close to the ideal picture given in the Jâtakas.

This ideal of a virtuous Buddhistic layman, the king in the old stories does not always follow. Very often we see in him an unrestrained tyrant guided by his own whims and caprices, "who oppresses and puts down his subjects by punishments, taxes, torture and robbery, as one pounds sugar in a sugar mill, who is as [p. 67.] odious to them as a particle of dust in the eye, as a particle of sand in the rice or as a thorn that has pierced the hand" (II. 240). To the virtues mentioned under *Dasarâjadhamme* of the idealised ruler there stand in opposition as many vices;

these form, as it were, a legend on the reverse side of the coin, the side which depicts the true picture of the king—drunkenness and cruelty (in the Khantivâdi Jâtaka, II. 3919; in the Culladhammapâla Jâtaka, III. 178 sq.), corruptibility (in the Bharu Jâtaka, II. 169 sq.), untruthfulness and unrighteousness (in the Cetiya Jâtaka, III. 454 sq.). Neither obedience to the written laws,[1] nor to the customs that have become law through tradition seems to have prevented the king from realizing his whims and desires. Only the virtuousness of his counsellors in spiritual and worldly matters (atthadhammânusâsaka amacca), whose spiritual superiority sometimes (as in the Kukku Jâtaka, III. 317 sq.) triumphs over the weaknesses of the ruler, might be in a position to curb his arbitrariness and tyranny. Where this opposite force was absent and the

---

[1] Written laws are mentioned often in the Jâtakas. In the Tuṇḍila Jâtaka the Bodhisatta after the death of the king of Benares causes a book to be written "on the right decision" (vinicchaye potthakaṃ likhâpetvâ II. 292) and exhorts the people to see this book for the decision of law suits. In the Tesakuṇa Jâtaka, the ministers make the succession devolve upon the *senâpati*, he gives up the royal dignity, causes the "doctrine of truthfulness" to be written on a gold tablet (vinicchayadhammaṃ suvaṇṇapaṭṭe likhâpetvâ V. 125) and orders the people to form their decisions in accordance with it. It may remain a disputed question whether we can infer from this mention of "law books" and "law tablets" in the Jâtakas the existence of written laws in earlier pre-Buddhistic times; none of these passages has any reference to the purpose of this story and both can be conceived as later additions.

ministers or the *purohita* only helped to carry out the desires of their ruler, there often arose circumstances which forced the people to take recourse to the only method available, namely, force, open rebellion. In the Padakusalamâṇava Jâtaka (III. 501 sq.) there is probably a germ of history; in spite of its legend- [p. 68.] ary garb it may have preserved the memory of actual facts. It is there narrated how a young Brâhmaṇa after he has discovered by magic the treasures stolen and concealed by the king and his *purohita* calls the king a thief in the presence of the assembled people and cries out:

"May the householders and citizens assembled here listen to me! What should be water is fire, where safety is expected, from there comes danger.

The king plunders the land as also the Brâhmaṇa, the *purohita*. Be on your guard; from your protector is your evil generated."

The people understand that the king who should protect them is himself a thief and in order to throw the blame from off his shoulders, has hidden the treasure and tries to discover the thief; they determine to kill the bad king so that he may not plunder them any more. With sticks and hammers they go out and beat the king and the purohita till they are dead.

The young Brâhmaṇa is elected king and placed in power.

Another example of such a violent removal of the unrighteous king is found in the Saccaṃkira Jâtaka (I. 326). Here also the king is driven out of the town by the enraged Khattiyas, Brâhmaṇas and other citizens and in his place a Brâhmaṇa is installed king.

Whether in this arbitrary, capricious and vicious despot of the Jâtakas we have to look for the true picture of the *râjan* of the older Buddhistic age, cannot be determined with certainty. Individual dispositions for giving the ruler unlimited power, now exclusively for his own ends, now for the good of his subjects come as much into view—though it should not be forgotten that we have to do not only in the literature but also in the history of India more with types than with individuals—as the attempt of the narrator to give the hoary legends as much an antiquated and primitive character as possible. In any case, this very little flattering picture of the *râjan* seems to me to come nearer the truth than the portrait of the ruler as sketched in other places

[p. 69.] and idealised under the influence of Buddhistic morality.

The already-mentioned ten duties of the king give us, little as they contain a true picture of the king, no idea of the essence of the kingly power, of the obligations or functions of the *rájan*, because they, as already said, contain universal prescriptions of morals applicable to the whole Buddhistic laity. From these *Dasarája-dhamme* the special obligations of the king demanded by his position as ruler are essentially different; the traditional duties of the ruler to which the kings of the Jâtakas also are subject, consist above all in the protection of the subjects from external and internal enemies and the safety of their person and property, as assured by punishment of all violation of these.

Frequent wars seem, even in the period described in the Jâtakas, to give the king an opportunity to exercise his duty as protector of the people. It is true he is no more the robber and plunderer, as the oldest epic narrative depicts,[1] who earns his livelihood by plundering expeditions; he lives no more permanently in the borders of his land, always ready to fall upon his neighbour, but lives with his court in a fortified town in the centre of his territory supported by regular taxes from the people. The people live in peace in their new residences and have the frontiers strongly protected; gradually, with growing civilization

[1] *Cf.* Hopkins, l. c., p. 76.

there come other interests into the foreground as the king's cares: the land is made fertile, cities are built, trade and commerce flourish. Nevertheless, there is no lack of warlike expeditions which are caused partly by the quarrels of the neighbouring kingdoms—as between Kosala and Kâsi (I. 262, 409)—but mostly by the rebellions of the intermediate bordering tribes. Of such insurrections we read very often (I. 437; II. 74); the aboriginal tribes driven into the mountains and probably subjugated only in name, gave the Aryan invaders surely much to do. Not
[p. 70.] always the troops stationed in the frontiers (paccante ṭhitayodhâ) are sufficient to quell the rebellion. After fighting several battles with the rebels, as narrated in the Bandhanamokkha Jâtaka (who are called *corâ* robbers), they send information to the king that they cannot carry on the war. Then the king collects an army (balakâyaṃ saṃharitvâ, I. 437) and takes the field.

In times of peace the principal work of the king seems to be to take part in the administration of justice, and indeed, from our texts we get the information that this participation was no merely formal matter. When in the Râjovâda Jâtaka it is said of the king, " He gave decisions in law-suits " (*vinicchayam anusási*, II. 2), it is clearly meant that the final administration of law rested with the king, that the final decision in law-suits as well as the final word regarding the punishment for breaking the law remained with him. With this there agrees what we learn from Pali texts about the manner of administering justice. According to the account given in the commentary on the Mahâ-parinibbâna Sutta concerning the administration of justice in Vesâlî, the chief town of the Licchavis, the process of law from the institution of a suit to its final decision was a considerably complicated affair.[1] But here also

[1] The meaning of the passage in question is, according to the English translation given by G. Turnour in the "Journal of the Asiatic Society of Bengal" Vol. 7, Part 2, 1838, p. 993, Note, this: When in ancient times a criminal was brought before the rulers of the Vajjis (*i.e.*, the Licchavis), they made him over at first to the *vinicchaya-mahâmattas*. These then tried him and if they were convinced that he was innocent, set him free. If they, on the other hand, held that he was guilty, they made him over to the *vohârikas*, without pronouncing any sentence. The latter examined the matter and set him free in case he was innocent; if, on the contrary, he was guilty, they took him to the *suttadhâras* (probably, they should be called *suttadharas*, "knowers of the Sutta, the law") who proceeded in the same way with him. From there he was taken to the *aṭṭhakûlakas* (probably, *aṭṭhakulakas*, by which, according to Lassen's supposition, a court consisting of eight heads of families is to be understood) who in their turn left the decision to the *senâpati*; from there, the accused was made over to the *uparâjan* and from him to the *râjan*. The latter then investigated the case and set the accused, if he held him innocent, at last free; if he, however, found him guilty he pronounced the judgment in accordance with the *paveṇipotthaka*, the "book of customs"—*Cf.* also Lassen, *Indische Alterthumskunde*, 2nd Edn., Vol. 2, p. 86 sq.

the final decision remained in the hands of the king. In the Jâtakas, where [p. 71.] apparently the more primitive conditions of a much earlier age, which presuppose a much more simple legal apparatus, are described, the criminal is brought direct before the king and generally sentenced by him without previously consulting the opinion of the ministers. An ascetic, who on a false suspicion of theft is arrested by the owners of the stolen property, is brought before the king and the latter pronounces the sentence without further examining the case: "Go and impale him" (IV. 29). Also in other narratives (for example, in the introduction to the Vaṭṭaka Jâtaka, I. 433, in the Avâriya Jâtaka, III. 232) the king alone pronounces the judgment; it happens, however, that a protest is made from the side of the minister of justice (vinicchayâmacca) against an unjust judgment of the king. Occasions for such protests frequently arose, especially, when charges were brought by men in high position and favourites of the king against common people. A typical example of this is afforded by the following narrative: "In ancient times"—so begins the Rathalaṭṭhi Jâtaka (III. 104. sq.)—"when Brahmadatta reigned, the Bodhisatta was his minister of justice (*vinicchayâmacca*). Once the

purohita of the king drove in his carriage to the village from which he used to collect his rents (bhogagâma) and when he came to a corner of the road he met a caravan. "Move your wagons out of the road, move them out of the road," he cried. As nobody yielded, he became angry and threw his spiked stick[1] at the driver of the nearest wagon. The stick struck the shaft of the wagon, returned and struck him on the forehead, so that there was a big bump. The
[p. 72.] *purohita* returned and complained to the king that he was assaulted by the drivers. The king who was seated in his court-room asked the drivers to be brought before him and pronounced the judgment, without inquiring into the matter: "You have assaulted the *purohita*, so that he has got a bump on his forehead; you must give up all your horses." Then the Boddhisatta said to him, "O great king, without inquiring into the matter you make these give up all their horses. There are, however, men who, when they themselves strike, say, "I am struck by another." Therefore, a ruler should not act without investigation; when he has heard a matter, he should act." With these words, he recited the verses;

---

[1] Patodalaṭṭhi, "stick for driving animals."

"Although he has struck, he says he is struck; although he oppresses he says he is oppressed.[1] He who speaks, first, O King, should not at all be believed.

Therefore, one hears, O wise man, the other also; when one has heard both sides, one acts, as is proper.

A lazy fellow, given to sensual indulgence is not good, an ascetic who does not control himself is not good, a king is not good who acts without investigation, a wise man who is angry is also not good.

The king should act after he has heard, and not before he has heard, O ruler! Honour and fame fall to the lot of him who acts after investigation, O King."

After the king heard the speech of the Bodhisatta, he decided rightly and in the right judgment blame was thrown upon the Brâhmaṇa.

From this one case in which the king, influenced by the *vinicchayâmacca*, revises an unjust judgment, to infer a general power of this minister to pronounce an opinion upon the

---

[1] The text has: Jetvâ jino ti bhâsati, "although he has conquered, he says, 'I am conquered;'" but what we are concerned with is probably derivatives of the verb 'jyâ,' to oppress, fleece, and jino is to be changed into jîno.

[2] *Cf.* Manu, VIII., 1: "A king who wishes to investigate a lawsuit should go to the court-room in a modest attitude with the Brâhmaṇas and ministers who know how to advise."

king's judgments, would be going too far. The right inference would be to suppose that the ministers, especially, the *vinicchayâmacca* and also the *purohita* and the *senâpati*, who, as we [p. 73] shall see, both took part in
[p. 73.] the administration of justice, advised the king and in some cases, had some influence upon his judgments. Also we are not in a position to draw a line between cases where the king alone pronounced the judgment and those which were judged by the ministers. That the entire province of the administration of justice did not lie in the hands of the king, although in the earliest times this might have been the case, is self-evident; the more complicated State organisation became, with a growing population and with the extension of territory, the more pressing must the necessity for a division of work have been felt, the more must the king have delegated his powers to the ministers. The legal life of the smaller towns and villages passed very much out of the direct sphere of action of the king and remained a matter for his representatives, as long as no appeal was made against the judgments of these to the king, looked upon as a higher authority. Quite in keeping with this, we also meet with a series of examples in the Jâtakas in which no mention is made of the participation

of the king in the administration of justice (II. 182; V. 229). In both the narratives, the question is of quarrels between two parties, of civil cases, not of the punishment of crimes.[1]

15. Criminal jurisdiction seems, according to the Jâtakas, to be exclusively exercised by the king. That any person other than the king can pronounce a sentence of death seems to be nowhere mentioned in the Jâtakas. Serious crimes, such as theft, adultery, bodily injury were punished by *râjâṇâ*,[2] *i.e.*, by the punishment inflicted by the king.

[p. 74.]

---

[1] Even the circumstance that in the Rathalaṭṭhi Jâtaka stress is laid on the participation of the king in the administration of justice with regard to the drivers against whom the *purohita* preferred a charge (*râjâ sayam vinicchaye nisîditvâ*, III. 105), signifies that under usual circumstances in cases of such little importance as the one in question, the king did not preside over the administration of justice. Still it is to be noted that Brahmanical law books did not alone assign to the king the task of personally conducting law-suits: "the Greek reports, the Indian epics, the inscriptions and numerous works of Indian princes on *vyavahâra* show that the Indian princes often exercised judicial powers in person." Jolly in the "Zeitschrift der Deutsch. Morgenl. Gesellschaft," Vol. 44, p. 344.

[2] The word denotes, according to its etymology, as it is a compound of the Sanskrit words râja and âjñâ, properly, "the king's command." Whether in the Pali, a special technical meaning is attached to the word, I cannot say. In the Culladhammapâla Jâtaka it is narrated that the king causes, with the help of the executioner, the hands and feet of the prince to be cut off. The executioner asks when he has carried out the order, "Have I, O King, executed the *râjâṇâ*" (*kiṁ deva katâ râjâṇâ*, III. 180). Here *râjâṇâ* probably means only "the king's

Beyond this power of inflicting punishment, the king's authority does not seem, according to the Jâtakas, to have extended to the person of the subjects. We read nowhere in our texts of any right which the king had to force his subjects to military or other service; on the contrary, the limitations of the king's power are distinctly pointed out, when the king in reply to the request of the *yakkhini*,[1] who was made his chief consort, to give her unrestricted power over the whole kingdom, [p. 75.] says, "My love, in no way do all the subjects of my kingdom belong to me, nor am I their lord (mayhaṃ sakalaraṭṭhavâsino na kiñci honti, nâhaṃ etesaṃ sâmiko, I. 398); only over those who rise

---

command." In other passages, on the other hand, the expression seems to be employed as a *terminus technicus*. A ferryman who has assaulted an ascetic and his pregnant wife is brought before the king and the latter, after he has pronounced the judgment, causes the *râjâṇâ* to be executed (III. 232). What the punishment consisted in, is not further mentioned; I suppose that either the capital sentence or some other serious corporal punishment, such as mutilation, is to be understood here. To this points also the introduction to the Vaṭṭaka Jâtaka (I. 438), where the son of a *seṭṭhi* who was suspected of having made short work of a prostitute, is brought for judgment by the *râjâṇâ*. The hands are tied behind his body and he is dragged in execution of the *râjâṇâ*. The whole town turns out in excitement as the report of the sentence upon the *seṭṭhi's* son spreads and a large crowd follows him beating the breast and mourning loudly. As the girl, however, in the meantime appears, the *râjâṇâ* is not executed, but the circumstances mentioned point to this, that the sentence was one of capital punishment.

[1] Skr. *Yakshini*, a female *yaksha*, a supernatural being, a demon.

against the king and do wrong am I lord. Therefore, I cannot give you unrestricted power over the whole kingdom."

Still the subjects of the king were not only reminded in times of war, when the king's army protected the frontiers of the land, and through the administration of justice exercised by him and by those authorised by him, of a power standing above them and surrounding and protecting them all; the people had duties which made them realize very clearly the fact of their being citizens of the State.[1] Whilst the king has for his care the securing of protection against external enemies and the preservation of internal order, the people also, as a counter-duty on their part, bear the cost of administration of the State, the army and the Court by payment of taxes. Similar conditions we have probably to suppose for the Vedic period; at least there seems no reasonable ground for understanding by the Vedic *bali* anything else than a fixed tax.[2] Probably,

---

[1] This supposition seems to me justified by the fact of a tax imposed upon the whole land and by the institution of the *gâmabhojakas* who represented the king in their village and collected taxes for him, and I don't understand how Senart will reconcile his theory with this fact when he denies the idea of the State to ancient India and never admits any beginnings of State-consciousness (*Revue des deux mondes*, Vol. 125 p. 348 sq.)

[2] For the Brâhmaṇa period the existence of taxes is certainly shown in the Aitareya Brâhmaṇa VII. 29, where the Vaiśya is characterised as "one who pays taxes to another (anyasya balikṛit), who is to be employed by another and taxed according to another's pleasure."

in the oldest times there were voluntary presents— according to Zimmer,[1] the only tax which the Vedas prescribed that the people should pay to the king—principally for meeting the cost of the king's Court, and when we find mention of the offer of such presents in the epics[2] and also here and there in the Jâtakas, this is to be considered a survival of the old custom. On the occasion of the coronation ceremony (chattamaṅgala), described in the Kummâsapiṇḍa Jâtaka, we find among the people surrounding the throne citizens with various kinds of presents[3] (*nânâvidha-paṇṇâkârahatthe nagaramanusse*). Petitioners expected obviously a favourable reception of their prayer when they did not appear before the king with empty hands. The Brâhmaṇa who goes to the king with the request that he will replace the second dead ox, gives

[p. 76.]

---

[1] *Altindisches Leben*, p. 166: "Fixed taxes the people didn't pay the king, they brought to him voluntary presents." Zimmer compares this with the old German conditions which are mentioned in Tacitus, Germania 15: "Mos est civitatibus ultro ac viritim conferre principibus vel armentorum vel frugum, quod pro honore acceptum etiam necessitatibus subvenit."

[2] *Cf.* Hopkins, l. c., p. 90 sq.

[3] The word *paṇṇâkâra* means, since it is derived from Skr. parṇa + âkâra, "having the form of a leaf" and points to the custom, which is still common in India, of carrying fruits, sweets, etc., in the leaves of the banana or some other tree. Originally used in connexion with such offerings, the word came to acqnire later the general sense "present." *Cf.* Childers, *Pali Dictionary*

him a present (*paṇṇâkâra* II. 166) with the words, "May the king be victorious."

In the age we are considering, the taxes formed in every case the principal sources of revenue of the king; they were an impost fixed by law, and were, if not brought voluntarily by the people themselves, collected forcibly by the king's officers (II. 240; IV. 224; V. 98). Still the Jâtakas contain, so far as I have seen, no fixed rule concerning the nature of these taxes nor concerning the amount of the king's share.[1]

[p. 77.] Only the fact that of the corn reaped a fixed portion fell to the king's share, appears from several passages. An over-conscientious *seṭṭhi* who has plucked from his rice field a handful of blades, in order to make out of them something with which to bind the twigs, has scruples about his conduct and reflects, "From this field I must give the king his portion (*rañño-bhâga* II. 378) and I have taken a handful of corn without making over

[1] According to Manu VII. 130, of the corn, an eighth, sixth or twelfth part belongs to the king. In X. 120, the eighth part is indicated as the lawful and permissible tax in peace times; in times of need, the king can take a fourth part (X. 118). According to Gautama, the tax of the agriculturists is a tenth, an eighth or a sixth part of the produce. According to Vasishṭha (I. 42), Baudhâyana, (I. 18. 1) Nârada (XVIII. 48) and Vishṇu (III 22), the sixth part is universally given as the lawful share and this is in agreement with what occurs in the epics where the king is repeatedly described as "shaḍbhâgin," "a sharer of the sixth part."

this portion." In the same passage of the Kurudhamma Jâtaka it is narrated how the tax-collecting official of the king (*doṇamâpaka*, properly, "measuring with the *doṇa*, a certain dry-measure") measures at the door of the royal granary the rice paid to the king (*râjabhâge vîhim minâpento*) and proceeds in this way, that he takes a grain out of the unmeasured heaps of rice and employs it as a marker. At that moment, it begins to rain. The official counts the markers and sweeps away with the words, "So much measured rice is there," the grains which have served him as markers and throws them over the measured heap. Then he rushes indoors and stands on the doorway. Here the thought occurs to him: "Have I thrown the markers over the heaps that have been measured or over those that have not been measured? If I have placed them over the heaps that have been measured, I have without any reason increased the king's share and diminished that of the owner (gahapatika)."[1]

The tax on the produce of the land mentioned here and consisting in a certain portion of the reaped corn constituted, according to the

[1] The story is told as an example of excessive conscientiousness. The official is seized with repentance at the thought that the grains which he swept away as markers, for the purpose of determining how much corn he has measured, from the unmeasured heap, were placed over the heaps that had been measured

lawbooks and epic exts, together with other natural products of the cow, [p. 78.] etc. the only taxes which could be collected from proprietor of land. Of a tax which was imposed on the land and which must be paid in the form of a rent, no mention is made here; the tax was fixed upon the annual produce. On the contrary, according to the Greek accounts, the agriculturists occupied the land as the king's tenants. The amount of the rent goes into the king's treasury, together with a fourth part of the produce as tax.[1] What do our texts say on this question? It seems as if the statements of the Greek messengers receive confirmation from the Jâtakas. Among the ministers of the king, as we shall see, the "surveyor" (rajjugâhaka amacca) occupies an important position; in the enumeration of the persons found in the court of the Kuru king, he is mentioned immediately after the house priest (*purohita*). Moreover, it is mentioned in the Kâma Jâtaka that officers of the king (râjakammikâ) come to a

---

[1] So also, according to Diodorus, II. 40.5, Strabo, on the other hand, only says that the agriculturists are tenants of the king and pay a fourth part of the corn as tax. Arrian speaks in extremely general terms of φόροι which the agriculturists had to pay to the kings or the autonomous states, without giving any particulars regarding the nature of the taxes and their amount.

village to measure the fields (*khettrappamâṇa-gahaṇatthâya*, IV. 169), whose owners (so it is said immediately after this) pray for a remission of taxes. Most probably these surveys were undertaken in order to fix the quantity of land and with this the amount of contribution which was calculated upon the land and which had to be paid, irrespectively of the annual produce, as rent to the king. No doubt this inference of the existence of rent, from the simple fact that the land was measured, is not perfectly valid. Surveys would be necessary, even if the tax consisted in a portion of the produce, simply to give the officials some means of calculating the average produce and thus checking the accounts of the occupiers of the land.

Who were these tax-paying tenants? It seems that even in the eastern lands the *Khattiyas* and the

[p. 79.]

Brâhmaṇas—this in spite of their wealth and in spite of the undisputed fact that the greater portion of the land was in their hands—were free from taxes, for in all passages in question the tax-payers are mentioned as belonging to the middle classes.[1] Thus, in the above-quoted Kurudhamma Jâtaka, *doṇamâpaka*, the royal

[1] The conditions described in the epic Hopkins characterises (l.c., p. 89) with the words: "The latter (the warriors) are *as a matter of fact* exempt from the taxes; the priests are so *by Divine law.*"

tax-collector, who measures the corn to be paid to the king, is afraid lest he should encroach upon the property of the *gahapatika*; to this class also belongs the *seṭṭhi* who is mentioned as the tax-payer (II. 378; IV. 169).

Exemption from taxes was occasionally obtained by pleading before the king. A *seṭṭhi* living in the frontier requests the brother of the king to send a letter to the king asking him to grant exemption, upon which the king grants him this (IV. 169).

The taxes are paid to the official who represents the king in the province allotted to him; in the village they are given to the *gâmabhojaka*, the village superintendent, who "enjoys the revenue of the village." If the subjects did not pay willingly or if the king wanted—as seemed often to happen, according to the instances narrated (II. 240; III. 9; IV. 224)—to harass the people by enhancing the taxes, he sent his officials who had to use force in filling the coffers of the king. These tax-collectors (*balipaṭiggâhakas*, *niggâhakas*, *balisâdhakas*), according to the Jâtakas, did not play an unimportant part in public life; how they were looked upon by the people seems to me to be indicated by the conclusion of the Gagga Jâtaka (II. 17), where the man-eating demon (yakkha) whom the Bodhisatta has subdued is given by the king the post of a *balipaṭiggâhaka.* In the Gaṇḍatindu Jâtaka the condition of a land ruled by an unrighteous king and plundered by his officials

[p. 80] is described. "Oppressed with taxes (balipîṭitâ, V. 98) the inhabitants lived in the forest like beasts with their wives and children; where there was once a village, there no village stood any more. The men could not, for fear of the king's people, live in their houses, they surrounded their houses with hedges and went after sunrise to the forest. In the day the king's people (râjapurisâ) plundered, at night the thieves." Sometimes the king's officers made common cause with the last-mentioned class, when these officers were really there to pursue and arrest this class. A minister, whom the king gave the position of a village ruler (*gâmabhojaka*) (I. 355) in a frontier village and who collected there the taxes for the king, came to an understanding with the robbers that he would go with his people to the forest and they would in the mean time plunder the village and share the spoils with him.

Besides the taxes, there were certain privileges of the king which he could use for filling his treasury. The principle mentioned in the lawbooks,[1] that unclaimed property belonged to

---

[1] *Cf.* the passages quoted in Foy's *Die königliche Gewalt nach den altindischen Rechtsbüchern*, Leipzig, 1895, p. 50.

the king, is seen also in the Jâtakas. If anybody dies without heirs, then his succession devolves upon the king. "Seven days and seven nights"—so we read in the introduction to the Mahyaka Jâtaka (III. 299)—"the army of the king took to bring the goods of people dying without heirs to the palace." Even cases where whole families leave their possessions, when, on renouncing the world, they pass into the homeless condition, occur in the Jâtakas, and this custom might, at a time when through the prevalence of pessimistic views the impulse to renounce the world was widespread, become a source of great income to the king. Still we have grounds for thinking that it was opposed to the moral principles of that age when the king made use of this right. In the Haṭṭhipâla Jâtaka it is narrated that the purohita and his wife after renouncing their entire worldly possessions go to the forest to join their sons who had already been in the homeless condition. The king hears this and resolves, "Unclaimed wealth [p. 81] comes to us" (*assâmikadhanam amhâkam pâpuṇâti* IV. 485),[1] and fetches the

[1] Similarly, in the Telapatta Jâtaka the king justifies his capture of the widowed *Yakkhinî*, saying, "Unclaimed property belongs to the king" (assâmikabhaṇḍaṃ nâma râjasantakaṃ hoti, I. 398).

money from the house of the *purohita.* The queen, however, explains to him, with the help of a parable, the wrong done by him.

As we, however, in our attempt to collect together the statements contained in the Jâtakas concerning the rights and duties of the king, have not hitherto been able to get an exhaustive account of the actual region of influence and sphere of power of the *râjan*, we must also examine the incomplete and partly contradictory details relating to the question of his succession.

In the Vedic age, the kingdom devolved either directly upon the eldest son of the king, or the new king was elected by the people.[1] The first case is what generally occurs even in the period described in the Jâtakas. Kingship was hereditary in the family (kulasantakaṃ rajjaṃ, I. 395; II. 116; IV. 124) and indeed, when there were several sons, it was the eldest who succeeded his father on the throne (I. 127; II. 87, 212), whilst the second son became the Viceroy (*uparâjan*). As a rule, only the sons of the eldest queen (aggamahesî), who must be of the same caste as the king and thus a *Khattiyâ*, seem to be legitimate; yet there are instances which make it probable that this legitimacy was not always considered a *conditio sine qua non* of

[1] Zimmer, *Altindisches Leben*, pp. 162, 172.

succession. In the already-quoted Kaṭṭhahâri Jâtaka the king makes the son born of a wood-gatherer (Kaṭṭhahâri) the Viceroy (*upạrâjan*) and after the death of his father, the latter succeeded to the throne.

If the king was without a male heir, then if he had a daughter, his son-in-law became [p. 81] heir to the throne; the son-in-law he sought either among his own kinsmen or among the members of another royal house.[1] In the Mudupâṇi Jâtaka (II. 323 sq.) the king makes his nephew his successor and explains to his ministers, "After my death my nephew will become king, my daughter will become his eldest consort (aggamahesî)." Later he changes his mind and informs his ministers that he will give his nephew another wife and marry his daughter into another royal house, in order to have as many kinsmen as possible. This intention is, however, frustrated by the cunning of these two lovers who at last carried out their desire and so we do not know how the succession would have taken place if the king had married his daughter to a foreign prince; probably, the

[1] In order to keep his previous promise, the king has to depart from this rule in the Devadhamma Jâtaka (I. 127) and in the Dasaratha Jâtaka (IV.124).

latter would have received the *uparajja* with the daughter.

If there is neither a male heir nor a kinsman who can succeed to the throne, the successor seems to be chosen by the ministers; election by the people, as represented in the Vedas and the epics,[1] is nowhere mentioned. The legends speak of a remarkable custom which in such cases was connected with the election of the successor. Seven days after the death of the heirless king, the *purohita* lets a car, the *phussaratha*,[2] be driven, after the funeral ceremonies are over (III. 238; IV. 39; V. 248). By beat of drums it is announced in the city, "To-morrow we shall drive a *phussaratha*." The five insignias of royalty are placed on the car and this is put in motion by the ministers who reflect, "It will come to the man who will become the king." The car then leaves the city and remains, as is often the case in stories, standing at one and the same place, namely, the gate of the park, where it rotates ready to be driven by the future king. This king is then soon found out by the *purohita*; he ascends the car and

[p. 83]

---

[1] Hopkins, l. c. p. 143.

[2] =Skr. pushparatha, car of flower, desire? Or is phussa=spṛśiya and pussaratha, "the car which is to be touched, *i.e.*, taken possession of"?

is anointed by the *purohita.* Have we to see in these legends the mythical form of an actual event, namely, the selection of a king by the *purohita,* or is the *phussaratha* nothing but a product of the rich imagination of the story-teller? To this no definite answer can be given, so long as our knowledge of *phussaratha* is confined to the Jâtakas; but I don't consider the possibility excluded, that when the king died without an heir and the ministers chose a successor from among themselves or from another royal house, the latter was conveyed to his residence in a manner similar to the ceremony described in the stories, and that people spread rumours about him that he was discovered as the right man by a miracle introduced by the gods.

When the election of the successor takes place in the way described, the new king is not, as before, a *khattiya,* nor the scion of a foreign royal house, but the usurper son of a seṭṭhi's daughter, in fact, the child of a poor woman born in the street (IV. 38). The legendary character of this narrative does not allow this to be taken as a proof that kingship did not lie always in the hands of the *khattiyas* but that persons belonging to other castes might occasionally be in possession of it. There are, however, some passages which seem to support such a theory. We have already met with of revolutions by which the reigning king is removed and in his place a Brâhmaṇa is put. In the Pâdañjali Jâtaka (II. 264) the chief minister (atthadhammânusâsaka amacca), probably also belonging to the Brâhmaṇa caste, of the deceased king, and not the weakminded prince, is anointed king by the ministers. Even the lawbooks speak of kings who do not belong to the Kshatriya caste and understand by these kings of low origin who have usurped the throne.[1]

[p. 84.] Such usurpations of the throne are mentioned in Indian history concerning historical personalities, as, for example, Chandragupta, the founder of the Maurya Dynasty who according to Brahmanical traditions was a Sûdra.

Did these usurpers change their caste when they ascended the throne? Did they become *ipso facto khattiyas* or did they continue to belong to their former castes? In the eyes of the Brâhmaṇas influenced by their caste-theory, they would remain what they originally were, whether they belonged to the Brâhmaṇa or the Sûdra caste. In reality, this question—especially, in the eastern lands and at a time when the caste idea had not been developed very clearly—had

[1] *Cf.* Foy, *Die Königliche Gewalt*, p. 8.

for the usurper very little significance, as he belonged to the ruling class, whether or not he was reckoned a *khattiya*, and by reason of this, as we have already seen, stood above this caste.

The ceremony which accompanied the accession to the throne was, according to the Jâtakas, the same as that which we know from the Vedas and the epics: The priest—generally, the *purohita* (III. 239; IV. 40)—consecrates the king and sprinkles water upon him (*abhisiñcati*). Whether this custom was also observed in the eastern lands seems open to question, on account of the superiority of the ruling class and its independence of the priestly caste. For, as a matter of fact, there lies in this act of *abhisecana*, though originally its significance may have been only a religious one, as an act by which the blessings of the gods were showered, or more correctly expressed, invoked by magic, upon the king, a certain dependence of the king upon the priest consecrating him. The refusal of the priest to perform this *abhisecana* could, under certain circumstances, call in question the succession of the right heir. Instances are not wanting in our texts which prove the possibility of the refusal to consecrate. In the Gâmaṇicaṇḍa Jâtaka it is narrated that the ministers, after they have performed the funeral ceremonies with great *éclat* and made funeral gifts, meet in the palace and tell the prince, because he is too young, that he can only be consecrated after he has satisfied their [p. 85] tests (kumâro atidaharo, na sakkâ rajje abhisiñcitum vîmamsitvâ tam abhisiñcissâma, II. 297). Here the question is, however, only of a delay in consecration; but in another case the investiture was not at all performed. "In ancient times" —so we read in the Pâdañjali Jâtaka—"when Brahmadatta reigned in Benares, the Bodhisatta was his adviser in worldly and spiritual things (*atthadhammânusâsaka amacca*, II. 264). Now the king had a son named Pâdañjali who was a good-for-nothing fellow. In course of time the king died. When the funeral ceremonies were over, the ministers said that they wanted to install the prince as king. The Bodhisatta, however, said, "The prince is a fool and a good-for-nothing fellow, we will first examine him and then install him as king." The ministers held a Court, gave the prince a place in their middle and made a wrong judgment, inasmuch as they gave a thing to the wrong owner. Then they asked the prince whether they had judged rightly. He bit his lips. The Boddhisatta thought, "The prince, I think, is a clever fellow, he knows that we have judged wrongly" and recited the first verse:

"Surely, Pâdañjali excels us all in wisdom; for he bites his lips and certainly sees through our game."

On the following day, another Court was held: this time, however, they judged rightly and asked the prince what he thought of their judgment. Again he bit his lips. Then the Bodhisatta understood that he was an out-and-out fool and recited the second verse:

"This man does not know right from wrong, or good from bad; beyond the biting of his lips he knows nothing."

The ministers concluded that the prince Pâdañjali was a fool and made the Bodhisatta king."

Had this priestly investiture been a condition of the validity of the succession, no small power in political matters would have been placed in the hands of the priests; on the other hand, this priestly influence, as well as the part of the ministers in the choice of the successor, [p. 86] seems to be confined to extraordinary cases—absence of an heir to the throne, minority or intellectual deficiency of the prince. The rule was that the father, according to the custom prevailing in the epic age[1], which was also recommended

[1] *Cf.* the passage quoted already from the Râmâyaṇa (II. 23, 26); further, Mhbt. XII. 63, 19:

sthâpayitvâ prajâpâlaṃ putraṃ râjye ca pâṇḍava
anyagotraṃ praśastaṃ vâ kshatriyaṃ kshatriyarshabha.......

in the lawbooks[1] placed the son in power in his lifetime which made the investiture by the priest a mere formality that had not much importance. It even happens that the king himself installs his son (rajje abhisiñci, IV. 96, 105); whether in this we are to see a taking away of the privilege enjoyed by the priest or whether the expression has lost its special meaning which has reference to the ceremony of investiture and acquired the general meaning "handing over the government," I cannot say definitely.

The handing over of the viceroyalty (*uparâjja*) to the eldest son seems generally to take place after the completion of his studies (I. 259; III. 123, 407); often power was made over immediately by the father to the prince, returned home from the University (IV. 96, 316; V. 177). Whilst we read in the Kummâsapiṇḍa Jâtaka (III. 407) that the prince Brahmadatta after he returned from Takkasilâ was made uparâjan by his father, to whom he had to furnish a proof of his ability and who was pleased with his performances, and that after the death of his father he succeeded him on the throne,

---

[1] Manu, IX. 323: "But (a king who feels his end approaching) shall give all his wealth derived from taxes to the Brâhmaṇas, hand over the reins of government to the son and seek death on the battlefield."

it is said in the Culasutasoma Jâtaka of Prince Sutasoma that after his return from Takkasilâ he received from his father the white umbrella (setacchatta, V. 177), the emblem of royalty, and ruled justly.

So long as the king's son is not grown up and in case the king has no male descendant, [p. 87] the eldest among the younger brothers of the king gets the *uparajja* (I. 133, kaniṭṭabhâtâ uparâjâ,[1] II. 367).

What duties and functions were connected with the office of a viceroy, the Jâtakas do not make clear; their statements are confined to the description of superficial things. On ceremonial occasions the *uparâjan* sits behind the king on the back of the elephant (II. 374), a seat which is otherwise occupied by the *purohita*. In the Kurudhamma Jâtaka it is further explained how the viceroy goes in the evening to do the king's work, accompanied by a large crowd from the street; "when he has driven to the palace he leaves on the yoke the reins and the spiked stick, in case he sleeps in the

[1] Both the expressions are connected closely with each other in the passage in question, a fact which Rouse in his translation (Cambridge, 1895, p. 251) has left unnoticed. Likewise, by each of the expressions *purohito brâhmaṇo, rajjugâhako amacco, doṇamâpako mahâmatto, nagarasobhaṇâ vaṇṇadasi* only one person is denoted, as appears from the verse which follows.

palace after dinner. At this sign, the crowd disperses, comes again the next day in the morning and waits till the viceroy comes out; also the driver who was in charge of the carriage at night comes the next morning with the carriage to the door of the palace. If, on the other hand, the *uparâjan* wants to return immediately, he places the rein and the stick in the carriage and goes to the palace to serve the king. This sign the people recognise as meaning that he will return immediately and wait at the gate of the palace." In reality, we have here a vivid picture of Court life in ancient India given in a few strokes; what, however, were the king's services which the *uparâjan* performed, we learn neither here nor anywhere else in the Jâtakas.[1] Also from the nature of our text we cannot safely trust to such statements, for whenever such statements occur, they appear only as incidental remarks. The narrator of a story is very little concerned

[p. 88]

with the actual political institutions; the events in the interior of the palace, in the chambers of the ladies, plots and palace intrigues occupy the foreground of his interest. In this the *uparâjan* naturally plays

---

[1] That, according to the commentary on the Mahâparinibbâna Sutta, the uparâjan had a share in the administration of justice, appears already from the remark made at p. 107 footnote.

an important part ; we read repeatedly of the king's fears that the *uparâjan* might become too powerful and dominate him, and of disciplinary measures taken by him to guard against such an eventuality. In the Succaja Jâtaka (III.67) it is narrated how the king sees his son on active service and how at the sight of him, the thought occurs to the king that he may probably injure him. He calls the prince and says to him, "My dear son, so long as I am living, you shall not live in the town ; remove your residence elsewhere and accept the reins of government after my death." Such banishments of the *uparâjan* do not seldom occur, according to the Jâtakas (II. 203, 229) ; also the fears of the king were not always without foundation, as the Thusa Jâtaka shows (III. 121 sq.) ; the sixteen-year-old prince plots against the life of the king ; he communicates his plan to his servants who strengthen him in his resolve : "You are right O King, what is the use of kingship if one gets it in old age ; you must in some way or other kill the king and take upon yourself the rulership." The king discovers all plots, binds the prince and imprisons him. What is remarkable, however—one may see in this a proof of how deeply-rooted the idea was in the people's minds that the son was the legitimate heir to the throne—is, that the story ends with the words, "After the funeral ceremonies of the deceased king were over, the prince was released and the reins of government handed over to him."

How far in addition to the *uparâjan* the remaining members of the ruling house participated in the administration does not appear clearly from the Jâtakas. Only, that standing next in rank to the viceroy, the *senâpati* was a kinsman of the king, we read from the *Devadhamma Jâtaka*, where it is said that the king

[p. 89]

gives his younger brother the *uparajja* and his step-brother the office of *senâpati*.

The less formal the participation of the king's relations in the administration was, the more must the state have lost the character of an absolute monarchy and approached that of an oligarchy. Whether we have to suppose the existence of oligarchies for the Vedic age, or whether in course of time, along with monarchies, States with an oligarchical form of government gradually developed themselves, I cannot decide.[1] As a matter of fact, according to Buddhist and Jaina sources, there were oligarchies in Buddha's time in Eastern India. "The proper constitution of the city of Vaiśâlî" which

---

[1] *Cf.* on the question, Zimmer, *Altindisches Leben*, p. 176. Foy, *Die Königliche Gewalt*, p. 6.

Lassen[1] mentions and of which he says that it is found nowhere else in ancient India, is in no way the only example of an oligarchical régime. According to the Jaina accounts,[2] there reigned, as subject States of Vaiśâlî, nine confederate Licchavi princes in Kośala and nine Mallaki princes in Kâśi land. The Pali texts deviate from this tradition in so far as they know of only one aristocratic confederacy of the Licchavis in Veśâlî and place the seat of the Mallas—I suppose that this is identical with the Mallakis of the Jainas[3]—at Kusinârâ and Pâvâ; also according to the Buddhist sources, the two princely houses are absolutely independent of each other. The Licchavis, the rulers of the Vajjis,[4] played, according to the Pali texts, an important part in the political life and gave the neighbouring king of Magadha much trouble; we learn from the Mahâparinibbâna Sutta that Ajâtasattu, the son and successor of Bimbisâra, wanted to exterminate the powerful Vajjis, and [p. 90] to guard against their attacks caused a fortress to be built by his ministers

---

[1] *Indische Alterthumskunde*, 2nd Edition, Vol 2, p. 86.

[2] Kalpasûtra, § 128 and Note. *Cf.* Jacobi, Das Râmâyaṇa, Bonn 1893, p. 106.

[3] As completely self-evident, I can't regard this, as Hardy has done (Buddhism, p. 92).

[4] The Vajjis = Skr. Vṛijis, were a race living north of the Ganges in Videha.

Sunidha and Vasakâra which later become Pataliputra, the capital of the Magadha kingdom. Of much less political significance was the family, from which Buddha himself was descended, the Sâkyas of Kapilavatthu; our source further mentions that they stood in a relation of dependence (*ânâpavattiṭṭhâna*, IV. 145) to the Kośala king.

In these free states we have also, it appears to me, to seek the πολεις αυτονομοι, of which Megasthenes[1] speaks. That by these republics are to be understood, seems to me hardly probable. What the Greek messenger saw and what he tried to express by the word αυτονομοι, was, in my opinion, only the fact that in the immediate neighbourhood of great monarchies, such as, the kingdom of Magadha, whose capital town Pâtaliputra itself was, individual cities or small states maintained their independence and were autonomous. That, moreover, the constitution of these small states was wholly different from that in the monarchies, I cannot accept; the difference consisted, in my opinion, only in the greater or less part which the remaining members of the royal families took in the government by the side of the king and by which they more or less limited his absolute power. A râjan stood even

---

[1] Arriani, *India*, Chapter XI. 9.

in Vesâlî and other free states at the head of the government, though he was only *primus inter pares*,[1] who had precedence over his kinsmen in the Council. The latter, however, whether in their position as *uparâjan* or *senâpati*, or as members of the Council, exercised no small influence upon the government.

---

[1] *Cf.* Oldenberg, *Buddha*, p. 101.

CHAPTER VI

THE KING'S OFFICERS

In the Jâtakas, where the king appears to us throughout as an absolute ruler, which he probably may have been in the great monarchies of the east, the advisory element of the administration is represented by the ministers (*amaccas*,. Of a participation of the people in the administration of the State, of a limitation of the kingly power through the will of the people, such as we find in the Vedas,[1] there is nowhere any talk in the Buddhist age. We must admit that under the stupefying influence of the climate and long peace, which followed the subjugation of the aboriginal races and which was only broken by occasional quarrels with the neighbouring kings or with races who were not completely subjugated and who lived in the frontier, the strength and political independence of the people decreased. The secure possession of an over-rich land did away with the necessity for individuals to serve the king with their arms and defend their home which was at first liable to frequent attacks ; as they felt themselves sufficiently protected by the king and his

---

[1] Zimmer, *Altindesches Leben*, p. 172.

strong army, they directed their thoughts towards increasing and improving their worldly possessions and ensuring the prosperity of the family. Through this the condition of the people improved, vast accumulation of wealth took place, agriculture, trade and commerce flourished. With this progress of civilization, there went hand in hand a development of the communal sense—as it did in Greece after the Persian wars ; where Indian thought, dissociated from worldly things subserved higher interests, it was mostly occupied with metaphysical questions, with anxiety for the welfare of the soul.[1]

The ancient power of the people manifesting itself in the *Samiti* was transferred to the council of ministers and here it developed into a factor which had an extraordinary, and under certain circumstances, even a dominating, influence. We saw above, in the discussion relating to the succession of the king, that the decision regarding the succession to the throne was often left to the ministers; we also find mention of the actual exercise of sovereign powers by the ministers ; besides the passage already quoted from the Gândhâra Jâtaka, it is mentioned in the Ghata Jâtaka also that the king, sick of worldly life, hands over the reins of government to the ministers (rajjaṃ amaccânaṃ niyyâdetvâ.

[p. 92.]

[1] *Cf.* Oldenberg. *Buddha*, p. 11 sq.

III. 170). Probably, the question here, as in the short absence of the king from the city mentioned in the Râjovâda Jâtaka (janapadaṃ pariganhissâmîti amacce rajjaṃ paṭicchâpetvâ II. 2), is only of a temporary direction of State affairs. Leaving aside such exceptional cases, the influence of particular ministers upon the course of internal and external politics depends upon the intelligence and energy of the then head of the State. Not every king could be so independent of his ministers, could behave so arbitrarily with them as the Magadha King Bimbisâra, of whom it is said in the Culavagga of the Vinaya Piṭaka (VII. 3.5), that he stripped some of his ministers (mahâmattas), who had advised him badly, of their offices, degraded other ministers with whose advice he was not satisfied, and promoted those, whose advice he approved of, to higher positions. In the Jâtakas even, we find examples of such an arbitrary treatment of ministers[1]; but there occur in contrast with them, cases where the king makes over the entire charge of government to a minister and willingly abides by his superior advice.

---

[1] Inconvenient councillors the king gets rid of, probably often on his accession to the throne, on which occasion, as mentioned in the Darimukha Jâtaka, he "examines the offices of the ministers and the duties assigned to them" (amaccânaṃ thânantarâni vicâretvâ, III, 239)

The court of the king consists in the epics of country nobles, the king's allies, the king's relations and feudatory kings; to these are to be added the priests who likewise belong to the King's Council but who seem to be only admitted by gradual stages into the knightly assembly.[1] We find analogical conditions in the Jâtakas, though only partially. As the *uparâjan* always is, so also is the *senâpati* sometimes a relation of the king, a *khattiya* (I. 133; IV. 168); of other offices which were also in the hands of the *khattiyas* we learn, on the other hand, nothing from the Jâtakas, nor do we find any conquered or friendly princes in the service of the king. As regards the share of the Brâhmaṇas in the administration, this is limited to individual cases. Wherever the question is of the king's officers, ministers and Brâhmaṇas are reckoned as separate classes and indeed, the latter, along with the other classes of people (the *gahapatis*, etc.), are set over against the ministers (*amacca ca brâhmaṇagahapati-âdayo ca*, I. 260). Thus we find this distinction in the Kumbhakâra Jâtaka, where it is described how, according to the Court etiquette, the mango is first eaten by the king, then by the ministers,

[p. 98.]

[1] Hopkins, l.c., p. 99.

then by the Brâhmaṇas, then by the *gahapatis*, etc. (III. 576). At the coronation ceremony, there stand round the throne of the king, at a distance from each other (*ekato-ekato*), the ministers, the Brâhmaṇas, the gahapatis, etc., as also the citizens and the dancing girls (III. 408). More clearly is the opposition between *amacca* and *brâhmaṇa* expressed in the Mahâmora Jâtaka: the ministers refer the king, when he puts a question relating to the meaning of a dream, as they themselves don't know how to interpret it, to the Brâhmaṇas with the words: "The Brâhmaṇas know it, O great king" (IV. 335).

From the quotations it is evident that by the expression *amacca*, no Khattiya or Brâhmaṇa is in general to be understood. But to what caste do the ministers belong, if they are not to be looked upon either as Khattiyas or as Brâhmaṇas? In my opinion, they do not always belong to the same caste; the *amaccas* form a class by themselves which is generally hereditary, and in consequence of this hereditary character, to which probably, as in the case of the Khattiyas, a specially developed class-consciousness is joined, possesses a certain, though distant, resemblance [p. 94.] with a caste. When asked about his *jâti*, a minister or some one belonging to him would perhaps have replied, if he was neither a Khattiya nor a Brâhmaṇa, "I come of a family of ministers" (*amaccakula*. II. 98, 125).

From this, however, it should not at all be inferred that not even occasionally did the Brâhmaṇa act as a minister of the king and in this way exercise some influence over him as well as over the government. Of the two ministers of Bimbisâra, already mentioned, one, Vassakâra, whom the king employs in the construction of a fortress and thus in purely worldly matters, belongs to the Brâhmaṇa caste. Also the *atthadhammânusâsaka amacca*, the "guide of the king in worldly and spiritual matters," repeatedly mentioned in the Jâtakas, seems always to be a Brâhmaṇa. In the Sattubhasta Jâtaka, this fact of belonging to the Brâhmaṇa caste is clearly stated; the Brâhmaṇa, who has gone to the court of the king of Kâsî after finishing his studies, receives the favour of the ruler and is loaded with honours by him. "The king"—so it is said further—"made him minister and was guided by him in worldly and spiritual things" (*atthañ ca dhammañ ca anusâsi*, III. 342). Regarding the particular functions of this *atthadhammânusâsaka amacca* we learn nothing definite from our sources; still we shall, I hope, not be wrong if we compare his position with that of the Chancellor in mediæval

European Courts which post was generally held by the clergy. Even the Indian "Chancellor" of that time seems sometimes to take into his own hands all the reins of government, for very often the *atthadhammânusâsaka amacca* is characterised as one versed in all branches of public life (sabbatthaka, II. 30, 74). In this "guide of the king in worldly and spiritual matters" of the Jâtakas we have to recognise the *amâtyamukhya* of the law-books, of whom it is said by Manu (VII. 141), "His first minister, who is versed in law, is wise, possesses self-control, and is of good family, he will put into this [p. 95.] position, if he is himself fatigued with matters concerning his subjects."[1]

Somewhat less general are the statements of the Jâtakas concerning the "leader of the army," the senâpati; of this officer they give us no clear picture but only a vague description. Often, as we saw, himself belonging to the ruling family, he seems to occupy a prominent place among the ministers, sometimes even the first place; in the Cullasutasoma Jâtaka, the King calls his ministers, having decided to renounce worldly life, with the senâpati at their

[1] In Manu VII. 58, the question is obviously of such a minister, who is here called the "best of all" (sarveshâṃ viśishṭa) and a Brâhmaṇa. *Cf.* Foy l.c., p. 68 sq.

head (*senâpatipamukhâni asîtiamaccasahassâni*, V. 178). Whether this office, conformably to its literal meaning—senâpati means "chief of the army"—was principally a military one, does not appear clearly from our texts; probably, in wars the senâpati occupied the next highest military post after the king.[1] In times of peace, he seemed to play a part which had little or nothing to do with the army; his chief work seemed rather to be the administration of justice. We read of a senâpati who in discharging his duties as a judge takes bribes (*viniccayam karonto lañcaṁ khâdati*) and thereby gives property to the wrong persons (asâmike sâmike karoti, II. 186).

Of a participation of the *senâpati* in legislation, the already-quoted passage from the Tesakuna Jâtaka speaks, where legislation in accordance with the Scripture is ascribed to him. After refusing the kingship offered to him by the ministers, he writes on a gold tablet, before he goes into the solitude of the forest, the laws to be followed in administering justice (*viniccaya-dhamma*, V. 125). "His opinion—[p. 96.] so it is said at the end—remained in force for forty thousand years."

---

[1] Besides the *senâpati*, another officer is mentioned in the Jâtakas whose title also points to a connection with the army, namely, the *mahâsenâpati*. The only passage where I have found this mentioned (Tesakuna Jâtaka, V. 115) gives us no clear idea about his functions only that he is a high officer, is what it stipulates.

Along with the circumstance stated here, that the senâpati was offered the kingship, it may be mentioned, as proof of the importance of his position, that the residents of the city, when their request for help is refused by the king, resolve to go to the senâpati, thinking, "The king cares nothing for the city, we will inform the senâpati" (V. 459 sq.)

Wherein, in particular, the judicial work of the senâpati differs from that of the minister of justice (*viniccayâmacca*), whose proper province—as his name implies—was the administration of justice, is not evident from the Jâtakas. According to the statement made in the commentary on the Mahâparinibbâna Sutta the *vinicchayamahâmattas* represented the first and lowest stage of judicial work; their judgment was only final in the case of acquittal; in other cases, the matter was referred to the *vohârikas*.[1] In contrast with this, the *vinicchayâmacca* appears to be an important personality; his protest succeeds, as we have already seen, in revising a wrong judgment

[1] The existence of these *vohârikas* = Sk. *vyâvahârikas*, I have not found in the Jâtakas; we meet them, however, in the Vinaya Piṭaka. In Mahâvagga, I. 40.3, the King Bimbisâra asks the *vohârika mahâmatta* what punishment he deserves who initiates a hired soldier into the religious order; in Cullavagga, VI. 4.9, they become the subject of a discussion between Anathapiṇḍika and the prince Jeta. Manifestly, we are to understand by the *voharika mahâmattas* "judicial officers."

pronounced by the king in favour of the priest.

Although, owing to the nature of our text, it is not everywhere possible to venture any general conclusion from any particular passage, one can mention the Kurudhamma Jâtaka (II. 380) as a proof of this, that the "ministers of justice" not only gave judicial decisions, but also advised on matters of law and morality. A prostitute received 1,000 gold pieces from a youth, and as he promised her that he would come back, made a vow that she would not receive the least thing from any [p. 97.] other man, even if it was only a grain of paddy. After she had waited in vain for three years for his return without breaking her vow and had become at last poor, she went to the court and asked the *vinicchayamahâmattas* for their advice: "My lords, it is three years since a man gave me money and went away; whether he is dead, I don't know. I have no means of livelihood, what shall I do?" They advised her to return to her former profession.

A very important personality for the king—the increase of king's wealth depended obviously in no small degree upon his work—was the rajjuka or the rajjugâhaka amacca, lit., "the rope-holding minister," that is, as appears from the description contained in the Kuru-dhamma Jâtaka, the "surveyor," the cadastral officer of the king.[1] As we saw in the account of the king's revenue, [p. 98.] the lands of the tax-paying subjects were measured, either to determine the amount of rent payable by them to the king or to determine from the extent of land the average produce to be brought to the king's storeroom. "Whether the minister himself

---

[1] Bühler shows in the "Zeitschift der D. M. G.," Vol. 47, 1893, p. 466 sq., the identity of this *rajjûka* with the *râjûkas* or *lajukas* mentioned in the inscriptions of Asoka, the highest officers of the Government.

The account of the rajjugâhaka amacca given in the Kurudhamma Jâtaka seems to be so simple, so obvious, that it is difficult to understand why Rouse in his translation of the Jâtakas (Cambridge, 1895, p. 257) takes the meaning "cart-driver" given by Childers (*Pali Dictionary*, under the word *rajju*). Doubts only arise regarding whether and in what way the *rajjuka* or *rajjugâhaka amacca* was engaged in fixing and collecting the taxes, whether he is to be conceived, as Bühler wants to do, as a "tax-officer who measures the field" (for the purpose of fixing the land tax). I don't consider myself compelled, as I have already said, to accept the inference from the measurement of lands to a "land-tax," and even the circumstance that in the Kâma Jâtaka (IV. 169), in immediate connection with the measurement of the field by royal officers, the question of remission of taxes occurs, does not seem to me to establish conclusively the existence of the land tax, for by *bali*, a tax on the produce, a fixed percentage of the crops raised, might very well be meant. Even the method of collecting the taxes noticed by us above gives us no fixed data by which to decide the question, as by the corn which was measured in front of the king's granary, we might understand as well a portion of the produce as an amount fixed for all time, a ground-rent. Against the supposition of such a ground rent there is first the circumstance that neither in the lawbooks nor in the epics is it even mentioned that the taxes which are

measured the lands, or whether officers acting under his supervision measured the fields, as the Kâma Jâtaka (IV. 169) shows, cannot be determined from the two mutually contradictory statements; what seems more probable is that the episode of the Kurudhamma Jâtaka owes its origin to the attempt of the narrator to give as ancient a colouring as possible to the events described by him.

It is, however, narrated how the *rajjugâhaka amacca* is one day busy in the province, measuring a field. He fastens a rope to a stick, and whilst he gives one end of the rope to the owner of the field, he himself holds the other end (and wants to put the stick on the ground). In this way the stick got into the hole of a crab.[1] He reflects, "If I push the stick into the hole, the crab will perish, if I place the stick in front, the king will suffer loss, if I

---

only to be paid in the form of a portion of the yearly produce are to be looked upon as rent of the ground; rather, the scruples of the conscientious *setthi* already mentioned, have a meaning when the question is of a percentage of the produce; for had he had to pay a ground-rent, he would only have injured himself and not the king. That, nevertheless, in some parts of India even in the older Buddhistic age a ground-rent was not collected, is surely not proved; it is rather probable that in different kingdoms, the mode of taxation was different.

[1] What is meant here, as Bühler, (l.c., p. 469) remarks, is the land crabs which one finds in many parts of India, especially, in damp places.

place it behind, the farmer will be injured, what is then to be done?"

By such considerations, however characteristic they may be of thinking influenced by Buddhistic morality, an officer can [p. 99.] hardly be guided; the scruples are represented in the narrative itself as examples of excessive conscientiousness. Rather, we have to suppose from the extremely ironical character of the Jâtakas, that frequent cheatings on the part of the royal surveyors may have served as an occasion for this narrative.

With the *rajjugâhaka amacca*, "the surveyor," the series of royal officers mentioned expressly as ministers (*amacca*) comes to an end; of the remaining numerous courtiers it is doubtful whether they are to be reckoned as belonging to the category of *amaccas*. In part, they are called, as well as the "taxing officers" (Doṇamâpaka), *mahâmattas*, "of great importance, esteem," an expression which is probably to be regarded as a designation of an office, similar to that of an *amacca*[1] but is perhaps only to be treated as a predicate, corresponding to our "grandee, magnate." Whatever that may be,

---

[1] Synonymously with *amacca* the word *mahâmatta* is obviously used in the passage of the Vinaya Piṭaka quoted above. The inscriptions also use the word in this sense. *Cf.* "Zeitschr. d. Deutschen Morgenl. Ges.," Vol. 37, pp. 267, 275.

this much seems to me certain, that the *mahâmatta* and the *amacca*, as well as the other courtiers, belonged to one and the same class, namely, that of "people in the king's pay and service," the *râjabhoggas*,[1] who are reckoned in the Pâtimokkha (Nissaggiya 10), along with the *khattiyas*, *brâhmaṇas* and *gahapatis*, as a special class. In the passage of the Pâtimokkha in question the matter is this: A monk has been given a valuable object through a messenger, in exchange for which he wanted garments; as givers of such a present, which only wealthy and aristocratic people alone can possess, there are mentioned in order, the king, [p. 100.] those in the king's pay, the Brâhmaṇa, the householder (râjâ vâ râjabhoggo vâ brâhmaṇo, vâ gahapatiko vâ). Comparison with this passage of the Pâtimokkha has made me suppose—of the tentative character of this supposition I am perfectly conscious—that by the word *râjañña*, mentioned in the Assalâyana Sutta,[2] which has already been noted, "royal

---

[1] *Râjabhogga* is explained in the Suttavibhaṅga, Nissaggiya 10-2-1 (Vinaya Piṭaka ed. Oldenburg, Vol. 3, p. 222) as "one who receives livelihood and money" (*yo koci rañño bhattavetanâhâro*). A similar idea is expressed by *râjabhaṭa* (Mahavagga, I. 40. 3 sq.; 66. 1; 76. 1), only *râjabhaṭa* seems to me to have a narrower meaning and to denote especially a mercenary soldier in the king's army.

[2] Ed. Pischel, p. 1389: Khattiyakulâ brâhmaṇakulâ râjaññakulâ uppannâ.

officers" are to be understood. Also here the highest classes of the population are enumerated, as in the Pâtimokkha, with only this difference, that the *gahapatis* are omitted; the first to be mentioned are the Khattiyas, corresponding to the *râjâ* of the Pâtimokkha, then—probably, through courtesy to Assalâyana,—in the second place and before the *râjaññas*, the Brâhmaṇas and thirdly, the *râjaññas*. I think these are identical with the *râjabhoggas* and that by this word "people in the king's service, high officials of the king, courtiers" are to be understood.[1]

---

[1] The etymology of *râjañña* speaks no doubt against this view. In Sanskrit *râjanya* means "princely, royal" and "one belonging to the royal family," and if *râjañña* in Pali preserved this meaning, the word *râjaññakula* must, as it is done in Pischel's translation, be translated by 'royal family.' But, as is well-known, Pali words have very often deviated from the Sanskrit etymology and that *râjañña*, at least in this passage of the Assalâyana Sutta, cannot have the meaning of the Sanskrit *râjanya* seems to me beyond doubt, because otherwise, the concept 'princely, royal' would be repeated twice, once through *khattiya* and a second time through *râjañña*. To describe Khattiyakula, as "warrior family" and to look upon the scale, khattiyakula, brâhmaṇakula, râjaññakula, as an ascending one, is opposed to the terminology of Pali texts of that time and that found in the Assalâyana Sutta, which was to understand by *khattiyas* the princely or royal families and to give in an enumeration of castes, the highest rank, the first and foremost position to the *khattiya*.

Perhaps it will be objected against me that I have attached too much importance to this passage of the Assalâyana Sutta and that probably the word *râjañña* is an error. This I cannot accept, for the same enumeration of the three *kulas* is repeated in exactly the same form three times and because the Buddhistic writers were particularly careful about their terminology.

By his profession, the "produce-measurer" stands next to the *rajjūgāhaka*; as befits his name *doṇamāpaka*,[1] lit., "one who measures with a dry measure," the task devolves upon him of measuring the produce given by the owners of land (gahapatis) as the portion of the king (*rājabhāga*). He is thus the proper tax officer of the king, whilst the *rajjuka* in my view had no direct connection with the collection of taxes. Whether or not his work as described above, can be called difficult or specially honourable, he must have been one of the important personages in the Court, for to him also the title *mahāmatta*, "of great weight, esteem," is given (II. 378). It is probable that even this narrative, like the account of the work of the surveyor, purposely describes the primitive conditions of former times, of which the people had only a faint memory, and that in reality, probably, in Buddha's time, only the title *doṇamāpaka* remained and not the work denoted by it, namely, measuring corn with one's own hands. This was probably assigned to an army of subordinate officers in which category we must also include the tax-collectors, and supervision of their work was only allotted to the high official.

P. 101.

---

[1] Abbreviated also in the form doṇa (II. 367).

A well-known figure in the epics and the classical Sanskrit literature, the chariot-driver (sârathi) of the king, meets us also in the Jâtakas (II. 377), but is pushed somewhat into the background, as compared with the other followers of the king at that time.

Likewise only occasionally do we find the keeper of the king's purse, the *heraññika*, (III. 193) and the superintendent of the king's storehouse, *bhaṇḍágárika* (IV. 43; V. 123) mentioned. The rare mention of these two officers does not, however, justify the supposition that they held an unimportant position in the Court; the bhaṇḍâgârika, at least, seems, according to the Nigrodha Jâtaka, where Pottika, the tailor's son, predicts to his friends that on the next da , one of them would be king, another
[p. 192.] *senápati*, he himself *bhaṇḍágárika*, to have played no unimportant part in public life, especially, in trade matters; for it is said at the end that the king makes Pottika who refuses to accept the office of *senápati*, a superintendent of stores and that the latter "is worthy of the regard of all guilds" (*sabbaseṇínam vicáraṇáraham bhaṇḍágárikaṭṭhánam*, IV. 43).

So in the lowest rank of the courtiers the doorkeeper, *dovárika*, seems to have been; we meet him, in the list of persons mentioned in the Kurudhamma Jâtaka as those of which the king's Court consists, as occupying the last place but one, being above the public women (*gaṇikâs*). And in the MahâpiṅgalaJâtaka, the doorkeepers are mentioned after the "subjects in general" (*amaccâ ca brâhmaṇagahapatiraṭṭhikadovârikâdayo ca*) (II. 241). It is true that he is called in the Sonaka Jâtaka "noble gatekeeper" (*ayyadovârika*, V. 250), but he might, as here, appear a noble and important personage to a poor wood-gatherer who wanted an audience of the king. According to the Mâtaṅga Jâtaka, his duty was to thrash Caṇḍâlas or similar vagabonds who wanted to peep at the palace, with sticks or bamboo posts, catch them by the throat and fling them on the ground (IV. 382). Also the treatment which the doorkeeper in the Mahâpiṅgala Jâtaka received during the lifetime of the cruel king does not indicate that he held a specially high rank. Whilst all people expressed jubilation and held festivities at the death of Mahâpiṅgala, one of the doorkeepers moaned loudly. On being asked by the new king why he alone moaned, whilst all else were making merry, and whether probably his father was good and kind to him, he replied, "I don't weep because Piṅgala is dead. For my head his death is a real happiness. For the King Piṅgala used, every time he went away from or came to the palace, to strike eight blows upon

my head with his fists as with the hammer of a blacksmith. So he will also, when he goes to the Beyond, oppress in hell the doorkeepers of Yama with blows from his fists, in the belief that he bestows them upon me, and then they will cry out, "He gives us much trouble," and send him back here. He will, I
P. 103. fear, come back and strike blows, as before, with his fists upon my head; it is for this reason that I weep."

Obviously, the *dovárika* had for his duty the closing of the gate of the city at night. According to the Kurudhamma Jâtaka, he announces thrice at the time of shutting the gate the closing of the city gate (probably, by blowing upon a horn); a poor man who had gone to the forest with his sister to collect wood and had thereby been late, he addresses as follows, "Do you not know that the king is in the city and that the gate of the city is closed at the right time?" (II. 379). Foreigners, who did not know their way about the city, he had to direct. In the Mahâassaroha Jâtaka the king promises the *dovárika* 1,000 gold pieces if he can take him to a man living in the frontier who would cause enquiry to be made about the house of Mahâassaroha.

Possibly, the person who closed the city gate was different from the palace door-keeper and was to be counted among the officers who had to look after safety and discipline in the city; still these also belonged probably to the class of *râjabhoggas*, the royal officers, as they were appointed and paid by the king and had to obey his orders. If a dangerous robber made the city unsafe, then the residents, as narrated in the Kaṇavera Jâtaka (III. 59), went to the king with the request that he would arrest the "great robber," upon which the king charged the *nagaraguttika* with the arrest and execution of this man. That he was appointed by the king is evident from the conversation between the king and the Caṇḍâla; jokingly, the king calls here the *nagaraguttika* the "king at night." Judging from the insecurity which on account of the frequent mention of robbers and thieves in the Jâtakas and other folk-literature must have existed in the Indian cities in ancient times, he was no small personage.

As the last of the royal officers who occupied a public office, the
P. 104. executioner, the *coraghâtaka*, must be mentioned[1] who came close to the *nagaraguttika* and who sometimes represent-

---

[1] Other persons of that time employed in the king's court whose work was of a private nature are treated of in the eleventh chapter.

ed him. According to the lawbooks[1] the office of the executioner was exclusively in the hands of the people belonging to the despised classes, Candâlas and Śvapacas; thus even in ancient India—at certain times and in certain places—this profession had the same contemptuous odour about it which it had in the Middle Ages when one pointed out the executioner among the "unholy people". The Jâtakas know nothing of such a contempt attaching to the position of the *coraghâtaka*; rather, parades and ceremonial processions in which he appeared in front of the king, point to a certain respect which the executor of the king's commands enjoyed. When summoned, he comes, a hatchet and a thorny rope in his hand, dressed in a yellow garment and adorned with a cross of red flowers, salutes the king and asks for his commands (III. 41; so also III. 179).

With the offices enumerated above, the great class of *râjabhoggas* is in no way exhausted; apart from the fact that even the Jâtakas do not touch all the circumstances of public life—they speak, for example, almost nothing of the gradations of rank in the army—it is to be reflected that the apparatus of government, although all threads of the centralised State

---

[1] Manu, X. 56; Vishṇu, XVI. 11.

government were spun round this one point, was not confined in the great monarchies within the capital of the kingdom; in order to hold such a vast territory, as the Magadha kingdom, under the sway of a single ruler, the king's power must have been represented by officers everywhere in the small towns and in the villages.

If the circumstances narrated in the Kharassara Jâtaka can be held typical, the superintendent of the village, the *gâmabhojaka*, was an *amacca* of the king; he collected the taxes for him (râjabaliṃ labhitvâ I. 354) and was punished by the king appropriately, as he with his own people went to the forest, leaving the villagers at the mercy of robbers.[1] Other narratives make the official character of the village superintendent still less (or not at all) clear. In the Kulâvaka Jâtaka (I. 198 sq.), the *gâmabhojaka* spoke ill of the villagers to the king; as, however, their innocence was proved, the king gave them the whole of the possessions of the slanderer, made him their slave and turned him out of the village. Of the appointment of a new superintendent, nothing is mentioned, rather the further course of the story seems to bring out that the villagers henceforth looked after their own

[p. 105.]

[1] In the introductory explanation, the king removes him and sends another *gâmabhojaka*.

affairs. Also when we read in other passages that the *gâmabhojaka* exercises judicial powers in the village, inasmuch as he settles quarrels and makes the guilty pay a fine (I. 483), that he issues prohibitions, for example, against the slaughter of animals (mâghâtaṃ kârâpesi, IV. 115) and against the sale of intoxicating liquors (*majjavikkayam vâretvâ*, IV. 115), that when through defective growth or flood, the crops fail and famine appears, he distributes meat to the villagers, whilst they on their part, have to promise him a portion of their next crops (II. 135), all these statements seem, indeed, to point to the position of the *gâmabhojaka* being one of power and honour[1] among the villagers but do not oblige us to see in him a king's officer. They rather seem to indicate an elected chief, to whom the village community itself gave the direction of the common affairs—a kind of self-government in the village [p. 106.] communities. That self-government prevailed in India in villages is extremely probable and in particular localities of India it may have continued up to

[1] This honour however, was not always shown, as the Gahapati Jâtaka shows: the gâmabhojaka who has committed adultery, is held by the hair by the husband, flung upon the floor of the house, and while he protests loudly against this, crying "I am the village superintendent" (gâmabhojako'mhi II. 135) is beaten to a jelly and driven out of the house.

the period described in the Jâtakas.[1] As the royal power grew, this, with the rest of self-government, was more and more reduced; in the Magadha kingdom, the village superintendent remained under the personal supervision of the king, as appears from a passage of the Vinaya Piṭaka (Mahâvagga, V. I. 1 sq.): to the King Bimbisâra, a contemporary of Buddha, the overlordship of 80,000 villages is ascribed (*asîtiyâ gâmasahassesu issarâdhipaccam rajjam kâreti*); he collects together the chiefs (*gâmikas*) of these villages and gives them instruction in worldly things (*diṭṭhadhammike atthe anusâsitvâ*). About two hundred years later, King Asoka arranged a system of inspection tours for supervising the work of the administrative officers. "For this purpose"—so it is said in the first edict [2]—"in accordance with the law (dhammate) I shall send every fifth year (an officer) who is neither harsh nor impetuous, but mild in his acts." This arrangement of Asoka agrees, as he probably himself wanted to indicate by the expression *dhammate*,[3] with the prescriptions of the lawbooks: in Manu it is said (VII. 120 sq.), after the gradations of rank

[1] The circumstance, among others, may be mentioned in favour of this supposition, that the village superintendents are only mentioned in the later lawbooks as king's officers. *Cf.* Foy., *Die königliche Gewalt*, p. 65.

[2] According to the translation given by Bühler in the "Zeitschrift der Deutschen Morgenländischen Gesellschaft," Vol. 41, p. 13.

[3] Bühler, l. c., p. 19.

among the administrative officers[1] are pointed out: "The business of these (officers), who are concerned with village matters and their special obligations, another officer
P. 107. (saciva) of the king will examine who is mild and extremely industrious. And in every city he should appoint as a supervisor to look after all affairs, a magnanimous, highly esteemed person who is like a planet among the stars. The latter should visit these officers serially; he should examine their work in their districts through spies specially selected (for this purpose)."

---

[1] Manu, VII. 115: He (the king) should appoint an officer over (every individual) village, so also over ten villages (dasagrâmapati), over twenty villages (viṃsatîśa), over one hundred villages (śateśa) and over a thousand villages (sahasrapati).

CHAPTER VII

THE HOUSE PRIEST OF THE KING.

Not properly belonging to the class of king's officers and yet partly entrusted with similar functions and surpassing them in many respects in importance and influence, the house priest of the king, the *purohita*, occupies an extremely peculiar position in the Court. We must, if we wish to arrive at a clear conception of the nature of the *purohita*, realize the historical evolution of his position of power.[1]

Even in the pre-Vedic times, intercourse with the gods was not permitted to everybody, but it required the intervention of "a certain person with special knowledge and special magical powers."[2] This privilege, this claim, based upon wisdom and supernatural powers, to be alone in communication with the world of demons and gods and to exercise influence upon it through sacrifice and magic, led to the institution of the office of a priest, an

[1] *Cf.* on this: Weber, *Indische Studien*, Vol. 10, p. 30 sq., Pischel and Geldner, *Vedische Studien*, Vol. 2, N. 1, p. 143 sq., Pischel in the *Göttingische gelehrte Anzeige*, 1894. Vol. 1, p. 420 sq. Oldenberg, *Religion des Veda*, p. 372 sq. For the epics, *cf.* Hopkins, *Ruling Caste*, p. 151 sq.

[2] Oldenberg, *Religion des Veda*, p. 372.

exclusive priest class, who through this privilege exercised a preponderating influence upon other classes of the population and even upon the ruling class. It is precisely the latter class which
P. 108. required the help of the priest, either in injuring its enemies or for protection against threatening evil.

Even the Khattiyas of the east, however much they may have excelled the Brâhmaṇas in wealth and power, felt themselves standing on the same level with them in spiritual matters and were in this one point compelled to give the priests a power over themselves, not indeed the Brâhmaṇa caste as such, for this had become through its worldliness something different in Buddha's time from what it claimed to be according to its own literature and what in fact it might originally have been, but individual representatives of this caste, and principally, the house priest, the *purohita*.

---

[1] From the later Sanskrit literature a passage of the Raghuvaṃśa (XI. 58 sq.) should here be quoted, where King Dasaratha, frightened by hostile wind and other strange natural phenomena, goes to his guru, the *purohita* Vaśiṣṭha, for advice; the latter removes his anxiety by explaining them as good signs. It is characteristic of the view which the poet has of the relation between the king and the *purohita* that the expression *krityavit* is used, by which Kâlidâsa wants to say that the king knew how he was to behave in such cases, that he chose the only right and possible way of escaping the threatening danger when he sought the help of his priestly counsellor.

The proposition of the Aitareya Brâhmaṇa (VIII. 24), that every king who wants to perform a sacrifice, must have a *purohita*, as otherwise the gods will not accept his offering, also held good in eastern lands, so long at any rate as sacrifice was held in esteem. A king without a *purohita* was even here inconceivable, before Buddhism called in question the efficacy of sacrifice and magical chantings. Not being himself in a position—just because he lacks supernatural powers, the exclusive right of the priestly class --to propitiate the gods and demons, nor knowing the means by which the future could not only be known but made to favour him, he took recourse to the magician priest for influencing the transcendental world, to the Indian Shaman. In executing his commission, the purohita must perform the sacrifice, along with Brâhmaṇas who act under him, in order to drive away the misfortune which accrues to the king through bad dreams (in the Mahâsaripa Jâtaka, I. 334 sq.), or through sinister moaning (in the Lohakumbhi Jâtaka, III. 43 sq.) ; if inexplicable natural phenomena, such as the flashing of the weapons, cause anxiety to the king, the *purohita* refers
P 109. them to the constellation of the stars ; arms and animals which the king uses, must be consecrated by magic formulæ (for example,

the state elephants through *hattisutta*, II. 46), so that their use may bring luck. If, however, all this was the business of the *purohita*, then the destiny of the king was placed in his hands : it lay with him whether the favour of the gods was to be invoked on behalf of the king, his sacrificial lord; it was in his power to do the opposite; to him the king must come if he wanted to know beforehand the result of any undertaking by means of any sign or constellation of stars; especially, when he did not trust himself to answer the question whether he had any chance of conquering his enemies in war or thought it necessary to seek the help of the gods.[1] This position of the *purohita* with respect to the king led necessarily to an extremely intimate personal relation between the two; under circumstances there might arise—when the king was weak and the *purohita* possessed great energy—a temporal power of the latter who as a matter of fact had originally nothing to do with administration. For both of these our text gives us instances.

The three priests who are considered specially holy in the epics, the *guru*, who has taught

---

[1] *Cf.* Weber, *Ind. Stud.*, Vol. 10, p. 31 : "If a king wants to defeat the army of an enemy, he must go to a Brâhmaṇa for help. If he gives his consent, he consecrates the war-chariot of the king with all sorts of incantations and thus helps him on to victory : so also when a king is banished." Ait. Br., VIII. 10; Vs. XI. 81.

the king in his youth, the sacrificial priest and the house priest[1] appear, according to the Jâtakas, to be united in the person of the *purohita*. He is the teacher, the *guru*, or, as usually said in our text, the

P. 110 *âcariya* of the king and is mentioned as such by the latter. "Give it to the *âcariya*"—with these words the king presents a costly carriage through his retinue to the *purohita* (II. 376). When the king, as narrated in the Sarabhaṅga Jâtaka, hears the *purohita* knock at the door with his nails, he asks, "Who is there," and at the answer, "It is I, O king, the *purohita*," opens the door and says, "Come in, my teacher" (*âcariya*, IV. 270). Also in the passage already mentioned of the Sarabhaṅga Jâtaka (V. 127), the king calls him several times *âcariya*. In answer to the purohita's question whether he had a good sleep, he replies: "How could I sleep well, my teacher, when the weapons flashed to-day all over the palace." The priest soothes his anxiety as he points to the birth of his son as the cause of this phenomenon. "What, however, my teacher, will happen to a boy born under such circumstances?" "Nothing,

[1] The three personalities do not appear even in the epics always sharply distinguished: *Cf.* Hopkins, *Ruling Caste*, p. 155.

O great king, he will become the best archer in the whole of India." "Good, my teacher, then educate him well and when he is grown up, present him to me."

Often the *purohita* is the teacher and guide of the king in his youthful days; in the Tillamutthi Jâtaka we read that the king makes the teacher who has taught him in Takkasilâ his *purohita* and looks upon him as if he was his father and follows his advice (II. 282). Still the *purohita* probably got the title of *âcariya*, not from his capacity as teacher of the prince; he rather figured, even after his pupil had ascended the throne, still as his teacher, for a king did not apparently consider his spiritual education over with the termination of his studies and let himself be taught further by his *purohita* and given instruction in the Vedas (Bârâṇasirâjâ puro-
[P. 111.] hittassa santike mante gaṇhâti[1] III. 28).

[1] That in this passage the Vedas are necessarily to be understood by *mante*, I won't maintain; magical incantations may also be meant here, a knowledge of which the king, as appears from other passages, had at heart. Of such magical incantations learnt by a Khattiya, there are mentioned in the Jâtakas: the magical incantations with the help of which one conquers the earth (*pathavijayamanta*, II. 243), the magic by which one can understand all tongues, even the tongues of animals (sabbarâvajânanamanta, III. 145), the magical incantation which helps to bring into view concealed treasures (*niddhinuddharaṇamanta*, III. 116).

This position as teacher made the *purohita* in many cases the fatherly friend and adviser of the king. What served to raise and consolidate the position of trust which the *purohita* held in the king's Court, was the circumstance that his office was ordinarily hereditary (I. 437; II. 47; III. 392, 455; *purohitakula*, IV. 200) and held by the same family for generations together. This circumstance further helped to bind the priest's family firmly with the ruling house. "For seven generations, the performance of elephant consecration (hatthimaṅgala) has been hereditary in our family,"—so complains in the Susîma Jâtaka (II. 47) the mother of the young son of the *purohita* whose holding this lucrative post the Brâhmaṇas dispute on the ground of his youth and ignorance of the Vedas and of the elephant book (hatthisutta)—"the old custom will pass out of our hands and our wealth will disappear." Sometimes, in consequence of this hereditary character of the office of the *purohita*, friendly relations existed betwen the king and the latter from early youth. The son of the *purohita* born on the same day as the king's son grows up with the prince; they wear the same clothes and eat and drink together; when they are grown up, they go together for study to Takkasilâ (III. 31). This friendly relationship continues even after the prince is given the *uparajja* after his return from the University. They continue to share the same food, drink and bed, and a strong mutual trust subsists between them, and as the prince, after the death of his father, ascends the throne, he wishes to give the post of *purohita* to his friend. It is true that in this case the *purohita*'s son prefers the homeless life, still it is narrated to us in the Susîma Jâtaka (III. 392) that directly on the commencement of the young prince's reign, the *purohita's* son steps into his father's office.

Thus intimately associated from youth onward, the *purohita* and the king remain also in later years inseparable com-
[P. 112.] panions. We meet them together in a game at dice (in the Aṇḍabhûta Jâtaka, I. 289); we see the *purohita* on festive occasions on the back of an elephant behind the king, who is seated upon its shoulder. The king bestows honour and riches upon him; of such favours we find repeated mention: thus, for example, we meet with the gift of a carriage (in the Kurudhamma Jâtaka, II. 376), of a village (in the Nânacchanda Jâtaka, II. 429). The last seems generally to be the source of livelihood of the *purohita*, for we read pretty often (III. 105, IV. 475) that he goes to his *bhogagâma*, that is, to the village from which he collects his rents.

As he shares the fortunes of the king, so also he shares the misfortune of his lord. When fleeing at night from an invaded town, the robbed king takes with him, besides the queen and a servant, only the *purohita* (III. 417). As he, as explained in the Padakusala-Mâṇava Jâtaka (III. 513 sq.), has plundered the land along with the king, he is killed, along with the latter, by the enraged populace.

But the *purohita* is not only the fatherly adviser, the friend and inseparable companion; he appears sometimes as an officer of a purely temporal character. Mention has already been made of his participation in the administration of justice; the Kiṃchanda Jâtaka describes to us a slandering, corrupt *purohita* who when sitting in Court makes unjust judgments (*kûṭavinicchayiko ahosi* V. 1). In better light the Dhammadbaja Jâtaka (II. 186sq.) shows the judicial work of the royal house priest. Here it is narrated how a man who is defeated in a lawsuit through the adverse judgment of a corrupt *senâpati* leaves the Court, wringing his hands and weeping and meets the *purohita*, as he proceeds to do the king's work. He falls prostrate before him and complains that he has lost his case: "Whilst people like you, my lord, advise the king in worldly and spiritual things the *senâpati* takes bribes and robs the rightful owner of his property." The *purohita* feels sympathy for him [P. 113.] and says to him, "Come, I will decide your case"; they go to the Court together where there is a great crowd assembled. The *purohita* reverses the judgment (*aṭṭam paṭivinicchinitvá*, II. 187) and helps the rightful owner to get his own property. The crowd praised him loudly, so that a great noise arose. The king heard this and asked what the matter was. "O king, the wise Dhammaddhaja has set right a wrong judgment and hence this shout of praise." The king was pleased and asked the *purohita*: "People say, my teacher, you have decided a lawsuit; is it true?" "Yes, O Great King, I have set right a thing wrongly judged by the *senâpati*." "Then you shall from to-day try lawsuits; that will bring pleasure to my ears and prosperity to the world."

That guarding the king's treasures was part of his duties, we learn from the Bandhanamokkha Jâtaka, where the priest who has fallen into disgrace and whom the king's people want to take to the place of execution, prays that he may be brought before the king, "for"—so runs his prayer—"I am an officer of the king (*aham rájakammiko*, I. 439) and have rendered him much service and I know where great treasures are hidden. The treasures of the king, I have guarded; if you don't take me to the king, much wealth will be lost."

Still all *purohitas* were obviously not content with the occasional care of state affairs; greediness and love of power would often lead them to use the influence which they had over the decisions of a weak and superstitious king in securing worldly prosperity. If an ambitious priest was in possession of complete mastery over the king's will, it was quite in the nature of things that he gave his thoughts to the acquisition of the highest position of power in the Court, that he tried to become the leader of the king in worldly and spiritual matters (*atthadhammânusâsaka*, V. 57) and as such, to take into his hands the whole direction of state affairs. If, as often happens, a minister or one of the remaining Brâhmaṇas has obtained that which is the highest aim of ambitious courtiers, in case the *purohita* is himself free

[P. 114.] from worldly cares, the latter is selected beforehand for the office of *atthadhammânusâsaka*. Not content with this, many *purohitas* aimed at something higher and tried to combine in themselves the office of the house priest of several kingdoms. Examples of this nature are found very often in Sanskrit literature; thus, in the Śatapatha Brâhmaṇa (II. 4, 4, 5), it is said of

Devabhâga Śrautarsha that he was the *purohita* of two kingdoms,[1] namely, those of the *Kurus* and the *Sṛiñjayas*. Such a *purohita* may have served as a model for the hard and cruel Piṅgiya mentioned in the Dhonasâkha Jâtaka. "I will" —so he thinks in his desire for fame—"make this king conquer all other kings in the whole of India; in this way he will become the sole king and I the sole house priest (*ekapurohita*, III. 159.)"

We must always, however, bear in mind if we want to get a right estimate of the position of the *purohita*, that such a position of worldly power was neither necessarily connected with his office as house priest nor determined by proper regulations; the political power of the *purohita* was purely individual and had its source wholly and solely in the personal influence which he obtained over the king through his function as sacrificer and magician. From this side, in all cases, was derived the chief strength as well as the chief activity of the *purohita*. We get no impartial estimate or complete picture of his work as a sacrificial priest—and, indeed, nothing else can be expected from the standpoint of the Jâtakas —our sources make the *purohita* only exhibit his

---

[1] Weber. *Indische Studien*, Vol. 10, p. 34.

priestly office from the standpoint of its lucrativeness. When in the Lohakumbhi Jâtaka (III. 45), at the beginning of a sacrifice,[1] the eldest pupil comes to the *purohita* and asks, "Is it not mentioned, O teacher, in our Vedas that the killing of a man is not a fortune-bringing act?", the latter replies: "You bring the gold of the king, we shall have meat. Remain silent." In a similar manner the *purohita* stops in the Mahâsupina Jâtaka (I. 343) the wise and learned scholar who likewise expresses misgivings concerning the killing of any living being, saying, "My son, much money will come to us in this way; you seem to me, however, to take care to save the treasures of the king." Whilst in both these narratives the sacrifice is meant to protect the king from threatening misfortune, in the Dhonasâkha Jâtaka the ambitious *purohita* helps the king through a sacrificial ceremony to acquire a city which is difficult to conquer. He proposes to his lord to pluck out the eyes of the thousand captured kings, rip up the bellies and take out the entrails and thus give a bali-offering to a tree god (III. 159 sq.).

[P. 115.]

---

[1] The question here is of a *sabbaçatukkayañña*, that is, a complete fourfold sacrifice, consisting of four elephants, four horses, four bulls, four men and four samples of other creatures, quails, etc.

Just as the sacrifice, so also other magical performances the *purohita* did for his own enrichment and worldly prosperity. The consecration of State elephants brought the *purohita*, according to the Susîma Jâtaka, always ten millions (*koṭi* II. 46), as all implements for consecration and the entire jewellery of the elephants fell to the lot of the performer of the *hatthimaṅgala*. That he made use of his skill to read the signs of the future to promote his own interest, was only too obvious; to make a king subservient to his will, he used to read out of the signs only that which conformed to his wishes. In the well-known story of King Sufferlong and his son Livelong[1] the *purohita's* reading of the signs plays a rôle which can properly be called by no other name than cheating, though it is not employed for a bad purpose. The Kosala king Dîghîti "Sufferlong" is defeated by his neighbour, King Brahmadatta, and driven out of his kingdom. Along with the queen he wanders from place to place and comes at last to Benares, the seat of his enemy Brahmadatta, where he remains in hiding in the
P. 116. house of a potter, dressed as a begging ascetic. Not long after

[1] This is found in the Mahâvagga of the Vinaya Piṭaka (ed. Oldenberg, Vol. I, p. 342 sq.). The conclusion of the narrative is also contained in the Jâtaka collection, namely, in the Dîghîtakosala Jâtaka (VII. 211 sq.).

his wife becomes pregnant; she gets the desires which pregnancy creates and wishes to see at sunrise a four-limbed[1] army ready for fight, in full equipment and standing upon a ground which promises luck and to drink the water in which the swords have been washed. She nârrates this to Dîghîti and explains to him that as he in his poverty cannot fulfil such an extravagant desire of hers she will die, since she cannot see her desire fulfilled. Now the *purohita* of King Brahmadatta is a friend of Dîghîti; to him goes the Kosala king and explains in what difficulty he finds himself placed. "Let me see the queen," replies the *purohita*, and as he sees the queen, he cries out "Verily, a Kosala king resides in your womb! Rest assured, at sunrise you will see a four-limbed army ready for fight, in full equipment and standing upon a ground promising luck, and you will get the water in which the swords are washed to drink." He goes to Brahmadatta and says to him, "O king, the signs (nimittâni) demand that there should be to-morrow at sunrise a four-limbed army ready for fight, in full equipment and standing on a lucky ground and that the arms should be washed." The Kâsi king orders his people to satisfy the *purohita's* requirements.

---

[1] Caturañginî senâ, *i.e.*, an army consisting of elephants, horses, chariots and infantry.

Thus the desire of the queen in her pregnant condition is fulfilled through the deceit practised by the *purohita*.

The activity of the *purohitas* who did not live in the king's Court but in the country seems really to be confined to magic, reading of signs and similar things. Here they stood with regard to the representatives of the king probably in a relationship similar to that of the house priest to the king. They, however, lacked all opportunity to develop any political capacity. These *purohitas* who were not in the service of the king are[1] also mentioned in Brahmanical literature, though rarely; still a verse of the Daśa-brâhmaṇa Jâtaka (IV. 364) refers
P. 117. to them and describes their work in these words:—

"Food brought from a distance some *purohitas* in the villages eat, many people ask them (the meaning of star constellations, etc.), they castrate animals, (happy) signs they read.

"Also (in the houses of these *purohitas*) there are slaughtered sheep, buffaloes, swine and goats. They are slaughterers, O great king, and yet they call themselves Brâhmaṇas."

---

[1] On the *purohita* in a wider sense, *cf.* Oldenberg, *Religion des Veda* p. 374 sq.

CHAPTER VIII

THE BRAHMANAS

We have placed the *purohita*, on account of his often purely worldly position, among the officers of the king but have emphasised the fact that the proper source of his political power is to be sought in his being a Brâhmaṇa, in his belonging to the Brâhmaṇa caste; with this we shall now deal minutely.

While we had to point out in the case of the *Khattiyas* that the expression "caste" did not strictly apply to them, either in the modern sense or in the sense of the Brahmanical theory, the case is different with Brâhmaṇas. They are no class and do not represent any special element of the Indian society which may be called the spiritual element, just as the *Khattiyas* represent the ruling element; also they do not represent a purely hereditary rank, as do, for example, the ministers of the king, for we shall see that the Brâhmaṇa and the priest are in no way identical. The Brâhmaṇas are a caste and that, too, almost in the sense in which they understand it in their own theory. Every one is a Brâhmaṇa by his birth,[1] not by his profession;

[1] So also a Brâhmaṇa is defined in the Vinaya Piṭaka (Nissaggiya X. 2.1): *brâhmaṇo nâma jâtiyâ brâhmaṇo.*

he may change his profession, he may P. 118. follow the most humble callings, still he remains a Brâhmaṇa, a member of his caste. What lends exclusiveness to this Brâhmaṇa society, what unites the Brâhmaṇas closely with one another and separates them from members of other castes is, firstly, the consciousness of being the premier caste, the only one which enjoys the privilege of offering sacrifice, as the only medium of communicating with the gods, and secondly, the contempt arising from this, of all people who are low by birth, whose contact is strictly prohibited, and finally, the observance of certain universal customs relating especially to *connubium* and the eating of impure food, the violation of which leads *ipse jure* to excommunication from the caste. Of course, the exclusiveness of the Brâhmaṇa caste exists only in idea. The great mass of. Brâhmaṇas, spread over the whole of Northern India in Buddha's time, does not constitute a well-organised body with a chief and a council; such an external organisation, as we find in the modern castes, seems wholly wanting in that age.[1] Also

[1] Only when the Brâhmaṇas live in villages which are exclusively inhabited by them and live in union, is the presence of any organisation thinkable. Such Brâhmaṇa villages (brâhmaṇagâma) are mentioned in the Jâtakas; II. 368; III. 293; IV. 276, further, Mahâvagga V. 13, 12; Digha Nikâya III. 1. 1; V. 1.

the jurisdiction to which the members of the Brâhmaṇa caste were subject is not to be looked upon as a formal court in which cases of violation of the caste rules were decided; it rather seems to consist in the pressure of public opinion which was strong enough to enforce the observance of the rules. If, for example, as in the cases cited above (pp. 31 and 33 of the original, pp. 42 and 44 of the translation), a Brâhmaṇa had partaken of the table leavings of a Caṇḍâla, he ceased to be a Brâhmana; in order to avoid the contempt of his former caste people, he gave up his residence or committed suicide (II. 84).

If we try to get a picture of this caste from a popular source, like the Jâtakas, we should not be surprised to find it different from that of the Brahmanical sources. Freed from his worldly conditions, the Brâhmaṇa appears to be placed, as it were, in an ideal world, as the centre of which he is regarded, standing above the gods, or at least, on the same level with them.[1] It is different with the Jâtakas which present to us the Brâhmaṇas as they are in their daily lives. We see him now as a teacher asking the new

[P. 119.]

[1] Manu IX. 316: "Who are the support of all worlds and gods, whose treasure is Brahmana (sacrifice, prayer, Veda)—who shall injure them, if he has any love for life?"

scholar about the honorarium he has brought, now he meets us behind the plough, now in the court of the king interpreting signs and dreams or predicting from the constellation of the stars the future of the newly-born prince, now as a rich merchant in the midst of his accumulated treasures, now at the head of a big caravan.

One may, however, object here that the Jâtakas, if they do not idealise, still commit the mistake that they give a prejudiced and contemptuous view of the Brâhmaṇas. Many narratives seem to justify this view, for in many cases the Brâhmaṇas are pictured as greedy, shameless and immoral and serve as a foil to the *Khattiyas* who play the part of the virtuous and noble humanity in stories. Such an intentional contrast appears to be fully evident in the Juṇha Jâtaka (IV. 96 sq.).

"In old times, when Brahmadatta reigned in Benares, his son "Prince Juṇha" studied in Takkasilâ. One night, as in darkness he quitted the house of the teacher to whom he was assigned, and went hurriedly to his residence, he met on the way a Brâhmaṇa, who was also likewise going home after finishing his begging tour, and as he did not notice him, he pushed him with his arms, so that the alms pot of the Brâhmaṇa broke in two. The Brâhmaṇa threw himself down on the ground, weeping loudly. Filled with pity, the prince returned, took him by the hand and raised him; the latter, however, cried: "You have broken my alms pot in two, my dear, give me my food." The [P. 120.] prince replied, "Brâhmaṇa, I cannot give you money just now, but I am the son of the King of Kâsi and am called Juṇha; when I ascend the throne, then come and ask the money from me." The prince completed his studies, took leave of his teacher and returned to Benares, where he showed his father what he had learned. The father rejoiced that he saw his son before his death, wished to see him also as king and made over the government to him which he as "King Juṇha" conducted justly. The Brâhmaṇa heard of this and reflected: "Now I will fetch the money for my food:" he went to Benares and as he saw the king on a festive occasion in the adorned city, placed himself on an elevated seat, crying, "Victory to the king." The king passed by, without noticing him. As the Brâhmaṇa knew that he remained unnoticed, he raised his voice and shouted:

"Hear my word, O ruler of men! With a particular object in view I have come here, Juṇha; one should not pass by a wandering, Brâhmaṇa, whom one meets on the way, it is said, (without noticing him), O best of men."

When the king heard these words, he pulled up the elephant with his diamond-studded hook and recited the second verse:

"I hear, I stand. Say, O Brâhmaṇa, on what purpose you have come here; tell me what you have come here to ask me, O Brâhmaṇa."

Upon this, the following verses were recited in the course of the conversation between the king and the Brâhmaṇa:

"Give me five rich villages, a hundred slaves, seven hundred cows and more than ten thousand gold pieces and two consorts of equal rank with me."

"Have you, O Brâhmaṇa, made any penance of great severity, or do you possess, O Brâhmaṇa, various magic incantations? Are any demons in your power, or have you rendered me any service?"

"I have not done any penance or magic incantations, nor are any demons in my power, nor do I remember having rendered you any service. It concerns only a former meeting."

"I see you for the first time, so far as I
[P. 121.] know. I have not known you
before this. Make clear to me
in reply to my question, when and where our meeting took place."

"In the beautiful city of the Gandhâra king, in Takkasilâ we lived, O King. There, in darkness, at dead of night, we met each other, shoulder to shoulder. There we both exchanged, O Prince, friendly words; this is the only time that we have met and we did not meet since or before."

"If at any time among men, O Brâhmaṇa, a meeting with another good man takes place, wise men do not ignore acquaintances resulting from casual meeting or long intercourse, nor do they leave out of account what is done before."

"Foolish men alone ignore such acquaintances as well as what was done before. Even great things which occur to fools come to nothing; for so are the fools, ungrateful by nature."

"The thoughtful, however, never allow transitory or long acquaintances or what was done before to disappear. Even a small thing which happens to thoughtful men does not go for nothing; for so are the thoughtful, mindful by nature."

"I give you the five rich villages, a hundred slaves, seven hundred cows and more than a thousand gold pieces and two consorts of equal birth with you."

"So it is with good men when they meet, O King, as it is with the moon when she meets the stars; she will be full, O lord of Kâsi, like myself, for I have received to-day what was promised at our meeting."

"The Bodhisatta," so ends the Juṇha Jâtaka, "heaped wealth and honour upon him."

As the shamelessness of a Brâhmaṇa is here ridiculed, so also in other passages, the greediness of the Brâhmaṇas gives the narrator a good opportunity for making fun of them. "The Brâhmaṇas are full of greed of gold" (brâhmaṇâ dhanalolâ honti, I. 425), so thinks the jackal in the Sigâla Jâtaka who ventured into the town at night and when he was sleeping was taken unawares by the breaking of the day and frightened by the inability to make good his escape without being noticed. He offers a Brâhmaṇa two hundred *kahá-* [P. 122.] *paṇas* if he can take him under his shoulders, concealed by his overcoat, out of the town. The Brâhmaṇa agrees, but is punished severely for his greed and in such a way that he cannot retaliate.

Especially, it is the Brâhmaṇas in the King's service whose greed is brought prominently into view. In the Susîma Jâtaka it is narrated that the Brâhmaṇas after the death of the *purohita*, who, as explained, got ten millions every time for the consecration of the State elephant, went to the king and told him that they wanted, as the purohita's son was still too young and knew neither the three Vedas nor the *hatthisutta*, to perform the elephant consecration themselves. The king agreed and the Brâhmaṇas were highly pleased to receive the money for the *hatthi-maṅgala*.

The power of the Brâhmaṇas to give an opinion by reading signs about the future of a man or the success of an enterprise had concealed in it the temptation to make this opinion depend upon the expected reward, and the Jâtakas make it probable that the Brâhmaṇas in many cases could not resist this temptation. An *asilakkhaṇapâthakabrâhmaṇa*, *i.e.*, a Brâhmaṇa who by fixed characteristics (for example, by scent) knows the goodness of a sword, says to people, who have simply paid him for this, "The sword has a lucky sign, it is luck-bringing" (*asi lakkhaṇasampanno maṅgalasamyutto* I. 455); if, however, he gets no reward for this, he declares the sword to be *avalakkhaṇa*, *i.e.*, as "possessing bad characteristics."

In the class of enemies whom the dog of Sakka dressed as a hunter should kill (IV. 184), are included the reward-seeking Brâhmaṇas :—

"If the Brâhmanas, knowing the Vedas, the sâvitrî[1] and the sacrificial litany, make offerings for the sake of the reward, then the dog must be let loose."

[1] The verse in the Rigveda (II. 62. 10): *tat savitur vareṇyam*.

Further, morality does not seem, according to the Jâtakas, to be in a good way with the Brâhmaṇas. We read in the Sambhava Jâtaka (V. 57 sq.) how the *purohita* Suchîrata is sent by his king, the ruler of the Kuru land, Dhanañjayakorabya, to the Brâhmaṇa Vidhura in Benares to bring an answer to the question relating to the *dhammayâga*[1] which he cannot himself answer. He does not go from Indapatta straight to Benares but goes to Vidhura after first travelling all over India without being able to get any answer from any wise man. Vidhura cannot answer his question, as he is occupied with other thoughts and sends him to his son Bhadrakâra. "My love," the latter replies to the request of the *purohita*, "I am in these days occupied in seducing the wife of another, my mind is full of it, so that I cannot answer your question, but my younger brother Sañjaya possesses a better understanding than I; ask him, he will be able to answer your question. But he gets nothing better from Sañjaya, for he also is

[P. 123.]

---

[1] *Dhammayâga* denotes literally an offering which suits the *dhamma*, the doctrine or the law. A special kind of offering is not to be understood by this, but rather, something like an "ideal offering which satisfies all requirements." In the answer which is finally ascribed to Sucirata, an offering in the Brahmanical sense is certainly not mentioned; for the Buddhist, even the *dhammayâga*, the ideal sacrifice, consists in virtuous life in accordance with the *dhamma*.

in love with the wife of another and swims the Gangâ every day to go to his beloved: "Evening and morning, when I swim across the river, death can swallow me: of this my mind is full." He points to him his seven-year-old brother and it is he who first answers his question.

Still, it would be wrong if we would infer from these examples a feeling in the Jâtakas hostile to the Brâhmaṇas. As everywhere in the Pali literature[1] the "true" Brâhmaṇa —that is, according to the Bud- [P. 124.] dhistic view, the Brâhmaṇa who attaches value not to birth, nor to the study of the Veda, nor to sacrifice, but only to virtuous conduct—is very much honoured. On account of the importance which is attached in Buddha's teachings to the virtuous life, there can be no

---

[1] So in the Brâhmaṇavagga of the Dhammapada (ed. Fausböll, p. 79): "Not the flowing pair, not the family, not the caste makes the Brahmaṇa. He who possesses truth, virtue, is happy and is a Brâhmaṇa" *Cf.* further the Brâhmaṇadhammika Sutta in the Sutta Nipâta (ed. Fausböll, p. 51 sq.) and the answer which in the Vinaya Piṭaka Buddha gives to the high-minded Brâhmaṇa in answer to the question regarding the characteristics of a Brâhmaṇa (Mahavagga I. 2-3): "The Brâhmaṇa who has removed all sins from himself, who is free from haughtiness, free from impurity and full of self-control, who has mastered science fully, who has fulfilled the duties of a saint, such a Brâhmaṇa can truly be called a Brâhmaṇa, for whom there is no more any desire for anything in the world."

question here of a hostile attitude of Buddhism towards the world-renouncing Brahmanical ascetics. The spirit of the Buddhistic writings and even of the Jâtakas is only against the external conception of Brahmanical duties (*brâhmaṇadhamma* IV. 301 sq.), as it is developed, for example, by Uddâlaka in answer to his father's question (see above p. 26 sq.). Whilst Uddâlaka understands by *brâhmaṇadhamma* going round the fire, sprinkling water and the setting up of the sacrificial fire, the *purohita* who sees the ideal of the Brâhmaṇa in the property-less, world-renouncing holy man, gives expression to the Buddhistic conception in these words :—

"Without land, without relations, unconcerned about the sensuous world, free from desires, immune from bad lusts, indifferent to existence, acting thus, the Brâhmaṇa attains peace of mind; for this reason one calls him virtuous."

That this Brâhmaṇa without property and without desires is even for the Buddhistic narrator a thoroughly honourable person, appears from numerous passages of the Jâtakas, for example, from the Saccaṃkira Jâtaka (I. 323 sq.), where with a hard-hearted and cruel prince an amiable and sympathetic Brâhmaṇa ascetic is contrasted. The frequent occurrence of *samaṇa* and *brâhmaṇa* together shows that the homeless ascetic and the Brâhmaṇa were for the Buddhist identical, just as for him the attributes of a homeless ascetic, propertylessness and desirelessness, inhere in the notion of a "true" Brâhmaṇa.

[P. 125.]

"Let virtuous ascetics and Brâhmaṇas (*sîlavante samaṇa-brâhmaṇe*[1] I. 187) sit in the stable of the (vicious) elephants and talk of the virtuous life" is the advice which the minister gives the king, as he hopes in this way to tame the elephant which has become wild through the plots of robbers. "Do you not know that you are a saint or a Brâhmaṇa" (*tava samaṇabhâvam vâ brâhmaṇabhâvam vâ na jânâhi* I. 305)—With these words the queen brings the sensual ascetics to their senses.

In my opinion, we have to distinguish between two kinds of Brâhmaṇas who, though they do not perhaps appear to be outwardly distinguishable in any way, are essentially different in nature[2] and have nothing in common

[1] Even in the edicts of Aśoka this juxtaposition of *samaṇa* and *brâhmaṇa* is found. In the fourth edict, among the duties laid down by Aśoka to be performed, proper conduct towards Brâhmaṇas and ascetics is mentioned (*bambhanasamanânam sampaṭipati*). *Cf.* Zeitsch d. Deutsch. Morgenl. Gesellschaft," Vol. 37, p. 255.

[2] A division of the Brâhmaṇa caste into different sub-castes, a combination of those excommunicated from their castes to form a new caste, as takes place in India to-day, is I think, not to be supposed for the older Buddhistic period, as we find no trace of it anywhere in Pali literature. Also that the Brahmanical lawbooks know nothing

with each other except the name and the fact of belonging to the same caste. We speak of the distinction between "proper" and "worldly" Brâhmaṇas. The first class corresponds closely to the ideal sketched in their own writings. Their life is usually divided into three or four stages, into which the life of a Brâhmaṇa is divided by the lawbooks and the observance of which, as is recommended here, appears to be looked upon as essential.[1]

The Brâhmaṇa goes, when grown up, to a teacher, studies here the Vedas, sets up then a household, renounces later worldly life and goes to the forest where he lives either as a hermit or surrounded by a host of pupils and ascetics and which he quits in course of time to take up the life of the ascetic and provide himself

[P. 126.]

of this, I would not with Senart (*Revue deux mondes*, Vol. 122, p. 98) explain by the attempt of the authors to represent the castes in their ideal integrity, but would rather conclude from this, that it is first in modern times, when the castes take more and more the character of professional communities, that the old unity of the Brâhmaṇa caste, although existing only in the idea, is lost.

[1] Âpastambh. II. 21.1 sq. "There are four stages of life (âśrama), the house-holder's stage, the scholar's stage, the stage of the ascetic and that of the hermit in the forest. Who lives in all these according to the prescribed rules, attains peace of the soul." Manu VI. 37 expressly states that going into the forest must follow the life of the scholar and that of the householder: "A twice-born who seeks to be freed from the world without studying the Vedas and without producing any son, sinks."

with food by begging (Bodhisatto Kâsiraṭṭhe brâhmaṇakule nibbattitvâ vayappatto Takkasilaṃ gantvâ sabbasippâni uggaṇhitvâ gharâvâsaṃ pahâya isipabbajjaṃ pabbajitvâ gaṇasatthâ hutvâ Himavantapadese ciraṃ vasitvâ lonambilascvanatthâya janapodacârikaṃ, caramâno Bârâṇasiṃ patvâ râjuyyâne vasitvâ punadivase dvâragâme sapariso bhikkhâcâraṃ cari. II. 85. Similarly also II. 394, 411; III. 147, 352). Here we have the four âśramas of the lawbooks—the period of life of the scholar, the period of life of the householder, the period of stay in the forest and the period of wandering as a beggar. The formula quoted, by which the mode of life of an "upright" Brâhmaṇa should be characterised, occurs in exactly the same words at the beginning of a large number of Jâtakas. Still on a more minute comparison we notice differences; sometimes the Brâhmaṇa renounces the world immediately after he is grown up, apparently without fulfilling the duties of the scholar and the householder, and becomes a homeless ascetic (I. 333, 361, 373, 450; II. 131, 232, 262); sometimes we read of the beginning of the householder's stage and later renunciation of worldly life without any previous stage as scholar (II. 41, 145, 269, 437; III. 45); sometimes, the adoption of the houseless condition—residence in the forest or wandering—takes place immediately after the completion of the studies (II. 72; III. 64, 79, 110, 119, 228, 249, 308; V. 152, 193). Between these two last stages of life, no distinction, as between two successive stages, is made anywhere in the Jâtakas, and it [P. 127.] is probable that in practice also no distinction between the two was made, as inclemencies of weather and the necessities of life compelled every ascetic at times to exchange residence in the forest for the mode of life of a wandering beggar. If we do not wish to suppose that the Jâtakas purposely vary the wording, in order not to use the same words always, in enumerating the different stages of life of a Brâhmaṇa—a supposition which is contradicted by the words which were wholly current in the then Pali literature and repeated to the point of weariness—we can, in my opinion, conclude from these variations that there was in reality no question of a schematic partition of the course of life of a Brâhmaṇa. Often might the four stages in the life of an orthodox Brâhmaṇa overlap one another and it rested with the authors of the lawbooks to try to make a model of this ideal in their theory: we should, however, be greatly mistaken if we would think of all Brâhmaṇas as given one and all to study and asceticism and suppose that they had divided their life into four stages and dedicated the last two to the occupation of a hermit and a wandering beggar.[1]

If we take into consideration this distinction between theory and practice brought about by the schematising influence of the Brahmanical lawbooks, there still arises a close approximation between the "proper" Brâhmaṇa of the Jâtakas and the Brâhmaṇa as we know him from the Brâhmaṇa texts and the lawbooks, and this, not because of the external division of life but through the fact that he fulfils the duties of a Brâhmaṇa and enjoys his privileges.

As the four duties of a Brâhmaṇa the Śatapatha Brâhmaṇa mentions
[P. 128.] (XI. 5. 7, 1)[2]: Brahmanical parentage (brâhmaṇyaṃ), suitable behaviour (pratirûpacharyâ), attainment of fame (yaśas) and teaching of men (lokapakti). We should not from the nature of our source expect that it should offer us any detailed illustration of this scheme, for this reason that the duties mentioned consist in part in the carrying out of things which lie beyond the range of vision

---

[1] Senart, *Revue des deux mondes*, Vol. 122, p. 102. The articles of Senart in the *Revue* quoted above (p. 8 Note, p. 3. Note in the original) have in the meantime appeared in book form under the title *Les Castes dans l'Inde. Les faits et le système.* Paris 1896. I shall refer henceforth to this edition.

Cf. Weber, *Indische Studien*, Vol. 10, p. 41, 69 sq.

of the Buddhistic narrator and of which he lacks any understanding. Thus, the Jâtakas contain no rules regarding sacrifice which together with study constitutes the duty of attainment of fame mentioned in the third passage; they only mention it, in order to exhibit its worthlessness and illustrate the swindling ways of the greedy Brâhmaṇas in filling their pockets. For the Brâhmaṇas to make profit out of the sacrificial ceremonies seems to have passed into a proverb current among the people. As a king at a sacrificial ceremony gives money to the Brâhmaṇas, so does the *senâpati* willingly give his wife to his lord—thus runs a verse in the Ummadantî Jâtaka (V. 221). Also for the fulfilment of the first duty, namely, *brâhmaṇya*, I cannot give any illustration from the Jâtakas themselves, but we can infer from the polemic against the value attached to birth which we come across here, and indeed, generally, in the Jâtakas, that even in the eastern lands, great importance was attached, at least in some cases, to pure birth on the part of the Brâhmaṇas. What is meant here by a true Brâhmaṇa we learn, for example, from a passage of the Nidânakathâ (I. 2), where it is said of the first Bodhisattwa, that is, Buddha in his first existence as Brâhmaṇa Sumedha, "Of good family, on both sides, on the father's side as well as on the mother's

of pure origin up to the seventh generation, faultless and irreproachable, so far as birth is concerned." They are the same words which appear elsewhere in the Pali canon[1] and in which in the Dîgha Nikâya (IV. 4) the Brâhmaṇas ask Soṇadaṇḍa to seek for his ancestor in the Samaṇa Gotama, while pointing out his Brahmanical origin. "Because you, O Soṇadaṇḍa, are of good family on both sides, there-
[P. 129.] fore, you should not seek the Samaṇa Gotama but Samaṇa Gotama must seek you."

That examples of virtuous Brâhmaṇas who were quite serious about the second duty, that of leading a proper life (*pratirûpacaryâ*), were not rare in the Jâtakas, has already been mentioned; here we will only quote the answer which in the Samiddhi Jâtaka (II. 56 sq.) the young Brâhmaṇa hermit gives with reference to the allurements of the nymph who reminds him that so long as he is young, he should enjoy life and not allow time to slip:—

"I don't know the time (of my death), the time is hidden from my sight: I will therefore lead the life of a beggar without enjoying; the (right) time (of a virtuous course of life) should not slip from me."

---

[1] See the passage of the Vâseṭṭha Sutta quoted below p. 220.

What is most explicit is the rule contained in the Jâtakas concerning study which constitutes, by the side of sacrifice, the third duty of the Brâhmaṇa, namely, attainment of fame (*yaśas*).

When the young Brâhmaṇa is grown up he leaves his paternal home and goes to a teacher.[1] As a rule, the time

[P. 130.]

for the beginning of studies is given as the end of boyhood: "After he was grown up (vayappatta)"—so it is said in the

[1] Another possible mode of life for which I find no analogue in Brahmanical sources is sometimes allowed to a young Brâhmaṇa by his parents. These kindled a fire (*jâtaggi*) on the day of his birth and kept it burning ever since. When the boy becomes sixteen years old, his parents say to him, "Son, we have kindled a fire on the day of your birth and have not allowed it to be extinguished; if you wish to lead a householder's life, learn the three Vedas; if you, however, wish to enter the world of Brahmana, take the fire into the forest and serve it, so that you may win the favour of Mahâbrahma and attain the world of Brahma." The agni-service mentioned here is probably identical with the "service of fire" (*aggiparicariyâ*), the third of the four false paths (*apâyamukhâni*), of which it is said in the Digha Nikâya (III. 2.3) that they don't lead to the attainment of the highest perfection in knowledge and mode of life.

For the explanation of the *jâtaggi*, the fire for a woman in child-bed (sûtikâgni), mentioned by Hiraṇyakeśin (Gṛihyasûtra II. 3) and which takes the place of the domestic sacrificial fire, should be pointed out here. *Cf.* Oldenberg, *Die Religion des Veda*, p. 338. The lawbooks know nothing of a fire kindled at the birth of a son; they speak, on the contrary, of a *vaivâhika-agni* *i.e.*, a fire kindled on the occasion of marriage which serves for the performance of domestic ceremonies, for sacrifices and for the cooking of the daily food, and consequently, requires to be kept permanently. Manu, III. 67.

Tittira Jâtaka (I. 431) and also in several other places (I. 436, 505; II. 52; III. 18, 171, 194, 228, 248; V. 193, 227)—"he learnt all sciences in Takkasilâ." In the Jâtakas, however, the Brâhmaṇa youth as well as the Khattiya was considered grown up when he had attained the sixteenth year.[1] This appears clearly in the Sarabhanga Jâtaka, where it is said of the purohita's son that in his sixteenth year he was extraordinarily beautiful and that his father sent him to Takkasîlâ on seeing the full growth of his body (*Sarîrasampatti*, V. 127). So also in the three Jâtakas where the parents give the son the option of either worshipping the "natal fire" (*jâtaggi*) in the forest or studying.

As in the case of the Khattiyas, so also in that of the Brâhmaṇas, Takkasilâ is always mentioned as the place where youths carry on their studies; more rarely, Benares is mentioned as the place of residence of a world-renowned teacher (II. 260; III. 18). This last appears, according to the Jâtakas—as already remarked—to be behind Takkasilâ in scientific importance,

---

[1] According to the lawbooks, the completion of the sixteenth year is the time by which the *sâvitrî*, *i.e.*, the ceremonial introduction into the caste through the utterance of the *sâvitrî*, must have been performed. The *upanayana*, on the other hand, the admission of the pupil into the doctrine and thus the beginning of the study, could very well take place in the eighth, sometimes even in the fifth year. Manu, II. 36 sq.

and is only resorted to, as a young Brâhmaṇa such as in mentioned in the Âsanka Jâtaka (III. 248) born in a Kasi village would otherwise hardly go to the distant city of the Gandhâra kingdom for purposes of study but would rather go to the chief town of his own land, to Benares.

As the chief subject of the study of the Brâhmaṇas, the Vedas occur naturally in our

[P. 131.] sources. "In the three Vedas thoroughly proficient"[1] (*tiṇṇam vedânam pâragû or pâram gato*, I. 38. 43. 166 etc.), "attained perfection in the three Vedas" (*tîsu vedesu nipphattim patto*, I. 285)—these are the invariable epithets of a true Brâhmaṇa. Instead of the three Vedas, the *mantas* are sometimes mentioned which the teacher makes his pupils learn (*mante vâcesi*, I. 402; II. 100, 260). "Formerly, I was a Brâhmaṇa like you studying the Vedas" (*mantajjhâyaka brâhmaṇa*, I. 167) says the goat, which remembers its former birth, to the Brahmanical teacher. Also when it is said generally of a Brâhmaṇa, "he learnt the science" (*sippam*

[1] It is noteworthy that everywhere in our text only three Vedas are mentioned. It appears to me that herein we have a proof that the Atharvaveda in the older Buddhistic age, although it existed as a collection—as appears from Sutta Nipâta, Verse 927, and was made use of by the Brâhmaṇas in the performance of magical rites—was not considered from the religious standpoint of equal worth with the other three Vedas.

ugganhi, III. 18; *uggahitasippa*, III. 249; V. 193), what is meant by it is the Brahmanical science καὶ' ἐ'ξοχη'ν, the study of the Veda. Still the three Vedas were manifestly not the sole subject which the Brâhmaṇas were taught during their student days; in several places "all the sciences" (*sabbasippâni*, I. 463; II. 53; III. 219) are mentioned as what the Brâhmaṇa has to learn and by this are to be understood, over and above the three Vedas, eighteen branches of science. The purohita in the Sabbadâṭha Jâtaka is versed in the three Vedas and eighteen sciences (*tiṇṇam vedânam aṭṭhârasannam sippânam pâram gato*, II. 243) and the *udicca-brâhmaṇa* of the Bhîmasena Jâtaka learns from a world-renowned teacher in Takkasilâ the three Vedas and the eighteen branches of knowledge (*tayo vede atthârasa vijjaṭṭhânâni*, I. 356. So also I. 463). Particulars about these *aṭṭhârasa vijjaṭṭhânâni* we don't learn from the Jâtakas themselves; still it is not improbable that they coincide approximately with the eighteen divisions which are mentioned in the Brahmanical systems and into which the Hindus still divide their sciences.[1]

---

[1] In a probably very modern work of an orthodox Brâhmaṇa, the Prasthânabheda (manifoldness of methods) of Madhusudana Saraswati, the following eighteen sciences are enumerated: 1. The four Vedas: *Rigveda, Yajurveda, Sâmaveda and Atharvaveda.* (2) The

[P. 132.] The scholars (antevasika) were not always placed in the same category, but were divided, according to the Tilamutthi Jâtaka, into two classes, namely, into the *Dhammantevâsika*, that is, such as during the day-time rendered service to the teacher (as remuneration for the instruction received) and prosecuted their studies at night, and the *âcariyabhâgadâyaka*, *i.e.*, those who paid an honorarium to the teacher; these live—as it is said in II. 278—like eldest sons in the house of the teacher. To the honorarium brought by the pupil, great importance is attached by the teacher. The meeting between the newly arrived scholar, a prince from Benares, and the teacher in Takkasilâ, narrated in the Tilamuṭṭhi Jâtaka, takes place in the following way: The young prince is informed where his teacher lives and meets him as he walks to and fro in

---

six Vedâṅgas (limbs of the Vedas), namely, śikshâ (phonology), kalpa (ritual), vyâkaraṇa (grammar), nirukta (word-meaning). chandas (metrics) and jyotisha (astronomical science of almanac-making); (3) The four Upângas (auxiliary members), namely, the purâṇas (stories of ancient times), nyâya (logic) mimaṇsâ (Vedic dogmatics) and the dharmaśâstras (law books). To these fourteen sciences mentioned even by Yâjñavalkya (I-3), Madhusudan adds four more Upavedas (auxiliary Vedas), namely, âyurveda (medical science), dhanurveda (military science). gandharvaveda (musical science) and arthaśastra (practical art of teaching). so that in the total, eighteen sciences arise. With these the âṭṭhârasa vijjaṭṭhânâni of our text are surely not wholly identical, because in these the three Vedas are not comprehended. *Cf.* Bühler, *Indian Antiquary*, 1894 p. 247.

front of his house after finishing his teaching work. When he sees the teacher, he takes off his shoes, removes his umbrella and stands saluting with respect. The former notices that the new arrival is fatigued with the journey and welcomes him cordially. After the young man has eaten and rested a bit, he approaches the teacher again, saluting respectfully and the teacher makes a minute enquiry about his antecedents. "Where do you come from, my dear," he asks him. "From Benares." "Whose son are you?" "The son of the King of Benares." "For what purpose have you come?" "For the purpose of learning the science." "Have you brought your teacher's honorarium (*âcariy·bhâga*) or do you wish to become a *dhammantevâsika*?" "I have brought honorarium for the teacher," replies the prince and places a purse containing one thousand gold pieces at his feet.

[P. 183].

This sum of one thousand *kahâpaṇas*[1] is always indicated as the amount payable to the teacher at

[1] Acc. to Manu III. 156, the teacher who teaches for a fixed fee belongs to the class of Brâhmaṇas excluded from participation in the soma-offering. Teaching for the sake of money was considered undignified: the scholar might at the end of his studies make a present to the teacher, the amount of which was determined by his capacity and could consist in land, in gold, in a cow, a horse, an umbrella, shoes, a chair, a seat, corns, clothes and even vegetables. Manu II. 245 sq.

the commencement of study. Of course, we cannot look upon such figures in our text as an indication of the amount of the honorarium, but we may perhaps draw the conclusion that the fees of the Brâhmaṇa teacher were not trifling. Even the poor Brâhmaṇa scholar who received a free education tried later to pay the teacher by earning the money jointly by begging (dhammena bhikkhaṃ caritvâ âcariyadhanaṃ âharissâmi. IV. 224); sometimes rich residents of the city, who took care to feed poor Brâhmaṇa youths, bore also the expenses of their teaching (Bârâṇasivâsino duggatânaṃ paribbayaṃ datvâ sippaṃ sikkhâpenti I. 239).

Of other teachers for whom the question of honorarium was less important, it is narrated that in order that they might remain undisturbed, they leave the city and go with their pupils into the forest. These have to take with them the necessaries of life (sesame, rice, oil, clothes, etc.) and must not build a cottage for themselves and the teacher far away from the street. The great reputation of the teacher protects them, moreover, from want, for not only do the relations of the scholars bring rice, etc., but
[P. 134.] even the inhabitants of the land provide them with the necessaries of life (III. 537).

The method of teaching must have been the same as that which we know from Brahmanical sources,[1] and that which is still in vogue in India; the teacher recites verse after verse and the scholar repeats what is recited. The same thing also is to be understood when in the Tittira Jâtaka it is narrated that the parrot consoles the scholars after the death of the teacher by saying that it will undertake their teaching and when they ask in astonishment how it can do this, replies, "I have listened when your teacher recited before you and have committed to memory the three Vedas." The parrot explains difficult (lit. knotty) passages one after another before the scholars (ganṭhiganṭhiṭṭhânam osâresi. III. 538).

Outwardly, the intercourse between the teacher and the pupil took place with the exhibition of the greatest respect on the part of the latter. As characterising the view that the teacher under all circumstances stands above the pupil, whatever may be the position of the latter, we have the Chavaka Jâtaka (III. 27 sq.), where, as already mentioned, a Candâla raises this protest against the king that he gives the *purohita* who teaches him the Vedas a low seat, whilst he himself occupies a higher one. The conduct of the king as well as of the *purohita* is characterised by the Candâla as *adhammika*, unlawful,

---

[1] Skr. kârshâpana. It means originally a certain weight and is used of copper, as well as of gold and silver coins, so that we get an idea of the value of 1000 Kahâpanas. *Cf.* Angus' Pali Dict.

contrary to the *dhamma*; we see that the prescription of the law books,[1] in accordance with which the scholar must always occupy a lower seat than the teacher, held good even in Eastern India.

Much of what has hitherto been said in discussing the relationship between the teacher and the pupil falls under the category of the duty occupying the fourth place in the scheme, the duty of *lokapatti*, properly, making the people ripe, *i.e.*, teaching them. The Brâhmaṇa fulfils this in accordance with the Brahmanical texts, in his threefold position as teacher, as sacrificial priest and as *purohita*.[2] As from the Jâtakas we learn nothing of

[P. 135.]

the sacrificial priest, in case he is not in the service of the king, whilst the *purohita* on account of his political position, is treated apart from his caste, the picture of the Brahmanical teacher has still to be completed by certain characteristics taken from the Jâtakas. Our text is full of passages which describe the Brâhmaṇas as "world-renowned teachers" (disâpâmokkha âcariya, I. 166, 239, 299, 317, 402, 436: II. 137, 260, 421; III.

---

[1] *Cf.* Weber, *Indische Studien*, Vol. 10, p. 129. Zimmer, *Altindisches Leben*, p. 210 sq.

[2] Âpastamba I. 2, 21; Vishṇu XXVIII. 12; Manu II. 198.

215), surrounded by a great crowd of scholars whose number is given as five hundred. The scene of their activity is cities like Benares and Takkasilâ; here they teach the Vedas and all the sciences and maintain themselves and their families, at the head of which they stand as *grihasthas*, on the honoraria they get from the pupils. Of other Brâhmaṇas we read that immediately after they finish their studies, they accept the homeless state and go to the Himalayas where they gather round them a host of ascetics and figure as their advisers and teachers.

We mentioned the Chavaka Jâtaka as an instance of the high esteem in which even in Eastern Buddhistic lands the position of the Brahmanical teacher was held. That, on the other hand, the people occasionally knew and condemned small defects of the "world-renowned men," we can gather from the almost proverb-like expression of our text, *âcariyamuṭṭhim na karonti* (II. 221, 250), *i.e.*, "they don't make the closed fist of a teacher, they keep nothing secret," as the teachers evidently occasionally used to do, in order that they might have something not known to the pupils. They might be afraid that the same fate might befall them as befell the Brâhmaṇa of the Mûlapariyâya Jâtaka (II. 260) with his five hundred pupils, who believed they knew as much as their teacher and for this reason no more went to him or answered his questions.

As they had to perform the duties of their position, so were the "true" Brâhmaṇas undoubtedly given certain privileges [1] even in the eastern lands. If their position was inferior to that of the Khattiyas who

[P. 136.]

did not think it worth while to leave their seat at the sight of a Brâhmaṇa and offer a seat to him, and even if the claim which the young Brâhmaṇa Ambaṭṭha makes in the Dîgha Nikaya (III. 1, 15), namely, that of the four castes, three—Khattiya, Vessa, Sudda—existed in order that they might serve the Brâhmaṇa, was not so absolutely valid as he thought, he never suffered from lack of *arca*, *i.e.*, proper respect. If in the enumeration of the castes, the Brâhmaṇas are placed second, still even to Buddha himself the Kaṇṇakathâla Sutta [2] ascribes the saying that along with the Khattiyas the Brâhmaṇas take precedence over the other castes, so far as visible marks of respect are concerned.

---

[1] As such there are mentioned in the Śatapatha Brâhmaṇa (XL. 5, 7, 1): 1. Arcâ (honour due to the Brâhmaṇas). 2. Dâna (presents to the Brâhmaṇas). 3. Ajyeyatâ (unmolestability). 4. Abadhyatâ (immunity from being killed). *Cf.* Weber, Ind. Stud. Vol. 10, p. 40 sq.

[2] *Cf.* above p. 18 sq.

Even the privilege of *dâna*, of receiving presents, the Brâhmaṇas of the Jâtakas enjoy in great measure. The liberality of the kings which probably laid the foundation for the wealth of individual Brâhmaṇas, seems to be even in the eastern lands, if not a duty, at least a recognised virtue. We have seen how willingly King Juṇha satisfies the by no means moderate demand of the Brâhmaṇa; in the Somadatta Jâtaka it is narrated that the king gives a Brâhmaṇa sixteen cows, articles of ornament and a village as a place of residence. The whole is described as a gift to a Brâhmaṇa (brahmadeyya, II. 166), an expression which indicates a standing custom and which we meet with elsewhere in Pali literature. In the Dîgha Nikaya mention is made in several places of villages which are given to Brâhmaṇas by kings as *brahmadeyya*.

But it is not only that the duty or custom of liberality towards the Brâhmaṇas falls upon the king; we read also of gifts which come to their share. As the Brâhmaṇa is still to-day in India[1]
[P. 137.] a personality upon whose favour much depends for the individual, as he requires him not only for

[1] *Cf.* Nesfield, *The functions of modern Brâhmaṇas in Upper India, Calcutta Review*, Vol. 84, 1887 p. 257 sq.

sacrifices but in all matters of daily life, such as protection against threatening evil coming from the stars, the ascertainment whether a day is good for a journey or for marriage or the consecration of a new house or new agricultural implements, so even in those times people tried to win the favour of the Brâhmaṇas whose services were required for similar purposes. People instituted festivities and invited Brâhmaṇa teachers with their pupils (brâhmaṇavâcanaka. I. 318) to them. Such a *brâhmaṇavâcanaka* given by a villager is described in great detail in the Citta-Sambhûta Jâtaka (IV. 391). Because it rained on the previous night and the roads were full of water the âcariya gives one of his pupils, along with others, the task of uttering benediction (*maṅgala*), to eat his own portion of the presents and to bring him (the âcariya) his portion. Before the pupils sit down to breakfast they bathe and wash their face; in the meantime, the people take the rice from the fire and set it down to cool. When the pupils gather together, they are given "guest-water" (dakshiṇodaka) and dishes are placed before them.

Whether the Brâhmaṇas enjoyed the remaining privileges which they claimed, according to the Brâhmaṇa texts, namely, complete *ajyeyatâ* (unmolestability) and *abadhyatâ* (immunity from execution) in the eastern lands, cannot be determined with precision with the very limited materials which the Jâtakas offer on this question. Most probably, the Brâhmaṇas were free from taxes, for whenever the question is of taxes, the *gahapati* is mentioned as the person who is taxed; on the other hand, the claim of the Brâhmaṇas to immunity from execution, even assuming that in ancient times it had more than a mere theoretical value, seems to have found only a local recognition. The Pali texts know of no privileged position of the Brahmanas in the eye of the law; rather the statement of

[P. 138.]

Madhura Sutta that a criminal, no matter whether he is a Brâhmaṇa or belongs to any other caste, would be executed, appears in a number of passages of the Jâtakas where one speaks of the execution of a Brâhmaṇa (for example, I. 371, 439).

Along with the "proper" Brâhmaṇas we meet with another sort whom I might call "worldly" Brâhmaṇas and by whom I believe that the Brâhmaṇa caste was chiefly represented in the eastern lands in Buddha's time. As the reason for this supposition, there is for me the circumstance that of one of the Brâhmaṇas hitherto described and conforming to the Brahmanical ideal, it is said with emphasis that he belongs to the north, or is of northern extraction, *i.e.*, is an *udicca brâhmana*[1] (I. 324, 356, 361, 373, 406, 431, 436, 450, 494, 505 ; II. 83 ; III. 232 ; V. 193, 227). By these *udicca brâhmaṇas* we have, in my opinion, to understand Brâhmaṇas living in Kâsi or Magadha land who traced their descent to Brâhmaṇa families living north-west of the centre of Buddhism, somewhere in the regions of Kuru and Pañcâla, attached great importance to this descent and tried by a strict observance of the caste-prescriptions to prove that they were true members of their caste. The pride with which the Brâhmaṇa, in reply to the Caṇḍâla's question to which caste he belonged, says, "I am a Brâhmaṇa from the north-west," (ahaṃ udicco brâhmaṇo II. 83), corresponds to the suspicion which seizes him that he has probably violated the caste-prescriptions. In

[1] Sk. *udicca* signifies as an adjective "living in the north" and as a substantive "the land lying in the north-west up to the river Saraswati," in the plural, "the inhabitants of this land." That by the *udicca brâhmanas* of our text is not meant, as I believe it does, "hailing from the north" but "Brâhmaṇas living in the north"—as Chalmers (Jâtaka translation, Cambridge, 1895, pp. 178, 274, 308, 317) appears to suppose—is for this reason improbable that the scene of action of these narratives, in which *udicca brâhmanas* occur, is the kingdom of Kâsi. Moreover, in the Saccaṃkira Jàtaka (I. 324) these very words occur : Bodhisatto pi kho tasmiṃ kāle Kâsiraṭṭhe udiccabrâhmaṇakule nibbattitvâ : "now even the Bodhisatta was at that time born in a northern (or north-western) Brâhmaṇa family in the kingdom of Kâsi."

the Mangala Jâtaka (I. 371 sq.) such an *udicca brâhmaṇa* is placed in direct [P. 139] opposition to a worldly Brahmana. The latter, a *sâṭakalakkhaṇa brâhmaṇa*, *i.e.*, a Brâhmaṇa who can read the future from signs which are found in articles of clothing, learns one day that a dress which was kept in a box and which he wants to wear, is eaten by a mouse. He reflects "If this dress which is eaten by a mouse remains in the house, there will be very great misfortune, for it is a very bad omen. Also one cannot possibly give it to a child or a slave, for whoever wears this brings ill-luck to the whole of his surroundings. I will throw it into a cremation ground, but I will not give it to any of my slaves, for he may desire to have it and keep it with him and thereby bring mischief. I will make it over to my son." He calls his son and after he has explained the thing to him, he enjoins him not to touch the cloth but to carry it with a stick and throw it away into the cremation ground; after this, he should wash his whole body and return. Shortly before the son reached the cremation ground, the Bodhisatta reborn as *udicca brâhmaṇa* had gone there and sat near the gate. As the young man threw down the cloth, he took it up. The young Brâhmaṇa narrated this to his father and the latter went to the

Bodhisatta and pressed him to throw away the cloth, as otherwise he would be ruined. The *udicca brâhmaṇa*, however, taught him that a cloth thrown into the cremation ground was good enough for him, that he did not believe in premonitory signs and that no wise man should cherish such superstitions.

Even in the Mahâsupina Jâtaka (I. 334 sq.) it is an *udicca brâhmaṇa* who explains to the king the true meaning of his dreams and the deceit practised by the Brâhmaṇas in his service.

This predominance of north-western Brâhmaṇas over those of the eastern lands forms a sort of complement to the statements which we find in Brahmanical sources about the Brâhmaṇas of Magadha—and in it I might see a further support for

[P. 140.]

my assertion that in north-eastern India in Buddha's time the orthodox Brâhmaṇas were not the chief representatives of their caste but Brâhmaṇas who were unworthy, as estimated by the Brahmanical view. The name of these is in the Brâhmaṇa texts (Aitareya Br. VII. 27) *brahmabandhu* and by this name the *mâgadhadesiya brahmabandhus* are expressly called.[1] The low opinion here formed

[1] Kâtyayana, XXII. 4. 22. Lâtyâyana, VIII. 6. 28. *Cf.* Weber, *Indische Studien*, Vol. 10, p. 99.

of the Magadha Brâhmaṇas may, in part, be due to the low estimate in which the western Brâhmaṇas held Magadha which was at a great distance from them and was not wholly Brahmanised; partly, also the Brâhmaṇas by their conduct may have acquired this bad reputation.

Unworthy Brâhmaṇas are in fact those whom we meet with in the Dasabrâhmaṇa Jâtaka (IV. 361 sq.)—unworthy, as judged by strict Brahmanical ideas, unworthy, also in the eyes of the Buddhists who were above caste-rules and who judged from the standpoint of their morality:

"In ancient times there reigned in the city of Indapatta in the kingdom of Kuru, King Koravya of the family of Yuddhiṭṭhila. He was advised by his minister Vidhûra in worldly and spiritual things. The king made large gifts, whilst he set the whole of India in motion, but not a single person among the recipients possessed the five moral qualities and they all led bad lives, so that the king got no pleasure from his liberality. As he krew that gifts had only effect when there was a right choice (of recipients), he determined to give only to virtuous people and ask the advice of the wise Vidhûra. When, therefore, the latter came to have an audience with him, he gave him a seat and asked his advice:

"Seek Brâhmaṇas, O Vidhûra, that are virtuous and learned, who eschewing sensual pleasures would enjoy my gifts; gifts, O friend,
we will make where what is
[P. 141.] given will bear rich fruit."

"Very difficult to find are Brâhmaṇas, O king, that are virtuous and learned, who, eschewing sensual pleasures, would enjoy your gifts.

"Verily, there are ten classes of Brâhmaṇas, O king. Hear when I distinguish and classify them clearly: Provided with sacks which are filled and bound with roots, they gather herbs, bathe and mutter aphorisms. Physicians (tikicchakas) they resemble, O king, even if they call themselves Brâhmaṇas; they are now known to you, O great king, to such we will go (with our gifts)."

"Strayed have they," replies King Koravya "from Brahmanism, they are not called (rightly) Brâhmaṇas; seek others, O Vidhûra, virtuous and learned,

Who giving up carnal pleasures would enjoy my gifts; gifts, O friend, we will give where what is given will bear rich fruit."

"Little bells they carry before you and ring, messages also they carry and they know how to drive wagons. Servants (paricârakas) they resemble, O king, they are also called Brâhmaṇas; they are known to you, O great king, let us go to such men." "Strayed have they, etc. (as above)."

"Carrying a waterpot and a bent stick they run behind the kings into the villages and the country-towns, saying—

'If nothing is given, we will not leave the village or the forests.' Taxcollectors[1] (niggâhakas) they resemble," etc. (as above).

"Strayed have they, etc. (as above)."

"With long nails and hair on the body, filthy teeth, filthy hair, covered with dust and dirt, they go out as beggars.

Wood-cutters (khâṇughâtas) they resemble,"

[P. 142.] etc. (as above).

"Strayed have they," etc. (as above).

"Myrobalans,[2] mango and jack fruits, vibhîtaka nuts,[3] lakuca fruits,[4] toothpicks, bilva fruits,[5] and planks, râjâyatana wood,[6] baskets

---

[1] As the tax-collectors sit down in front of the gates of the tax-payers and do not leave until the tax is collected, so the Brâhmaṇas do not cease begging till they are paid.

[2] Haritaka and âmalaka are the fruits of *terminalia chebula* and *embliers officinalis*. Both were used as medicines. The sale of fruits and herbs was forbidden to the Brâhmaṇas in Manu X. 87. Honey and ointment also were among the articles which the Brâhmaṇas were not allowed to deal in.

[3] The fruit of *Terminalia Bellenica* Roxb. The kernels of these are odoriferous.

[4] A tree belonging to the Citraen order, the unripe fruits of which are used as medicines.

[5] *Artacarpas Lacucha* Roxb.

[6] *Buchanania Latifolia* ?

made of sugar, scents, honey and ointment, the most diverse wares they sell, O Lord."

"Tradesmen (vâṇijakas) they resemble," etc. (as above).

"Strayed have they," etc. (as above).

"Agriculture and trade they carry on, they breed goats and sheep, their daughters they give away (for money), marriages they arrange for their daughters and sons.

"The Ambaṭṭha[1] and vessa they resemble," etc. (as above).

"Strayed have they," etc. (as above).

"Some purohitas eat food brought from outside, many people ask them (regarding omens), animals they castrate and lucky signs they prepare."

"Sheep are also slaughtered there (in the houses of the purohitas), as also buffaloes, swine and goats; slaughterers (goghâtakas) they resemble," etc. (as above).

"Strayed have they," etc. (as above).

"Armed with the sword and the shield, axe in hand, they stand in the roads of the *vessas* (*i.e.*, in the business streets), lead the caravans (through roads exposed to robbers).

"Cowherds (gopas) they resemble and *nisâdas*, etc. (as above)."

---

[1] Skr. Ambashtha, name of a race. According to the Brahmanical caste-theory, son of a Brâhmaṇa by a woman of the third caste.

"Strayed have they," etc. (as above).

"Building huts in the forest,

[P. 143.] they make nooses; hares, cats, lizards, fish and tortoises they kill.

Hunters (luddakas) are they, O great king, even they," etc. (as above).

"Strayed have they, etc. (as above).

"Others lie for love of money under the bed of kings; the latter bathe over them after a soma offering is ready.[1]

"Bathers (malamajjanas) they resemble, etc. (as above)."

"Strayed have they, etc. (as above)."

An appendix attached to the Dasabrâhmaṇa Jâtaka gives a sketch which in the Vâseṭṭha Sutta (No. 35 of the Sutta Nipâta)—indirectly at any rate—is made of worldly Brâhmaṇas. Between the two youths Vâseṭṭha and Bhâradvâja a dispute arises as to whether a person is a Brâhmaṇa by birth or by act. Whilst

---

[1] The verse describes in aphoristic brevity the celebration of a sacrificial bath by which the king on the occasion of a soma-sacrifice instituted by the Brâhmaṇas, becomes free from blame and sin. He sits—so explains the commentator—on a platform adorned with the precious stones and bathes on it, whilst Brâhmaṇas stand below it. By this the impurity and blame of the king pass over to the Brâhmaṇas standing below who then sit on the platform at the termination of the sacrifice and are washed off all blame by other Brâhmaṇas. As rewards they receive the costly bed and the whole jewellery of the king. On the sacrificial bath and its original meaning, *cf.* Oldenberg, *Religion des Veda*, p. 407, sq.

Bhâradvâja maintains, "when anybody is of high birth on both sides, on his mother's side as well as on his father's, is of good family up to the seventh ancestor, blameless and irreproachable in respect of birth, he is *ipso facto* a Brâhmaṇa," Vâseṭṭha sees true Brahmanism in virtue and in good works. As they cannot convince each other, they resolve to have their dispute settled by the samaṇa Gotama. The latter points out in his answer, that in contrast with other living beings who are divided into several species, human beings are not distinguished by external characteristics; the differences among men lie only in their names.

[P. 144.] "For he who earns a livelihood by cattle-breeding—know this, O Vâseṭṭha—is an agriculturist and no Brâhmaṇa.

"And whoever among men gets a living through a many-sided skill in arts—know this, O Vâseṭṭha—is an artist (sippika) and no Brâhmaṇa. And whoever among men ekes out a living through service which he renders others—know this, O Vâseṭṭha—is a servant (pessika) and no Brâhmaṇa. And whoever among men lives by trade—know this, O Vâseṭṭha—is a tradesman (vânija) and no Brâhmaṇa.

"And whoever among men lives by skill of arms—know this, O Vâseṭṭha—is a warrior

(Yodhâjîva) and no Brâhmaṇa. And whoever among men earns a living as *purohita*—know this, O Vâseṭṭha—is a sacrificer (Yâcaka) and no Brâhmaṇa. And whoever among men gets his rents from villages or lands—know this, O Vâseṭṭha—is a king (râjan) and no Brâhmaṇa."

Both the quotations show that the Brâhmaṇa caste constituted an extremely parti-coloured society and was anything but a body of priests who studied or taught the Vedas and offered sacrifices to the gods. Whether all the professions mentioned therein were followed by them, is another question. Especially, the picture given by Vidhura may be a prejudiced and exaggerated one, and it is also to be considered that the purohita only says, "They resemble physicians, servants, collectors of taxes, etc.," and not that they were actually so. Nevertheless many details receive confirmation through other passages of the Jâtakas, where a subjective colouring on the part of the narrator is out of the

[P. 145.]

question for this reason that the statements concerning caste and profession are made parenthetically and are of secondary importance for the flow of the narrative.

According to the commentary of Sâyaṇa on the Aitareya[1] Brâhmaṇa, six categories of

---

[1] Ed. by Kâśînâtha Śâstrî Agâśe (Ânandâśrama Sanskrit Series, No. 32, Part I), Poona, 1896, p. 74.

Brâhmaṇas are distinguished in the Smṛiti of Sâtâtapa. These, although Brâhmaṇas by birth, are not worthy of being so, and in the first place, among these improper Brâhmaṇas, the servant of the king (rajabhritya) is reckoned.[1] Probably, the sense of this passage is not directed against the service of the king as such—the work of the *purohita* did appear in the eyes of the Brâhmaṇas as a perfectly legitimate occupation—but against such services as are attributed to the Brâhmaṇas in the Dasabrâhmaṇa Jâtaka. Surely, we must leave to Vidhûra in this case the responsibility for his statements, as further materials from which one might conclude that the Brâhmaṇas really had those low occupations which Vidhûra attributed to them, are not to be found in the Jâtakas. It is with difficulty that such individuals as figured as servants, messengers, carriage drivers of the king—although they might be found in particular cases—can be looked upon as the type of Brâhmaṇas in the king's service.

In the first place, the king employed Brâhmaṇas even in the eastern lands—at least in the old Buddhistic age—for sacrifice; for whenever, in general, a sacrifice was made Brâhmaṇas must be present who made the gods

---

[1] *Cf.* Weber, *Indische Studien*, Vol. 10, p. 100.

willing to accept the offerings. That, however, the practice of making offerings was in full bloom in Buddha's time, appears certainly from the criticism which is offered in the older Pali texts to the Vedic cult of sacrifice. It cannot have been a difficult problem for Buddhism to discredit sacrifice among the people, if it has had no other meaning than that which is ascribed to it in the Jâtakas. Here it preserves completely its sacerdotal character and is lowered [P. 146.] to the rank of a magic art for protection from threatening evil. In the Mahâsupina Jâtaka the king makes an offering in order to prevent the effect of evil dreams. The Brâhmaṇas and the *purohita* come in the morning to the king who sits in his place full of thoughts of death and reflects on the sixteen dreams, and ask him if he has slept well. "How could I have slept well, my teachers," answers the king, "when towards morning I dreamt sixteen great dreams. Since then I have been full of fear; tell me, my teachers, what they signify." Then he narrates to them his dreams and asks what will happen to him in consequence of these. The Brâhmaṇas wring their hands. On the king asking, "What are you wringing your hands for?" they reply, "The dreams are bad, O great king." "What will result from them?" The Brâhmaṇas reply that of the three evils—injury to the kingdom, injury to life, injury to property—one will happen. "Is there any means of preventing it, or is there none?" "In truth, the dreams are so extraordinarily frightful that there is properly no means of preventing their consequences. However, we will find some preventive means; for if we could not do this, what would be the use of all our learning?" They advise the king to perform a complete fourfold (sabbachatukkena) sacrifice. Full of fear, the king says, "So is my life in your hands, my teachers; make haste and look after my welfare." The Brâhmaṇas are highly pleased at the prospect of gold and feasts. They console the king, saying that he should not have any anxiety and go out of the city where they prepare a place for the sacrifice (yaññâvâṭa). After they have brought a number of quadrupeds to the place of sacrifice and have also collected a number of birds, they move about busily to and fro to bring this and that.

In the Lohakumbhi Jâtaka, it is not dreams which frighten the king but moans from the four sons of the king condemned to live in hell who in a former existence led a loose life. Here also the Brâhmaṇas advise a fourfold sacrifice (sabbacatukkayañña,
[P. 147.] III. 44) in order to avert the impending misfortune and the king orders

immediately to take four elephants, four horses, four bulls and four men and of all other creatures, quails, etc., any four samples and in this way to institute a complete fourfold sacrifice. When the king later learns the true cause of the moan, he causes the place of sacrifice to be destroyed.

The conclusion of this Jâtaka as well as similar narratives—for instance, the story of the prince who terminates a sacrificial ceremony in his kingdom by a tournament and further, the prohibition of the slaughter of animals in the Ayakûṭa Jâtaka (III. 146)—point to this, that with the spread of Buddhistic doctrines the cult of sacrifice gradually declined. For the older age, however, quite apart from the fact that the origin of such stories is to be traced rather to the tendency of Buddhistic doctrines against the killing of living animals than to actual facts, we have to suppose an adherence to the practice of sacrifice for this reason, that we see Brâhmaṇas always appearing among the king's retinue.

But the kings required the Brâhmaṇas not simply for sacrifice. Manifestly not less important for them was a service the performance of which is even to-day in India an affair of the Brâhmaṇas,[1] namely, the prediction of

[1] *Cf.* the remark made below.

the future. Although the king in difficult cases, especially, when he had to decide on war and peace, first betook himself to his *purohita*, there remained also for the other Brâhmaṇas in his court enough opportunity for displaying their supernatural wisdom. Whether the king will take the field or not, whether the king remaining in the city or the king besieging him will attack, whether the king besieged in his city or the one who is outside will win—with such prophecies the Brâhmaṇas used to earn their livelihood, according to a Buddhist treatise, called Mahâsîla, on the "right conduct" (sîla) of a *samaṇa* or Brâhmaṇa (Digha Nikâya II, 58).

[P. 148.] On the birth of a king's child, it seems to have been a standing custom to have the future of the child predicted by Brâhmaṇas. Signs (lakshaṇa) in the body of the newly-born served to the Brâhmaṇas versed in reading signs (Lakshaṇa-kusalâ Brâhmaṇâ, I. 272; aṅgavijjapâṭhakâ, II. 21; lakshaṇapâṭhakâ, II. 194; nemittika-brâhmaṇâ, IV. 79; nemittâ, IV. 230) for the deciphering of the future.

Also in interpreting the whims of the queen during the period of her pregnancy, eth Brâhmaṇas had to show their skill. In the introduction to the Thusa Jâtaka (III. 121) King

Bimbisâra asks the fortune-teller (nemittika) what the whim of the queen, who wants to suck the blood from his knee, has for its significance. The fortune-teller's reply is that his son will kill him and take the kingship into his own hands. On the day of naming, the child is called, on account of this, Ajâtasattu, *i.e.*, one who though unborn is still an enemy (of his father).

As at the birth of a child, so also on other occasions, the Brâhmaṇas know how to find out from the physical signs of any ordinary mortal what is hidden from view. As *aṅgavijjâpâṭhakas*,[1] they are in a position to judge from the external appearance not only the future of a man but also his worth, his character. For this reason, the king sends Brâhmaṇas, as narrated in the Ummadantî Jâtaka (V. 211), to the house of the father, a rich seṭṭhi who offers his extremely beautiful daughter, Ummadantî[2] to him, in order that they may examine the offered beauty. In a most charming manner it is described how the

---

[1] = Skr. aṅgavidyâ + pâṭhakâ, "versed in the science (of the signs) of the body, chiromancy."

[2] = Skr. Ummâdayantî, "causing one to lose one's senses, become distracted." Her beauty was, as said in the course of the Jâtaka, of such a nature that ordinary men (puthujjanâ) when they saw her could not preserve their self-control.

Brahmanas perform their mission. Whilst they, after an honourable reception, are engaged in eating their porridge, Ummadantî appears, decked with all her jewellery. The effect of the sight of her makes it impossible to entertain any favourable opinion of the strength of character of the Brâhmaṇas; they lose their self-control and seized with passion, forget that they have not yet finished their meal. [P. 149.] Some put their food on their head instead of into their mouth, others put it into the arm-pit, others, again, throw it towards the wall, in short, all lose their senses. When the girl sees their conduct, she cries out, "These should examine me for my signs! Seize them by the throat and drive them out." The ejected Brâhmaṇas report angrily to the king, "O king, the woman is a witch, she is not suitable for you."

We notice clearly enough that ridicule is thrown upon the incapacity and treachery of the Brâhmaṇas in the words of the narrative. To see in such things, as fortune-telling, interpretations of dreams, etc., only lying and deception, shows that these stories are a product of their age and their land. Originating in the circles of the common people in whose religious thought superstition occupied a large place, they retain traces of their origin notwithstanding complete rejection and deprecation of superstitious ideas. But in the hands of the Buddhist monks to whom the above-named arts appear as endangering " right conduct " and as unworthy of a samaṇa or Brâhmaṇa, they receive a transformation which is directed against the conduct of the Brâhmaṇas practising these things for the sake of their own profit. Often these, according to the account of the Jâtakas, made their prophecies to a certain extent depend upon the gifts falling to their share; thus we read in the Kunâla Jâtaka how the dream-readers are bribed by the jealous wives of the king and predict before the latter that the dreams of his principal consort signify evil for him, to avert which he must place the queen in a ship and leave it at the mercy of the waves. In the opening chapter of the Pañcâvudha Jâtaka it is narrated how the parents of the new-born prince on the day of the naming ceremony please the Brâhmaṇas by granting all they desire before they ask him about the signs which indicate the future (brâhmaṇe subbakâmehi santappetvâ lakshaṇâni patipucchiṃsu, I. 272).

Along with the signs in the human body, other means are mentioned in the already quoted chapter of the Dîgha
[P. 150.] Nikâya which contains a complete list of superstitious practices, which

serves the Brâhmaṇas for purposes of fortune-telling. The question here is of prophecies from things, like cloths eaten by rats, pieces of cloth, etc., of fortune-telling from the flights of birds, the crowing of the raven, from interpretations of certain signs in precious stones, sticks, clothes, swords, arrows, bows, weapons, in women and men, boys and girls, male and female slaves, elephants and other animals; there is further mentioned here the prediction of coming natural phenomena, such as solar and lunar eclipses, falling meteors, earthquakes, etc., and the reading of the future from such events and from the position of the stars. In the Jâtakas we come across various Brâhmaṇas who are occupied in practising such "common arts (tiracchâ navijjâ) and swindling trades" (micchâjîva) as are indicated in the Mahâsîla; we have already been acquainted with the asilakshaṇapâthakabrâhmaṇa who predicts from the smell of a sword whether its use will bring luck or not, and the sâṭakalakshaṇabrâhmaṇa who sees an unlucky omen in a cloth eaten by rats. Even the art of interpreting the stars—to which probably even a Buddhist will make no objection—was, according to the Nânacchanda Jâtaka, practised by the Brâhmaṇas in such a manner that it deserved the name of "a swindling trade." The king is attacked at night by robbers and listens, while the former purohita of his father, now removed from office, who reads the stars in a neighbouring street, says to his wife, "My lady, our king has fallen into the hands of enemies." "My lord, what does the king matter to you; the Brâhmaṇas will become aware of it." The king succeeds in escaping and as he returns he hears the purohita inform his wife of his escape through the position of the stars. At daybreak the king summons the Brâhmaṇas and asks them if they observed the stars at night. "Certainly, O king." "Was the constellation favourable or unfavourable?" "Favourable, O king." "Did no eclipse occur?" "No, O king." The king orders the former purohita [P. 151.] to be brought and asks him likewise whether he observed the stars at night and whether he noticed any eclipse. "Yes, O king, last night you fell into the hands of your enemies, you were free, however, in a moment." "This is a reader of the stars (nakshattajânanaka), as he ought to be," cries out the king, removes the other Brâhmaṇas from his service and from that day onward keeps the *purohita* to himself.

Sacrifice and fortune-telling seem, however, to have been both not so valuable as a third art which was likewise a privilege of the Brâhmaṇas, namely, magic. We have heard above (p. 120) what the king replies to the Brâhmaṇa, manifestly shocked at his shameless demands:

"Hast thou, O Brâhmaṇa, performed a difficult penance, or dost thou possess, O Brâhmaṇa, various magic incantations; are any demons obedient to thee or dost thou know any service rendered to me?"

As sacrifice and fortune-telling, so also the three herein-mentioned things from which the Brâhmaṇa, according to the view of the king, could have found a justification of his unlimited claims—asceticism, magic incantations and power over demons—are a work of supernatural powers. Through the magical power of asceticism (tapas) the Brâhmaṇa could obtain ascendancy even over the gods which it lay in his hands to use for the king. What a great rôle asceticism plays in Brahmanical literature, how here, especially, in the epics, its influence as transcending all bounds is described, is known.[1] Buddhism preaches asceticism[2] in its

[1] *Cf.* L. V. Schoeder, *Indiens Literatur und Cultur*, Lpg. 1887, p. 388 sq.

[2] "What separated Buddha above all things from most of his rivals was his rejection of penances in which these recognised the path of emancipation. We saw how according to tradition Buddha himself in the age in question, through which he lived as a boy, knew self-mortification in its severest form and perceived its worthlessness in himself. What drives earthly thoughts away from the soul is not fasting and bodily penances but work for its own sake, above all, the struggle for

dogma and even in the Jâtakas, the self-chastising Brâhmaṇas are attacked and ridiculed.[1] But asceticism with its magic influences has found recognition even among the Buddhists in a somewhat different form and consequently, also has found entrance into our story-literature. In place of penances there appears the holiness resulting from vision by whose power wonderful things are achieved and even gods are tranquillised and forced to give up their seat in heaven.

[P. 152.]

As we don't find asceticism—perhaps even for this reason—mentioned among what are called in the Mahâsîla "low arts and swindling practices," magic incantations, the knowledge of which among the Brâhmaṇas was taken for granted by King Juṇha, were looked upon as such by the Buddhists. The long list of magic incantations enumerated in the Mahâsîla shows that the most ancient practice of magic was widely prevalent among the Brâhmaṇas; of some of these *mantas* and their employment we read even in the Jâtakas. In the Vedabbha Jâtaka (I. 253) we meet with a Brâhmaṇa who being in possession of the knowledge of *vedabbhamanta* can bring

knowledge and for this struggle one creates the force only out of an external life which is as far removed from sensuality as it is from self-denial or even self-created pain." Oldenberg, *Buddha*, p. 178.

[1] See above (p. 23).

about a rain of precious stones at a certain position of the stars; another Brâhmaṇa knows the magic practice with the help of which one conquers the earth (paṭhavijayamanta, II. 243). In the same category as the knowledge of these magic formulæ belong sciences, mentioned likewise in the Mahâsîla, like knowledge of people and animal languages, which are ascribed in the Maccha Jâtaka to the purohita, (so pana sabbarutaññu hoti, I. 211) and further, the *vatthuvijjá*, *i.e.*, the art of knowing through supernatural signs the correct position of a house, a cloth, etc. In the Suruci Jâtaka the king who wants to build a palace for his son summons the teachers of this art (vatthuvijjâcariyas, IV. 323) and lets them find an auspicious place for the building.

To magic incantations the Brâhmaṇas owe also the power over demons ascribed to them in the Juṇha Jâtaka. The ancient belief in an innumerable number of small super-terrestrial beings, who as tree or snake [P. 153.] gods endanger the life of man, frighten him as man-eating or child-robbing demons or torture him as disease-bringing spirits, occupies naturally in our narratives, which reflect the conceptual world of the lower people, an important place and the art of making these beings harmless or useful through magic practices—a privilege of the Brâhmaṇas as old as the belief in the demons itself—received also in Buddha's time no small recognition among the people. These people who had power over demons are called in the Pali texts *bhûtavejjas*, knowers of the science of the spirits (bhûtavijjâ), exorcists; such a bhûtavejja we come across in the Padakusulamânava Jâtaka: the thief who sees an old woman in the hole where he has placed his stolen bundle, believes that she is a *yakkhini* and calls a *bhûtavejja*. The latter enters the hole and recites a magic verse (mantaṃ karonto, III. 511). The art of exorcism was chiefly employed where the question was of freeing the "possessed" of the evil spirit dwelling in them. "Some cure men bitten by snakes, the wise cure people possessed by evil spirits," so it is said in a verse of the Kâmanîta Jâtaka and the method of cure used by the wise Brâhmaṇas (paṇḍitas) is mentioned in the commentary: making sacrifice (balikamma), incantations for preventing threatened evil (parittakaraṇas) and herbs (osadhas). "Physicians they resemble," says Vidhûra in the Dasabrâhmaṇa Jâtaka of these herb-gathering and verse-uttering Brâhmaṇas, and it is probable that not only certain branches of the curative art, such as, exorcism practised upon a person bitten by a snake and expulsion of evil spirits, were practised by the Brâhmaṇas, but that the medical

profession in general, which among most people separated itself from the beginning from the spiritual, was in ancient times even in India principally a matter for the Brâhmaṇas. Still there occur in the Jâtakas, side by side with the Brâhmaṇa physicians (vejjabrâhmaṇa, II. 213), some who are simply called *vejjas* (I. 455; III. 202; *visavejjakula*, I. 310; *vejjakulâni*, III. 145) and who probably at a later period, through the unity of a hereditary profession,
[P. 154.] were bound together to form a caste by themselves.

Allied to the magic exorcists by the nature of his work is the Brâhmaṇa snake-charmer (ahiguṇṭhikabrâhmaṇa IV. 457) of the Campeyya Jâtaka. He has learnt the *âlambanamanta* in Takkasilâ from a world-renowned teacher and earns a living by making snakes rendered harmless by means of herbs and magic incantations, dance in villages, market towns and the residences of kings.

As this snake-charmer exhibited his art not only in the court of the king but also among the people, so also the other "worldly" Brâhmaṇas with whom we have hitherto had to do, and as functions of whom we have come to recognise sacrifice, prophecy and magic, are not exclusively employed in the service of a king. As little then as to-day, when the sign-reading and prophesying Brâhmaṇa is an indispensable personality[1] for every Hindu, do the Brâhmaṇas scorn to give man, where they can, the benefit of their wisdom for the sake of reward.

[P. 155.]

In the Nakkhatta Jâtaka we become acquainted with a "family ascetic" (kulûpaka âjîvika, I. 257) who is asked by a family living in the city, who wants to marry the son of the house to a country girl, on the day fixed for the marriage whether the position of the stars is favourable. Angry at the circumstance that the day was chosen beforehand and that people consulted him afterwards, the Brâhmaṇa determines to spoil the festivities and

[1] On the importance of the modern astrologer, the *jyotishi*, see Nesfield, *Caste System*, p. 58 87. It is said there among other things, "The first thing which a father after the birth of a child does, is to go to the jyotishi and tell him as accurately as he can the hour of birth. The jyotishi questions the stars and casts the horoscope by which the destiny of the child is determined." "In the case of illness or other misfortune, the astrologer is asked whether an evil star is in the ascendant which may have brought about the misfortune. When the answer is in the affirmative, as is naturally always the case, then the man seeking advice is told that he must make a gift of money or make some other present to propitiate the hostile star, and as the astrologer is the recognised exponent of the feelings and wishes of the star, he estimates what one would not otherwise have supposed, the gift required for the propitiation of the hostile star. This then constitutes a portion of the astrologer's dues." For bringing about betrothals and marriages, the services of the astrologer were indispensably necessary. When the family barber or *napit* had chosen a boy whom he considered eligible for a girl of the same caste, then no negotiations could be concluded between

says, "To-day the constellation is unfavourable; if in spite of this, you perform the marriage, it will bring you evil." The people believe in him and remain at home. Those who were in the country waited in vain for them and finally reflected: "They have fixed the marriage for to-day and have not yet come: what do we care any more for them?"—and married the girl elsewhere. Next day the townspeople came to fetch the girl. The country people received them with the words, "You townsmen are a shameless people, you fix the day and don't take the bride. As you did not come, we have given her to somebody else." "We asked the ascetic and did not come because he told us that the stars were unfavourable; give us the girl." "As you did not come, we have given her

[P. 156.] to somebody else, how can we

---

the parents before the astrologer was asked whether the stars of the boy were not hostile to those of the girl. As if this was not sufficient, he must also find out what were the castes of the boy and the girl in their former existence. If both belonged to the same caste, the betrothal contract can be made, provided that the stars are not in other respects hostile. If it happens, however, that the caste of the boy in a former existence was lower than that of the girl, then betrothal is not permitted." "For all events which can take place in the life of a man or a woman, the astrologer must select an auspicious day—for marriage, for every part of the marriage ceremony, for the commencement of a journey, for the placing of the first plough on the ground, etc. A woman cannot wear a new set of bracelets before she knows that the stars are favourable and an orthodox Brâhmaṇa will not put on a new garment until he has ascertained that the day is auspicious on which he wears it for the first time."

marry a girl already given away a second time?" When they were quarrelling in this way among themselves, a wise man residing in the town appears who has occasionally business in the country. The townsmen narrate to him the story and believed that he would pronounce a judgment in their favour that they could not come on account of the sign of the stars. He replied, however, "What does the look of the star matter? the possession of the girl is the lucky star" and recited the verse:

"As he looked for favourable stars, fortune moved away from the fool. Fortune is the look of the star of fortune, what should the stars matter?"

The townspeople had to go away without the girl, disappointed.

Still instances of such a (so to speak) private use of their supernatural skill was not so common among the Brâhmaṇas of the Jâtakas that we could suppose that their services were as much sought by the people of that time, were as indispensably necessary, as in India of to-day. We rather get from our sources the impression that as a rule, the court of the king was the meeting-place for the Brâhmaṇas, where they could best exhibit the arts and sciences learnt by them during their student days. To bring prosperity again to his family, the young Brâhmaṇa of the

Somadatta Jâtaka goes to Benares and joins the king's service after he has studied in Takkasîlâ and on his return finds his parents in poverty (II. 165). As this Brâhmaṇa youth, so also probably, the other Brâhmaṇas in the court, have received a scientific training and have deviated less from the customs prescribed for their caste by the Brahmanical theory than the members of the Brâhmaṇa caste with whom we are here concerned, than the Brâhmaṇas employed in civil professions.

"Agriculture they carry on, goats and sheep they breed," so Vidhura in the Dasabrâhmaṇa Jâtaka protests against the Brâhmaṇas, a protest which was wholly justified if we are to follow the Pali texts. The land-cultivating and cattle-rearing Brâhmaṇa is here such a permanently recurring figure[1] that it seems probable that in the Buddhist

[P. 157.]

countries land was mostly in the possession of the Brâhmaṇas.

[1] Besides the passages cited from the Jâtakas, we find, for example, the Brâhmaṇa agriculturist mentioned in the Sutta Nipâta (ed. Fausböll, p. 12), where it is said of the Brâhmaṇa Kasibhâradvâja, that at the time of sowing he tills his soil with 500 ploughs. In the Brâhmaṇa village (brâhmaṇagâma) which is mentioned as his place of residence, Brâhmaṇa agriculturists must have lived, just as also probably the Brâhmaṇa villages mentioned in the Jâtakas are to be looked upon as principally occupied by agriculturists. In the Suttavibhaṅga, Pâcittiya XIX. 1 and in the Bhikkhunivibhaṅga, Pâcittiya IX. 1. (Vinaya Piṭaka ed. Oldenberg, Vol. 4, pp. 47, 266) mention is made of the barley fields (yavakhettas) of a Brâhmaṇa.

Land-cultivating and cattle-rearing Brâhmaṇas are also not uncommon in Western India; the law-books recognised certain exceptional cases when this occupation was permissible for a Brâhmaṇa in cases of dire necessity.[1] For that was a time when liberality towards Brâhmaṇas was a clear-duty of the king and the amassing of wealth and the possession of land by the Brâhmaṇas were necessary consequences of this. Nevertheless, in the western lands the circumstance that the Brâhmaṇas tried to maintain at any cost their premier position among the castes, the position of an age-long holy and (through the privilege of offering sacrifice) premier caste, worked itself in this way, that this occupation, which was reserved, according to the theory, for the Vaiśyas, was followed by private individuals and as quietly as possible, probably, also by means of leases. To cultivate the land, plough in hand, could not be a worthy thing for a Brâhmaṇa, because with a plough the killing of living beings was unavoidable.[2]

Things were different in the eastern lands. Through the liberality of the Khattiyas in possession of great land, there were no such strict caste-rules restraining individual conduct and this would lead to a limited or cautious use

---

[1] Manu X. 116

[2] Manu X, 83 sq.

of the goods presented. At every step we find Brâhmaṇas driving the plough in the Jâtakas and not only such as had their lands cultivated by slaves or day-labourers but also small farmers who worked their fields themselves. We read of a Brâhmaṇa who goes along with his son to the field and ploughs it, whilst the boy collects the weeds and burns them (III. 163); another Brâhmaṇa unyokes his oxen after ploughing and begins to work upon his land with a spade (V. 68). The poor Brâhmaṇa farmer of the Somadatta Jâtaka who ploughs with two oxen complains, as one of his oxen is dead, that he cannot any more drive his plough (*kasikammaṁ na pavattati* II. 165).

[P. 158.]

The big Brâhmaṇa landowners have their fields cultivated by their slaves or by day-labourers. Of a *kassakabrâhmaṇa* who is in possession of 1,000 karîsas[1] it is narrated that he goes with his men to the field and supervises their ploughing (III. 293). The Brâhmaṇa mentioned in the Sâlikedâra Jâtaka (IV. 276) possesses likewise a field of 1,000 karîsas on which he has sown rice. When the crop is cut, he makes the hedge thick and places his own men (attano purisâ) to guard one-half of his

[1] A certain superficial measure = four *ammaṇas's*; *cf.* Childers, *Pali Dictionary.*

property by assigning fifty karîsas to one, sixty to another, while the remaining five hundred *karîsas* he puts in charge of a hired labourer (bhataka) who is punished for every loss.

More frequently than the *Kassakabrâhmaṇa* we meet in the Jâtakas with the figure of the rich Brâhmaṇa (brâhmaṇo aḍḍho mahaddhano, IV. 15; brâhmaṇo aḍḍho mahaddhano mahâbhogo. IV. 22; dve brâhmaṇâ asîtikoṭidhanavibhavâ. IV. 28), whose wealth is given as 800 millions (II. 272; III. 39; IV. 28, 237). The *mahâsâlakulas* mentioned in the Jâtakas, that is, families of great wealth and influence, are all Brâhmaṇas (II. 272; IV. 237, 325; V. 227). About the manner in which such great wealth arose and whether it was employed in business or money [P. 159.] transactions, our sources say nothing; the narrator mentions the immense wealth of the Brâhmaṇas as a rule only to show in its proper light their great renunciation of worldly goods or their boundless liberality. Still it seems to me we can suppose that by these rich Brâhmaṇas big landholders or princely merchants are to be understood; for through presents alone such enormous riches could hardly have accumulated in Brâhmaṇa families; it is also not probable that these could be amassed without recourse to money transactions carried on from generation to generation, as narrated in the Kaṇha Jâtaka (IV. 7).

Moreover, we make the acquaintance of such a Brâhmaṇa merchant-prince in the Mahâsutasoma Jâtaka who being in possession of great wealth engages in trade, as he sends five hundred wagons from the east to the west (sampannavibhavo brâhmaṇo pañcahi sakatasathi vohâraṃ karonto pubbantato aparantaṃ sañcarati V. 471). Along with this, we also read of Brâhmaṇa tradesmen who roam about the country, selling their wares. A hawker like this is the father of the Bodhisatta of whom it is said in the Gagga Jâtaka that he was re-born in a Brâhmaṇa family in the kingdom of Kâsi and that in his sixteenth year his father gave him a bundle of water-pots which they used to sell in the villages and the country markets (II. 15).

To engage in trade when necessity requires it, is also permitted by the Brahmanical lawbooks; but a number of things is mentioned which it does not become a Brâhmaṇa to deal in, such are, among other things, fruits, roots, medicinal herbs, honey, oil and spirituous liquors.[1] If we believe in the words of Vidhûra already quoted, it was precisely these and similar

[1] Manu X. 86-89; Gautama VII. 9 sq.; Âpastamba I. 20. 12.

things with the sale of which the Brâhmaṇa tradesmen were principally concerned.

If agriculture, cattle-breeding and trade were looked upon by orthodox Brâhmaṇas as respectable professions and even as permissible occupations for a member of their own caste, other callings, the adoption of which by the Brâhmaṇas is likewise mentioned in the Jâtakas, belonged undoubtedly to the class of despised professions, which were practised as a rule by the lower classes of the population. It is true we don't find any more in our text Brâhmaṇas of whom Vidhûra says in the Dasabrâhmana Jâtaka that they drive the caravans of tradesmen through dangerous places. On the other hand, the Brâhmaṇa hunter mentioned by him is represented in the Cûlanandiya Jâtaka by a young Brâhmaṇa who lives in a frontier village, hunts in the forest with his bow and earns his livelihood by selling the hunted beasts (II. 200). Still it is expressly added in this case that the Brâhmaṇa youth who has studied in Takkasilâ takes up this profession which is followed, as we shall see, by especially despised people, for example, the Nishâda, because he cannot earn a livelihood by any other means. In the Phanaanda Jâtaka, a Brâhmaṇa carpenter (brâhmaṇavaḍḍhaki, IV. 207) is mentioned who brings

[P. 160.]

wood from the forest and earns his livelihood by making wagons and lives in a carpenter's village (vaḍḍhakîgâma) outside the city. The proximity of the forest from which they obtained the wood —a purely economical reason—may have been the cause of the carpenters living apart, outside the city; perhaps also this isolation had a social meaning and had its ground in the meanness of the profession which exposed it to the contempt of fellowmen and necessitated isolated residence in a village outside the city.[1] It is doubtful, however, whether this contempt spread even to the Brâhmaṇa carpenter in whom his high caste served as a counterpoise to the meanness of his profession.

With the Brâhmaṇa agriculturists, merchants, hunters and carpenters we leave the solitary height upon which is enthroned the Brâhmaṇa, who is raised according to his own

[P. 161.]

theory above all other members of society, and descend to the motley groups of people where the care for material existence drives out all spiritual interests and throws into the shade the question relating to birth and caste. Or, shall we suppose that even here the Brâhmaṇa,

---

[1] On the low social position of the carriage-builder (rathakâra) and the isolation of contemptible classes, see the last chapter.

remembering the special rights and duties, arising from his belonging to the Brâhmaṇa caste, separates himself clearly from the rest of the population, that along with his (so to speak) civil occupation he has practised sacerdotal functions and in that way has secured a certain superiority over other classes? The Jâtakas give no instance from which such a double function can be inferred. Something must have been said somewhere in our sources of one of these Brâhmaṇa agriculturists or tradesmen which related to specifically Brahmanical functions and stamped him as a Brâhmaṇa. The poor Brahmana farmer of the Somadatta Jâtaka (II. 165) whom his son forces at great pains to commit to memory a verse and who at the decisive moment says before the king exactly the opposite of what he wants to say, does not give one the impression that he can help his neighbours with advice in spiritual things.[1] We have to suppose in that age gradations and contradictions within the Brâhmaṇa caste similar to those which India of to-day shows, where a wide gap separates the proud priests of Benares and the pandits of Bihar in their spotless garments from the potato-cultivating Brâhmaṇas

[1] With another *kassakabrâhmaṇa* (III. 293) the care which he bestows upon the purification of his mouth is perhaps regarded as a sign of his Brahmanhood.

of Orissa, half-naked farmers whom no one would think of as belonging to their caste, if the ornamental piece of Brahmanical thread round their neck had not proclaimed this.[1]

He, however, who does not think the *argumentum ex silentio* sufficient as a proof of this proposition, should be reminded of the relation in which, according to the Pali canon, the worldly Brâhmaṇas stand to the Buddhist monks. Of
[P. 162.] an opposition, no trace is to be found; the Brâhmaṇas stand in friendly relationship with the monks: they give them shelter, invite them and entertain them.[2] Even in the Jâtakas the intercourse between the Brâhmaṇas and Buddha—of such a thing mention is of course made only in the commentary—is throughout represented as friendly; the Brâhmaṇa agriculturist occurring in the introduction to the Kâma Jâtaka (IV. 167) exchanges friendly words with Buddha when he comes to his field; at the sowing season he even promises that when the corn will be ripe he will give handsome alms to his order. Such a relationship is only conceivable if we suppose that these Brâhmaṇas are

[1] *Cf.* Hunter, Gegether, Vol. 6, p. 193.

[2] Setavibhanna, Pârâjika IV. 8. 11 : 9. 3. Pacithiya XXXV. 1. Sehtiya 51 (Viraya Piṭaka, W. Oldenberg. Vol. 3, 10, 103 ; Vol. 4, pp. 81, 197.

distinguished from the Buddhistic laity by nothing except their Brâhmaṇa birth, that they further did not care much either for their Veda study or their sacrifice—these special duties of a "correct" Brâhmaṇa—the performance of which would certainly have erected a barrier between them and the Buddhist monks.

CHAPTER IX

The leading middle class families

There was always, however, even for the worldly Brâhmaṇas, a circumstance which prevented their being entirely merged in the mass of the population, namely, their Brahmanical birth and their belonging in consequence to the Brâhmaṇa caste. The attempt to marry within their own caste and thus prevent a mixing with the lower elements which we showed above from the Jâtakas, would alone have sufficed to erect a barrier between these Brâhmaṇas and the rest of the population.

Much less sharply pronounced, there appears to us another line which, according to the theory of the Brâhmaṇas, divided in Indian [P. 163.] society the Aryan Indians from the mass of dark-coloured aborigines.[1] We can suppose that at a very early

[1] Even from Brahmanical literature we get the impression that Indian society divided itself into two groups, namely, into Brâhmaṇas and Kshatriyas, on the one side, and Vaiśyas and Śûdras, on the other, and that irrespective of the distinction based upon Aryan birth, the last two classes formed in the eyes of the two higher ones, a conglomerate mass with which neither the Brâhmaṇa nor the Kshatriya came much in contact. *Cf.* Hopkins, *The Mutual Relations of the Four Castes, according to the Mânavadharmaśâstram.* Imag. Diss., Leipzig, 1881, pp. 78, 82.

age a mixture between the Aryan and non-Aryan elements of the population took place —a supposition which will only be improbable when we look upon the Aryan Indians, belonging neither to the Kshatriya nor to the Brâhmaṇa caste, as enclosed within fixed bounds and united to form a caste. The Indian caste-theory comprised them under the third caste, the caste of the Vaiśyas ; as their occupations and duties, there are mentioned in Manu (I. 90), "cattle-breeding, distribution of alms, sacrifice, study, trade, lending money at interest and agriculture."

Now we meet with the expression Vessa (=Skr. Vaiśya) in Pali texts but only in passages where we have to do with theoretical discussions about the caste-question which, as mentioned above, prove nothing for the real existence of a caste called Vessa. Nowhere do we notice in the Jâtakas—where we should expect to find it first, seeing that they get their materials so often directly from the people—an indication that as a matter of fact a caste which did not comprise Aryans belonging either to the Brâhmaṇa or the Kshatriya caste, did exist. A caste, in the sense of the Brahmanical theory, the Vaiśyas never became even in the western Brahmanical lands; originally, in the oldest Vedic age, a name for the class of cattle-breeding and land-cultivating Aryan settlers, it served later the purpose of the theorising Brâhmaṇas to bind together the unlimited number of social groups.

An expression which is exactly similar in meaning to the word Vaiśya and likewise comprehends a definite class of [P. 164.] people, is the word *gahapati*[1] so very common in Pali literature. According to its etymology, it means "householder, head of a household," and denotes generally, if not always, a landlord or merchant-prince of high birth and wealth. We shall not be mistaken if we see in these *gahapatis* in part the gentry of the land, the lower land-owning nobility, in contrast with the nobility which is related to princely houses, the Khattiyas, and in part the high and rich middle class families of the big cities which can be compared with the patricians of the imperial and industrial cities of the Middle Ages. Like the khattiyas, the gahapatis also seem to have distinguished themselves from the great mass of the population by a certain consciousness of position and by pride in their Aryan descent. The son of the *seṭṭhi gahapati* Yasa is called in the Mahâvagga (I. 7. 7) *kulaputta*, a youth of high birth, good family. Such a *kulaputta* must, whenever

---

[1] =Skr. *grihapati*.

possible, marry in an old and rich family; the parents take care to avoid a *mesalliance* and bring for the grown-up son a girl of good family (Bodhisatto Bârâṇasito avidûre gâmake gahapatikule nibbatti. Ath' assa vayappattassa Bârâṇasito kuladhîtaraṃ ânesuṃ II. 121). In the court of the king the *gahapatis*, on account of their importance and wealth, played a significant part: either along with the ministers and Brâhmaṇas mentioned in the third place, or along with the last, they appear permanently in the retinue of the king.[1] At the coronation of the king there are represented: ministers, Brâhmaṇas, heads of households, citizens, gatekeepers, etc. (amaccâ ca brâhmaṇagahapatiraṭṭhikadovârikâdayo ca. II. 241).

This passage, where the raṭṭhikas (=Skr. *râshtrika*, inhabitant of a kingdom, subject) are mentioned along with the *gahapatis*, shows that the concept *gahapati* is in no way identical with what, according to the Brahmanical caste-theory, is to be understood by *Vaiśya*; for to this caste, which embraces all Aryan Indians with the exception of Kshatriyas and Brâhmaṇas, the *raṭṭhikas* would have to be looked upon as belonging,

[p. 165].

[1] Not only in the Jâtakas but also in other Pali texts, for example, Mahâvagga I. 22. 3 (Vinaya Piṭaka ed. Oldenberg, Vol. I, p. 35).

as well as the citizens (negamas) and farmers (jânapadas), who in another place (in the Nigrodhamiga Jâtaka I. 152) are counted among the "householders" as subjects of the king. For the Indians, subject to the influence of the (Brahmanical) theory and inclined to schematise, the *gahapatis* appear nevertheless as a caste, as, in fact, the third caste, corresponding to the Vaiśyas of the Brahmanical system, as in the enumeration[1] of castes they very often appear in the third place after the *khattiyakulas* and the *brâhmaṇakulas*. A justification of such a schematism lay in this, that this class also through the value it attached to pure descent and through the prohibition of unequal marriages, liked to form a close body and showed a faint resemblance with the Brâhmaṇa caste in this, that the jâti of a *gahapati* was hereditary, that a *gahapati* who through the loss of his fortune was ruined and was forced to maintain himself by following lower occupations, still remained always a *gahapati*. We read of one such *gahapati* who deals in vegetables (pannikagahapati, III. 21;

---

[1] Thus, in the already cited narrative of the *chabbaggikas* which is identical with Cullavagga, VI. 6. 2. *Cf.* further Mahâparinibbâna Sutta V. 24 (Journal of the Royal Asiatic Society, Vol. 8, p. 242): *Anandakhattiyapaṇḍitâ pi brâhmaṇapaṇḍitâ pi gahapatipaṇḍitâ pi abhippasannâ*; Mahâvagga, VI. 28. 4 (Vinaya Piṭaka, ed. Oldenberg, Vol. I, p. 227): *yadi khattiyaparisam yadi brâhmaṇaparisam yadi gahapatiparisam yadi samaṇaparisam avisârado upasamkamati.*

IV. 446), of another poor *gahapati* who maintains himself and his mother with difficulty by working as a hired labourer (III. 325).

But this hereditary character of the position, combined with a special value attached to purity of blood do not in my opinion suffice to make the *gahapatis* appear as a caste; in our eyes they can only be regarded as a special class, as a special rank and not as a caste, the characteristic marks of which are lacking: apart from marriage within the limits of the class, we don't see any common customs, not to speak

[P. 166.] of any judicial powers, which would punish any transgression of caste-rules by exclusion from society.

Almost in the same sense as *gahapati* is the expression *kuṭumbika* used; this also denotes members of the citizen class, as a rule like *gahapatis*, wealthy citizens at the head of a household (kuṭumba). Connection with such a kuṭumbika family appears to have been considered suitable by the rich and aristocratic families: a leading citizen (nagaravâsi kulaputta I. 196) seeks the daughter of a *kuṭumbika* living in a village for his son. The *kutumbikas* living in the town engage in trade, according to the Jâtakas. Thus, in the Sâlaka Jâtaka it is said of the Bodhisatta that he is reborn in a *kuṭumbika* family and maintains his livelihood by dealing in corn (dhaññavikkaya II. 267). Several times mention is made of money-transactions which the *kutumbikas* who are residents of a town carry on with the country. Over and above the *kuṭumbika* from Sâvatthi, mentioned in the *paccuppannavatthu* of the Succaja Jâtaka (III. 66), who goes with his wife into the country in order to collect debts, there is mentioned in the Satapatta Jâtaka a *kuṭumbika* who lends a villager 1,000 kahâpaṇas (II. 388). The sons of another *kuṭumbika* determine after the death of their father to administer his goods and collect his assets; they go to the village and return after they collect 1,000 kahâpaṇas.

The most important and aristocratic representative of the gahapati class is the *seṭṭhi*.[1] Although he appears to us, at least according to the Jâtakas, in the court of the king in whose service he is, we have not yet counted him among the king's officers, because he does not properly belong to the class of *râjabhoggas*, officers of the king, but a gahapati does[2];

[1] = Skr. śreshṭhin which is generally rendered by "the chief of the guild."

[2] The office of a seṭṭhi seems to be permanently occupied by a *gahapati*. Nowhere is it mentioned that a member of another caste or class, such as, a rich Brâhmaṇa has held this position. If not in the brief form *seṭṭhi*, of the *seṭṭhi gahapati* mention is made, in Vinaya Piṭaka, Mahavagga I. 7. 7; VIII. 1. 9, 13; Cullavagga VI. 4.1 sq.

he appears to play a double part, an official and a private part. In the Vinaya Piṭaka the *seṭṭhi* plays an important private rôle; he appears throughout as a respectable tradesman enjoying a special position of honour among the members of his profession; such, for instance, was preeminently the much-quoted generous worshipper of Buddha, Anâthapiṇḍika. Still it is to be considered that in the Culavagga (VI. 4.1) it is said of him that he is the brother-in-law of "the seṭṭhi of Râjagaha"—an expression which in itself refers to an official position; also that Anâthapiṇḍika believes that his brother-in-law has invited King Bimbisâra to a banquet, speaks in favour of this supposition. Of the same *seṭṭhi* of Râjagaha it is said expressly in the Mahâvagga (VIII. 1. 16) that he rendered various services to the king as well as to the tradesmen (bahûpakâro devassa c'eva negamassa ca). In the Jâtakas the *seṭṭhi*, as already said, stands mostly in close proximity to the royal court. For the management of the finances of the State, for paying the army and the officials, for military operations, public buildings, etc., the king obviously consulted the opinion of a business man familiar with the trade affairs of the land; on the other hand, the commercial community

[P. 167.]

must also have tried to have its interests represented in the court and to watch carefully legislation and administration. Two purposes the *seṭṭhi*, the official "representative of the commercial community" at the king's court, served. In his official capacity he goes to the king's public audience (râjupaṭṭhâna. I. 269, 349; III. 119, 299; IV. 63), as said in another place, three times a day (divasassa tayo vâre râjupaṭṭhânaṃ gacchati III. 475); in this capacity he takes (formal) leave of the king when going out on a journey, and obtains the permission of the king when resigning his office or when he wants to renounce the worldly life and become a homeless ascetic (pabbajjaṃ me anujânâhi II. 64)

Just as his social rank[1] was hereditary, so also the office (seṭṭhitthâna) of the father passed as a rule on to the son (I. 231, 248; III. 475). Reborn in a *seṭṭhi* family, the Bodhisatta when

[P. 168.]

[1] Of seṭṭhi families mention is also made in the Vinaya Piṭaka. Mahavagga I. 9. 1 has—seṭṭhânuseṭṭhinaṃ kulânaṃ puttâ. Whether by this *anuseṭṭhikula*, the 'highest after the seṭṭhi families,' as the expression is rendered in the translation of Rhys Davids and Oldenberg (*Sacred Books of the East*, Vol. 13, p. 110), is meant, appears doubtful to me, as, according to the Jatakas, the *anuseṭṭhi*, in the same way as the *seṭṭhi*, seems to have held a fixed post in the royal court. In the Sudhâbhojana Jâtaka (V. 384) the *seṭṭhi*, when he goes to the king, calls on his way on the *anuseṭṭhi* in order to take the latter with him.

he is grown up, sets up a household and obtains after the death of his father the position of a "representative of the commercial community" (seṭṭhikule nibbattitvâ vayappatto kuṭumbaṃ saṇṭhâpetvâ pitu accayena seṭṭhitthânaṃ patvâ IV. 62).

Details of the duties and functions connected with this office we cannot obtain from our source. Possibly the king required him in order to exercise supervision over trade in accordance with the prescriptions of the lawbooks [1] and for the purpose of controlling through him the administration [2] of the laws relating to trade societies and guilds. Perhaps, along with this, he required of him personal service, management of money affairs, superintendence of the king's treasury; in any case,

---

[1] Manu VIII. 401 sq: "He (the king) shall fix the sale price as well as the purchase price of all market commodities after carefully considering the place of their origin, their destination, the period of warehousing, the probable profit and loss. Every five days or at the expiry of a fortnight, the king shall fix the prices in the presence of experienced men."

[2] Manu VIII. 41: "Versed in the law, he (the king) shall examine the laws of the castes and lands, the laws of guilds (sreṇi-dharma) and the laws of families and (so) fix the law for each of these (groups)—*Cf.* Hopkins, *Ruling Caste*, p. 81: "Such associations" —namely, trade associations and guilds—" had their own rules and regulations which were under the supervision of the king; the king could (according to the theory) neither sanction law nor himself give laws which were opposed to the recognised laws or those sanctioned by custom."

he seems by virtue of his immense wealth to have become indispensable to [P. 169.] the king, as we find him constantly in his retinue. Out of the daily intercourse friendship sometimes grew between the king and his seṭṭhi, and just as was the case with the *purohita*, the fact of the office being hereditary in the same *seṭṭhi* family may have contributed towards making this family intimately connected with the ruling house. In the Aṭṭhâna Jâtaka (III. 475) the heir presumptive and the son of the *seṭṭhi* of Benares are playmates and are taught and educated in the house of the same teacher. Also after the prince has succeeded to the throne, the son of the *seṭṭhi* lives in his neighbourhood and later, after the death of his father, when he himself becomes seṭṭhi, he goes three times daily to the palace of the king and talks with him until nightfall. "Where is my friend?", cries the king as one day he misses the seṭṭhi.

In this official position as "a representative of the commercial community" the seṭṭhi does not appear always even in the Jâtakas, but appears here at times as a private gentleman, as a rich and influential merchant prince. A seṭṭhi living in Benares engages in trade and drives a caravan of five hundred wagons (I. 270); in the province (*paccante* I. 451; IV. 169) the seṭṭhis living in the country (janapadaseṭṭhi IV. 37) for whom an official position is manifestly improbable, are mentioned in several places. How far these tradesmen differ from others, for example, from the caravan leaders (satthavâha), to be mentioned later, especially, whether they exercised any supervising functions with regard to these as "masters of the guild," does not appear from the Jâtakas; what we learn from our source is confined to a description of their wealth and their influence. The wealth of a seṭṭhi is given, like that of the rich Brâhmaṇas, uniformly as eight hundred millions (asîtikotivibhavo seṭṭhi, III. 128, 300, 444; V. 382), a statement which has very little value as a judgment concerning actual conditions, as, on account of the very little care which the Indians show for correct, or even approximately correct, numbers, any other great number would have had the same meaning, as we do not know what coin is to be added to this

[P. 170.] figure. Somewhat more accurately the wealth of a seṭṭhi is indicated, when in the Visayha Jâtaka (III. 129) it is narrated that Sakka, rendered uneasy by the charity of the seṭṭhi, destroys his entire wealth—money, corn, oil, honey, sugar, etc., even his slaves and hired labourers. As belonging to the household of a seṭṭhi, there are mentioned in another place, besides wife and child, servants (parijana) and the headsman (vacchakapâlakâ). The cowherd of a seṭṭhi drives the cattle of his master into the forest when the corn begins to ripen, erects a stall for the cow and gives the milk from time to time to the seṭṭhi. If we add that occasionally the rice fields of a seṭṭhi are mentioned, it follows that we have to look upon the seṭṭhis not only as tradesmen but also as cattle-rearing and land-cultivating owners of the soil.

On account of the great wealth at his disposal, his influence manifestly extends outside the sphere of work of his own business ; it is true we do not find it expressly stated that he lends money at interest ; we may, however, very well suppose that he gives the inn-keeper who "lives by him" (taṃ upanissâyo eko varunivâṇijo jîvati, I. 252) sufficient means with which to carry on his trade in spirituous liquors. Even the tailor who lives with a seṭṭhi (seṭṭhiṃ nissâya vasantassa tunnakârassa, IV. 38) may have stood in a similar relation to the master of the house.

The desire to preserve wealth and respectability in the family may have strengthened the inclination and practice in seṭṭhi families of marrying within their own *jâti* and led to frequent marriages among themselves. The

seṭṭhi of Râjagaha, mentioned in the Nigrodha Jâtaka, brings for his son the daughter of a *seṭṭhi* living in the country (IV. 37). The slave of the *seṭṭhi* of Benares succeeds, as narrated in the Kaṭâhaka Jâtaka, in winning by means of a false letter the hand of the daughter of a *seṭṭhi* friendly to his master and living in the frontier. The letter which the slave has written himself and which he hands over to the business friend of his master begins with the words: "The bearer of this letter is
[P. 171.] my son N. N. I consider it desirable that our children should marry with each other" (âvâhavivâhasambandho nâma mayhaṃ tayâ tuyhañ ca mayâ saddhiṃ patirûpo, I. 452).

Hand in hand with this regard for equal marriage and purity of blood, there goes in the the Khattiyas and the proud Brâhmaṇas, as well as in high seṭṭhi families, a deep contempt for people who are low either by profession or by race; especially, does this "caste-spirit" make itself felt with regard to the class of Caṇḍâlas, the pariahs in the then Indian society: We saw above what a shock the *seṭṭhi's* daughter gets when she learns that she has seen a Caṇḍâla and how very anxious she is to prevent the evil effects of this sight by washing her beautiful eyes.

The wealth and respectability of the *seṭṭhi* families brought it about naturally that the sons of such a family received a careful education ; it even appears from our source that they, partly at any rate, fulfilled the universal duty, according to the law-books, of the three higher castes, namely, that of studying the Vedas. The two sons of the *seṭṭhi* mentioned in the Nigrodha Jâtaka were sent to Takkasilâ to a teacher by the Seṭṭhi of Râjagaha and he paid the teacher 2,000 as honorarium (IV. 38) ; the already-mentioned young *seṭṭhi*, occurring in the Aṭṭhâna Jâtaka, is instructed along with the prince by the same teacher (III. 475). It is true in both these cases it is only said that the youths "learnt the science" (sippaṃ ugganhiṃsu) ; still I think it probable that even in this passage by *sippa*, religious study is to be understood, because, as already said, among the disciples of Buddha the sons of rich and respectable families were in large measure represented—a fact which in my opinion is to be attributed principally to the participation of these circles in the spiritual activities of that age.

If these *seṭṭhi* families who were united through the common consciousness of rank, through the custom of contracting marriages with their own jâti and preventing mixture with the lower castes, and further, through a common hereditary profession, present [P. 172] an appearance not wholly dissimilar to that of caste, there arise from the great mass of the people other social groups which through the appearance of another factor, external organisation, represent a still more sharply defined unity, namely, the associations of tradesmen and manufacturers comparable to our mediæval guilds.

CHAPTER X

THE GUILDS OF TRADESMEN AND MANUFACTURERS

The existence of trade associations which grew partly for economical reasons—better employment of capital, facilities of intercourse—partly, for protecting the legal interests of their class, is surely to be traced to an early period of Indian culture. When we read in the Dharmasûtras that the agriculturists, tradesmen, cattle-breeders, usurers (kusîdin) and manufacturers have their own special laws for their class which are authoritative for the king,[1] we can infer from this with some certainty the organisation of trade and particular branches of it; in the later law-books, mention is expressly made of guilds (sreṇi). Thus, it is said in Manu VIII. 41, that the king has to examine and determine the laws of the guilds. In the epics also the guilds appear as an important factor not only of the industrial but also of the political life.[2]

Still there is the question whether the economical conditions, as they are [P. 173.] described by Manu and in the epics, represent the view of culture unfolded by

---

[1] Gautama, XI. 21: deśajâtikuladharmâścâmnâyair aviruddhâḥ pramâṇaṃ kṛishivaṇikpaśupâlyakusîdakâravaḥ sve sve varge.

[2] Hopkins, *Ruling Caste*, p. 81 sq.

the Jâtakas, whether they can at once be assigned to the period of the older Buddhism. The systematised commercial law, as we find it in Manu, the rules relating to loans at interest, the institute of experts in sea-borne trade, the duties upon river-borne and sea-borne merchandise, all this presupposes a stage of economical development which appears to me to be centuries later than the stage of culture depicted in the Jâtakas.[1]

It should not, however, be said that we have here the first beginnings of commercial transactions; undoubtedly, the statements contained in the Jâtakas relate to oversea trade as well as to brisk inland trade. When in describing a caravan passing through sandy deserts, its march is compared with a journey through the sea (saṁuddagamanasadisam eva gamanaṃ hoti. I. 107), when it is narrated that one entrusts the lead to a "land tax-collector" (thalaniyâmaka) who directs the caravan with the help of astronomy, we find clearly expressed here acquaintance with navigation and the knowledge of the

[1] The opposite view is taken by Dahlmann in his book on the Mahâbhârata. According to him, there is "an extraordinary agreement between the culture-period represented in the Jâtakas and the Pali canon and that of the Mahâbhârata"; "the blossoming of economical life," as described here, is, in his opinion, "in full agreement with the picture of culture in Manu." Jos. Dahlmann, *Das Mahâbhârata als Epos und Rechtsbuch*, Berlin, 1895, pp. 166, 180.

starry heavens required for this. Also another thing which the Indians employed, like the seafaring Phœnicians and Babylonians of ancient times, for finding the direction during navigation, we find mentioned in the Jâtakas, namely, "direction-giving crows" (disâkâka); they showed the navigators, when they lost sight of the land, as they flew towards the land, in what direction the coast was to be found. On the high seas such a "compass" could not surely be of much use to the sailors—for this reason it is narrated of the merchants in the Kâsi kingdom who have a *disâkâka* on board their ship, that they suffer shipwreck in mid-ocean (III. 267)—
[P. 174.] but it is very useful for navigation along the coast. This, and not navigation in the open sea, is, I think, throughout meant when the Jâtakas speak of oversea trade. The disappearance of the coast after several days' navigation is especially brought into prominence and stated as a cause of shipwreck. "Five hundred tradesmen"—so it is said in the Paṇḍara Jâtaka (V. 75)—"went on a sea-voyage and suffered shipwreck on the ocean, as on the seventeenth day no land was to be seen; all on board, not one excepted, became the food of the fish." On the whole, we shall do well if we accept a bit cautiously this supposition of an extensive oversea trade. If there

really was regular trade[1] between India and countries like the Babylonian kingdom—whose name exists in the form *Bâveruraṭṭha* (III. 126)[2] —we should certainly have heard occasionally from the Jâtakas of the products of this land, of its inhabitants and their customs. The existence of the mere name shows that the city was known by name in the age to which our source relates; probably, Indian sailors went to Babylon and spread reports on their return home about the city and its wonders, so that from that time onward in every story in which the ship-wrecked played a part, the name of the city of *Bâveru* appeared, the mention of which served to make the listeners expect something wonderful. But oversea trade is not so frequently mentioned in the Jâtakas that one can talk of a *Samuddavāṇija* as a typical figure.

The plentifulness of great navigable waterways in Northern India allows us to assume an early development of internal maritime trade; still I have found it mentioned in only one place in the Jâtakas. In the sale of a ship's cargo mentioned in the Cullakaseṭṭhi Jâtaka (I. 126), the question is of wares unloaded at a port in the neighbourhood of Benares. The hero

---

[1] *Cf.* Dahlmann, Das Mahâbhârata, p. 179.

[2] To the category of the quoted passages (I. 107; III. 126, 267; V. 75) belongs further the designation of a narrative (IV. 158) as Samuddavâṇija Jâtaka.

of the narrative, a youth of good but poor family, learns from a sailor [P. 175.] friend that a big ship has arrived at the port. He hires for eight kahâpaṇas a vehicle and drives with great pomp to the port. Here he buys the ship's cargo on credit and gives his signet ring as security; then he erects a tent close to the ship and after he takes his seat within it, he gives an order that if tradesmen want to see him they should only be admitted after a threefold notice. On the news of the arrival of the ship about a hundred tradesmen from Benares come to buy the cargo. They are told: "You cannot buy wares any more, for a great merchant who lives at such and such a place has bought them by advancing a deposit." When they hear this, they go to the youth and are admitted by the servants to his presence after a threefold notice in the way mentioned above. Everyone of the hundred tradesmen pays one thousand in order to receive a portion of the ship's cargo and finally in order to buy off his partnership, they pay each one of them for the rest of his goods a further 1,000. Thus the youth returns to Benares with 2,00,000 in his possession.

In the culture-period depicted in the Jatakas, overland trade seems to have far

surpassed in importance sea-borne trade. The tradesman who goes about the country with his caravan is in fact a typical figure in our narratives and, according to the statements in these, caravan traffic cannot have been small, either with regard to the distance traversed or with regard to wares carried. Big trade routes cross the land in all directions and carry on an exchange of goods between the several and (judged by their products and necessities) widely different parts of India; there was, especially, manifestly brisk trade between the eastern and the western parts. We read in the Apaṇṇaka Jâtaka of a caravan-leader (satthavâha, I. 98) who goes from the east to the west with 500 wagon-loads and then returns. Tradesmen residing in Benares travel to Ujjani[1] in order to carry
[P. 176.] on trade (II. 248). Also from trade relations between Kasmir and Gandhâra kingdoms, on the one side, and Videha land, on the other, we learn, as narrated in the Gandhâra Jataka, that the king of Videha inquires of the tradesmen about the health of his friend, the king of Kasmîra and Gandhâra (III. 365).

About the nature of the goods carried, the statements of the Jâtakas speak in a very

---

[1] = Skr. Ujjaini, the capital of Avanti.

uncertain voice. The narrator speaks mostly of five hundred wagons laden with valuable goods and leaves us to exercise our conjecture regarding the contents of these loads. Probably, the packages of the tradesmen contained cloths, for according to the Tuṇḍila Jâtaka there were in the neighbourhood of Benares fields sown with cotton[1] (kâppâsakhetta III. 286) and this cotton was probably in Buddha's time chiefly used in the manufacture of goods in Benares.[2] On the other hand, cotton industry appears to have flourished in certain places in the west, as in the Mahâvagga of the Vinaya Piṭaka ; Sivi cloth (Siveyyaka dussa VIII. 1. 29) is praised as specially valuable.

Famous were also the horses of the west, above all, the stèed of Sindh (sindhava. II. 288); according to the Jâtakas the kings of the eastern lands were provided mainly with horses brought from the north or the west; we meet very often in our texts with horse-merchants

[1] Cotton is even now found in places to the west of Benares as far as Agra. *Cf.* Table 13 in Bartholomew's *Hand Atlas of India*, Westminster, 1893.

[2] In the Mahaparinibbâna Sutta (V. 26) it is said that the mortal remains of a world-ruler were covered with folds of new cloths and torn cotton, and the commentator adds as an explanation of the expression *vihata kappasa*, "The cloth of Benares (Kasikavattha) on account of the fineness of its texture, absorbs no oil."

who come from the north (uttarâpathakâ assavâṇijâ) and sell their horses in Benares (I. 124; II. 31, 287).

The insecurity of the road made the business of a *satthavâha* at that time very troublesome and dangerous. Organized bands of robbers—in the Sattigumba Jâtaka a village containing five hundred robbers is mentioned (coragâmaka IV. 430), at its head stands the "oldest among the robbers (corajeṭṭhaka II. 388)—lay in wait for the travelling tradesmen, especially in the forest, and forced them to employ armed men who for a salary led the caravans through the dangerous places.[1] Still the tradesmen were compensated for the troubles and dangers of caravan traffic by the great profit which, according to the Jâtakas, they made; in the Vaṇṇupatha Jâtaka it is stated that the caravan-leaders got twice or thrice their dues on the sale of their wares (bhaṇḍaṃ vikkiṇitvâ dviguṇaṃ catugguṇaṃ bhogaṃ labhitvâ, I. 109).

[P. 177.]

---

[1] The business of these forest-guards (aṭaviârakkhika, II. 335) formed a profession by itself which was hereditary in the family and favoured an organisation similar to that of the guilds of tradesmen and manufacturers in this, that at the head of a number of forest-guard families there was a leader (ârakkhikajeṭṭhaka). As we have seen above, even Brâhmaṇas were driven into this profession according to the Dasabrâhmaṇa Jataka.

If, according to the details given, trade exhibits in the Jâtakas, if not that stage of development which it shows in Manu, at least a high stage of growth, we should not be surprised at the mention of guilds (seṇi) in our text. It seems doubtful to me, however, whether from the few passages in which it is expressly mentioned, we can infer an organised guild life. Apart from the already-quoted passage from the Nigrodha Jâtaka, where it is said of the Royal storekeeper that he is worthy of the esteem of all guilds (sabbaseṇînaṃ vicâraṇâ-rahaṃ bhaṇḍâgârikaṭṭhânaṃ IV. 43), we find these also mentioned elsewhere (*sabbaseṇiyo* I. 267, 314) but without any statement which allows any inference concerning their constitution or organisation. The *paccuppannavatthu* of the Uraga Jâtaka gives some indication of a more developed guildhood; mention is here made of a "guild quarrel" between two ministers in the service of the king and at the head of the guilds (seṇipamukha). For the older period, the period depicted in the Jâtakas themselves, we can only speak with certainty of the presence of professional unions among the trading classes.

[P. 178.] The families in which wholly fixed branches of trade were hereditary formed professional unions. At their head stands a leader (jeṭṭhaka) about whose powers we learn no details, whose existence, however, indicates in itself an organisation of different branches of trade. Thus we read of the leader of the *caravan drivers* (satthavâhajeṭṭhaka, II. 295); if we add to this the hereditary character of this profession—which is sufficiently indicated by such expressions as "family of caravan-drivers" (saṭṭhavâhakula, I. 98, 107; II. 200) and "son of a caravan-driver" (satthavâhaputta, I. 99, 194; II. 335), who on his own account, again, is a caravan-driver—then we have in my opinion two criteria which point to the existence of a close order of caravan-drivers. From the criterion of hereditariness alone, it seems somewhat bold to infer a compactness and a certain organisation of the branch of trade in question; mention is made of the hereditary character of the profession of a grain merchant (dhañña vânijakula, III. 198); the business of a green-grocer was also hereditary in the family (paṇṇikakula, I. 312).

In individual branches of the tradesmen's profession, their small stability may be the reason why we don't read anything of a close organisation; thus, nowhere is mention made of an organisation of sea-faring traders. Also the more frequently-mentioned tradesmen who cry out their wares in the streets of the city—a pedlar dealing in pots and pans (kacchapatavâṇija I. 111) sells his goods with the cry " Buy waterpots, buy waterpots "—or go about the land (II. 109) with a donkey on which they place their wares, can hardly have enjoyed the privilege which the membership of a guild conferred.

In general, the details cited only prove indistinct traces of professional unions within the trading classes, only the first beginnings of a guildhood. With the gradual development of trade relations, the significance and inner compactness of the guilds deepened, and being similar to the castes on account of the traditional orga-
[P. 179.] nisation and the hereditariness of membership, they gradually got, in course of time, as certain rules and customs with reference to marriage and interdining were developed, the appearance of real castes, especially, the Brâhmaṇa caste, till they finally became the modern trading classes.

But even to-day, we don't find in the trading class such a strict caste organisation as in other departments of economic life: the greater flexibility which the trading profession demands by its very nature, in contrast with other professions, the changes to which it is subject, seem to have stood in the way of a strict schematic organisation of this professional branch.

More sharply pronounced appear in our text the divisions within the manufacturing classes according to the individual branches of the profession. Here appear circumstances which greatly favour a combination and organisation of particular unions. For manufacture, the hereditariness of the profession, which for trade was originally nothing more than a mere custom, was of essential importance; under the direction of his father the son is introduced to the technicalities of the profession which he is to adopt, from his early youth, and the manual skill, the talent for a particular handicraft, is inherited and increases from generation to generation. The taking up of a profession other than the ancestral one was manifestly unheard of among the manufacturers; not a single exception to the rule do we find mentioned anywhere in our source. "Son of a smith" (kammâraputta, is in the Pali texts (Sutta Nipâta, verse 83; Mahâparinibbâna Sutta, iv. 14) used as a synonym for a smith. Along with the families of smiths we find also other families of artisans in the Jâtakas; the hereditary character of the manufacture of pots is exhibited in the Kacchapa Jâtaka, where it is said of the Bodhisatta that he was reborn in a potter family (Kumbhakâra-kula, II. 79) and maintained his wife and child by manufacturing pots. Similarly it is said in the Kumbhakâra Jâtaka: "The Bodhisatta was re-born in a potter family in a village lying in front of the gate of Benares; when he grew [P. 180.] up, he became a householder and receiving from his wife a present of a son and a daughter, he maintained his wife and children by manufacturing pots." With a stone-grinder family also we become acquainted in our text: the Bodhisatta born in it understands his handicraft thoroughly when he grows up, as mentioned in the Babbu Jâtaka.

More even than the hereditariness of the profession there was another factor which contributed to the organisation of particular branches of trade,[1] namely, the local union and isolation which the different handicrafts, according to the Jâtakas, undoubtedly experienced. In the city, fixed streets were the place of residence of fixed tradesmen; for example, ivory-carvers (dantakâra) had a street to themselves. It is narrated how a man

[1] For the supposition of a local union of different branches of trade the Jâtakas give no ground. A passage in the Mṛicchakatika of Sûdraka allows the conclusion that the Seṭṭhis lived in a special part of the town by themselves; as in the second act the Vasantasenâ asks her escort Madanikâ whether she knows the name of her (Vasantasenâ's) beloved one, Madanikâ replies evasively, in a joking spirit, "He lives in the quarters of the big tradesmen" (seṭṭhicattare paḍivasadi).

reaches Benares and going about the town comes to the ivory-carvers' street and sees how ivory things are made by them in various forms (dantakâravîthiṃ patvâ dantakâre danta-vikatiyo kurumâne disvâ, I. 320). In another passage also the street of the ivory-carvers is mentioned: A poor man who lives in Benares sees how in the street of the ivory-carvers, ivory rings, etc., are made (dantakâravîthiyaṃ dantavalîyâdaṁ karonte disvâ) and asks, "Will you buy tusks from me if I bring some?" As they answer in the affirmative, he kills elephants, takes out the tusks and maintains his livelihood by their sale.

Some trades were followed not inside but outside the town, although mostly in its proximity, and in villages which were occupied by members of one and the same profession. Such tradesmen's villages are often
[P. 181.] mentioned as being in the neighbourhood of Benares: "Not far from Benares"—so it is said in the Alînacitta Jâtaka (II. 18)—"lay a carpenters' village" (vaḍḍhakigâma). There lived five hundred carpenters. They proceeded by river to a forest, prepared the wood for use as material for the construction of houses, constructed various kinds of one-storeyed, two-storeyed buildings, etc., and made sign-posts with all pieces of wood, beginning

with posts. Then they take the wood to the shore, put it on board the ship and go down stream to the city. Here they make houses for everyone who desires it, take the money, and return home and make new materials with it.

Such a village in the neighbourhood of Benares and occupied only by carpenters, occurs again in the Jâtakas (II. 405; IV. 159); in the last passage it is said that a thousand families lived in the big village (kulasahassanivâso mahâvaḍḍhakîgâmo).

The potṭers also seem to have lived outside the town in a village by themselves; at least mention is made of one potter family who lives in a village in front of the gate of Benares (Bârânasinagarassa dvâragâme kumbhakârakula, III. 376).

More wonderful than these manufacturers' villages in the immediate neighbourhood of a big city which could find an easy market for their products and also could have their needs, such as clothes, implements, supplied, from the City, is the existence of such professional villages in the middle of the flat country. We read in the Sûci Jâtaka of two smiths' villages lying side by side, of which one consists of a thousand huts (sahassakuṭiko kammâragâmo III. 281). From the neighbouring villages, people go to this village in order to provide themselves with axes, hatchets, ploughshares, spikes and other implements. When one reflects what a difficulty such a local isolation creates in the economical relations, one will see in these manufacturing villages not a phenomenon of secondary importance, but a highly important factor and one that is characteristic of the physiognomy of the social life of that time. The power of traditional customs which suit the spirit of the Indian people inclined to schematism, has created and maintained here a new impetus which is stronger than the practical need which obviously points to a variety of professions within the same common life. However much the origin of professional communities may have to be traced, as we have to do in the case of the Russian village communities, to the close relationship of the villagers with one another and to the equal right of all in the common property,[1] on the Indian soil, the maintenance of such a remarkable institution seems to have been due principally to the inborn tendency towards organisation, classification, schematism in the minds of the Indians. As the Brâhmaṇas worked together in villages in which foreign, especially, lower, elements were not tolerated, so, following their example, social

[P. 182.]

[1] *Cf.* Senart, *Les castes dans l' Inde*, pp. 197, 229.

groups, united by community of profession, separated themselves from one another and helped to create the manifoldness of modern caste-life.

As with the guilds of tradesmen, so can we also in the case of the manufacturers, infer from the institution of the elders (jeṭṭhakas) the presence of a certain organisation. Such elders stand at the head of the smiths (kammârajeṭṭhaka or jeṭṭhakakammâra),[1] garland-makers (mâlakârajeṭṭhaka III. 405), and carpenters (vaḍḍhaki IV. 161). It appears that the number of manufacturers combined into a guild having a common leader could not exceed a certain figure; at least, it is said, in the last-named passage of the Samuddavâṇija Jâtaka, that in a village inhabited by a thousand carpenter families, every five hundred families had a head (kulasahasse pañcannaṃ pañcannaṃ kulasatânaṃ jeṭṭhakâ dve vaḍḍhaki ahesuṃ). Whether the elder had either by law or by custom any recognised authority over the members of his union, is not mentioned; his office seems to have been an honorary one which was held by specially skilled manufactures and not always by the oldest in point

[P. 183.]

[1] *Kammâra* is used of blacksmiths as well as of silversmiths, (Dhammapada 43) and, as here, of goldsmiths. The latter are called in other places (I. 182; V. 438) *suvaṇṇakâra.*

of age. The elder seems to have occupied a peculiar position in the royal court. "The senior among the hundred smiths"—so it is said in the Sûci Jâtaka (III. 281)—"was a favourite of the king, blessed with wealth and property." In another place it is narrated that a prince asks a kammârajeṭṭhaka to come to him and commissions him to make a female figure out of a quantity of gold (V. 282).

The three conditions mentioned: local division of different kinds of work, hereditary character of branches of profession and the existence of an elder: seem to me to indicate clearly an organisation of handicraft which can be compared in many respects with our corporations in the Middle Ages. Also in these tradesmen's corporations of ancient India the principle finds application, which has already been mentioned in connexion with the guilds of tradesmen: the more in the course of centuries the caste theory—even in Buddhist lands—obtained currency, the greater the exclusiveness of, and respect for, the leading castes, the more did the manufacturers' corporations become incorporated in the caste-order. After the example set by nobility and the Brahmanical caste, they surrounded themselves with limitations by which a common bed and a common table were forbidden with members of castes who on account of the lowness of their race occupied a lower stage of human society than they themselves. That many of the manufacturers mentioned above occupied a comparatively low social position admits of no doubt and was, in my opinion, the chief reason why they separated themselves from the rest of the population and thereby had in ancient times the appearance of being something akin to a caste: the corporations of the manufacturers fall—partly, at any rate—undoubtedly under the category of the despised castes which will be treated of in a later chapter.

CHAPTER XI.

Casteless professions.

But from these despised and shunned portions of the population the guilds of tradesmen and most of the manufacturers with which we have had hitherto to do, are far removed. Between these there is a multiform and chaotic society which resists more or less every attempt at classification and about which there can be no talk of an organisation according to castes in that age. To this belong the great number of manufacturers standing outside their corporation and exclusively in the service of the king—namely, contractors and artists, the wandering dancers and musicians who move from village to village, showing their skill, and the tramps who consider every means good which helps them to earn their livelihood, and further, the herdsmen, huntsmen and fishermen living in the country, in the forest and in mountains, and finally, the mass of labourers and slaves.

In the lawbooks we find the rule that the kings could make the artisans work one day in the month for him;[1] the Jâtakas know

---

[1] Manu VII. 138; X. 120.

nothing of this; on the other hand, artisans are mentioned who seem to have worked only for him. In the Kusa Jâtaka there appear three distinct artisans in the pay of the king in the following order: a court potter (râjakumbhakâra V. 290)—we meet with one in the Cullakaseṭṭhi Jâtaka (I. 121), where it is described how he seeks on horseback to burn pots for the royal court—a basketmaker (râjupaṭṭhâka naḷakâra. V. 291) in the king's service and a court gardener (râjamâlakâra V. 292). The designation of these as "court purveyors" seems to me to refer to a special position which raises them above their otherwise low or even despised rank and makes improbable their being members of a corporation, in the same way as in the case

[P. 185.]

of the barber working in the royal court whose occupation as barber ranked certainly among the lowest professions. This court barber was no unimportant person in the king's court, he sometimes even stands in friendly intercourse with his employer.[1] "Friend," (samma kappaka I. 137) so addresses the king in the Makhâdeva Jâtaka his barber, while asking the latter to inform him if he finds any grey

---

[1] Upâli, the barber of the Sakyas, seems in the Cullavagga of the Vinaya Pitaka (VII. 1. 4) to be a personal friend of the Sakyas. *Cf.* Oldenberg, *Buddha*, p. 158, Note.

hair on his head. The many small personal services for which people wanted him—as such there are mentioned in the introduction to the Sigâla Jâtaka (II. 5), shaving the beard, curling the hair, placing the dice-board in position, etc.—seem to have made him indispensable for the king, the royal ladies, the princes and princesses. Also the position of a court barber is sometimes described as highly lucrative: in the Makhâdeva Jâtaka it is narrated that the Videha king when he renounces worldly life gives a village to his barber which brought him 100,000 (satasahassuṭṭhânaṃ gâmavaraṃ. I. 138).

Even the king's cook (rañño sûda V. 292) does not hold an insignificant position in the royal household, at least not in that of a king who was such a "gourmand" as King Bhojanasuddhika,[1] whose dinners cost, according to the description in the Dûta Jâtaka (II. 319), 100,000 every time and consisted of a hundred different dishes. Still in the Kusa Jâtaka, the occupation of a cook is described as one to be practised by slaves or hired labourers (dâsakammakarehi kattabbaṃ. V. 293).

A special office in the royal court was that of the estimator (agghakâraka. I. 124;

---

[1] Literally, "one who is very particular, scrupulous with regard to eating." *Cf.* the expression used in the Upasâḷha Jâtaka (II. 54) of a Brâhmaṇa, namely, *susânasuddhika*, which signifies something like „scrupulous, superstitious with regard to the cremation ground."

agghâpanikaṭṭhâna. I. 126) whose work consisted in estimating the value of elephants, horses, precious stones, gold, etc., and in paying the owners of wares their proper
[P. 186.] price. In the Suppâraka Jâtaka the work of an estimator was given to a blind fisherman who exchanges his work for service in the Court. He determines as valuer the things which are most heavily taxed. Thus he knows by merely touching with the hand that a carriage which should serve the king as a State carriage is built with the wood of a perforated tree or that a costly garment is eaten by mice at one place; he receives, however, from the king only eight kahâpaṇas for every valuation. Not willing to accept a payment which according to him is suitable for a barber (imassa dâyo nahâpitadâyo. IV. 138), he leaves the service of the king and returns to his fisherman's village.

Besides the men who had to look to the daily needs of the king and his Court, a whole army of skilled men of every kind surrounded the person of the king in the courts of the powerful princes of that time. Thus, we come across musicians (gandhabba I. 384; II. 250), dancers and singers (nâtaka IV. 324; naccagitâdisu kusalâ, II. 227); elephant tamers (hattâcariya, II. 221) and archers (dhanuggaha, II. 87; V.

128). Whilst, moreover, these skilled men in ancient India, as we shall see, were of little respectability and the arts practised by them were mostly unprofitable, the artists in the service of the king did not seem to have been from the pecuniary point of view in a bad way. An archer demands from the king an annual salary of 100,000 (ekasaṃvaccharena satasahassaṃ, II. 87). The king agrees to this; on the other hand, the old archers (porâṇaka-dhanuggaha) consider the salary too high. Still better paid is another *dhanuggaha*; he receives daily 1,000 (devasikaṃ sahassam labhitvâ râjânaṃ upaṭṭhahi, V. 128) and incurs in this way the displeasure of the rest of the king's servants. These figures, though, as everywhere in Indian sources, bad as a statistical material, point to a respectable and lucrative profession. Probably the archer was entitled to high salaries, as he could render the king valuable services, whether in hunting or in war.

About the salaries of the other Court artists there are found in the Jâtakas only a few general statements. [P. 187.] An old musician (gandhabba) informs the king that his pupil wants to serve him and adds, "Fix the nature of the salary" (deyyadhammam assa jânâtha, II. 250), to which the king replies, "He shall get one-half of your salary." To this the pupil, however, does not agree; he demands equal salary, as he knows his art quite as well as his teacher. A musical tournament ordered by the king ends the matter in this way, that the vanquished scholar at a sign from the king was belaboured with stones and clubs and killed, whilst the teacher receives much money from the king and the residents.

Similarly in the Upâhana Jâtaka mention is made of a pupil of an elephant tamer (hatthâcariya, II. 221) who demands the same salary as his teacher. The king announces by beat of drum, "To-morrow a teacher and his pupil will both exhibit their skill in elephant-taming; who wants to see must come to the palace." The night before the performance, the teacher instructs the elephant to commit all kinds of mistakes, so that when given the order "Go forward," it goes backwards, and when ordered to go backwards, it goes forward, etc. The consequence is, that next day, as the elephant does the reverse of what it is ordered to do by the pupil, the angry crowd kills him by throwing stones and beating him with sticks.

That many of the artists mentioned here, especially, the archers, belong as much to the class of "Court people" as, for example, the executioner or the gate-keeper, I do not consider impossible.

Like the latter, they were paid by the king; like these they were attached to the king's service which they could not quit against the wish of their master. Whoever among them—like the court barber in the Gaṅgamâla Jâtaka—wants to lead the homeless life, must get the permission of the king (râjânaṃ pabbajjaṃ anujânâpetva, III. 452). But they are distinguished from the râjabhoggas or râjaññas, by which I understand only the "royal officers," by their purely private character. They hold no public position and their work is [P. 188.] confined to personal service which they render to the king and his family.

On account of the comparatively great respectability and the high salary which the Court artists enjoyed, the effort of most of the artists was to get into the king's service; as, however, this fell to the lot of only a very few, others tried to serve under rich private persons. Very often we meet with artists in the service of young tradesmen whom they help, along with other parasites, to squander their paternal property: jumpers, runners, singers, dancers, etc., receive each one of them 1,000 from the squandering and pleasure-seeking seṭṭhi's son (laṅghanadhâvanagîtanaccâdîni karontânaṃ sahassaṃ dadamâno, II. 431) and make him in a short time a beggar. In contrast with these parasitic artists, there were many who earned their bread with difficulty by catering for the amusement of people at festivities. We read of a dancer (naṭa III. 507) who lives in a village not far from Benares and goes with his wife into the town, where he gets money through dancing and singing which accompanies his lyre (vîṇâ). As, however, such festivities, in spite of their frequency, formed only an occasional break in their daily life, the dancers led at other times a thoroughly miserable life, as did the dancing family (naṭakakula, II. 167) in the Ucchiṭṭhabhatta Jâtaka in which the Bodhisatta was reborn. This family maintained itself by begging and even the Bodhisatta had no other way of earning a livelihood than through alms.

It seems to me that by this *naṭa* or *naṭaka* we are not to understand actors, as in later times, for in our text dramatic performances are nowhere described. A sort of pantomime which is performed by two dancers is no doubt described; probably, in this we are to look for a fore-runner of the later Indian drama. "At that time there were"—so it is narrated in the Suruci Jâtaka (IV. 324)—"two skilled dancers, named 'Dull ear' and 'White ear'; they tried to make the king laugh. One of these, 'Dull ear,' set up at the gate of the palace a big tree called Atula, threw

[P. 189.]

a ball of rope and climbed, after attaching the rope to a branch of the tree, the Atulamba tree with the help of the rope. The tree of Vessavaṇa[1] is also called Atulamba. Now the servants of Vessavaṇa arrested him, hacked his body to pieces and let these pieces fall. The other dancers joined the pieces together and sprinkled them with water, upon which the dancer revived and danced in a garment of flowers. The other dancer, 'White ear' set up a funeral pyre and went with his followers into the fire. When he disappeared and the funeral pyre was burnt out, people sprinkled water upon the ashes. On this, the dancer rose with his followers and danced, decked in a garment of flowers."

If the dances described here are more than a creation of the narrator's fancy, jugglery must have reached in ancient India a comparatively high stage, as their explanation can only be sought in mirrors which give the spectator the illusion of a person climbing the rope or going into the fire. That the concave mirror, this most important instrument in modern magic, was known in ancient India, is in itself undoubtedly highly improbable. Still a passage in Śaṅkara's commentary on the Vedânta,[2]

---

[1] Skr. Vaiśravaṇa, patronymic of Kubera.

[2] Quoted by Deussen, *System des Vedanta*, p. 322.

where reference is made to jugglery exactly similar to the first trick in our text, presupposes likewise the use of a mirror: "The highest God"—so runs the passage—"is only as much different from the acting and enjoying individual called *Vijṇânâtman*, created by ignorance, as the magician climbing a rope with shield and sword is different from the same magician really standing on the ground."

It is in an illusion of the spectator that probably the trick of the sword-eater consists, of whom it is narrated in the
[P. 190.] Dasaṇṇaka Jâtaka that he swallows a sword thirty-three feet long and having a sharp edge.

We make the acquaintance of a special kind of dancers in the "jumpers," the *laṅghananaṭaka* of the Dubbaca Jâtaka, namely, an acrobat who knows how to jump over a number of lances sunk in the ground and placed one behind the other. The Boddhisatta who is born in an acrobat family, learns from a *naṭaka* the art of jumping and tours with his teacher exhibiting his art. "His teacher, however"—so it is said further (I. 430) —"knew how to jump over four lances, not over five." Now one day he appeared in a village and placed, while he was drunk, five lances on the ground, one behind the other, with the intention of jumping over them. Then the

Boddhisatta said, "You don't know the art of jumping over five lances, my teacher; take away one lance, for if you try to leap over the five lances, you will be pierced by the fifth lance and die." "You don't know what I can do," answered the teacher in a drunken fit, and leaps, without paying heed to his pupil's words, over the four but is fixed by the fifth, as the *madhuka* [1] flower is fixed on its stem, and falls to the ground crying loudly."

In the same category of touring jugglers who exhibit their art in the court of princes or in festivities for the entertainment of the people, the snake charmers (ahiguṇṭhika) of our text are to be placed. Of such an *ahiguṇṭhika* it is said in the Sâlaka Jâtaka (II. 267), that he has trained an ape to which he has given an antidote [2] and which he then
[P. 191.] allows to play with a snake and that in this way he earns a livelihood. Another snake charmer has likewise

---

1 Bussia latifolia.

2 Osadha=Skr. aushadha, herb, medicine. It appears that in ancient times the snake tamers used to make themselves and the animals which they allowed to play with the snakes proof against snake-bite through some plant juice. On the other hand, the practice, so common among Indian snake-charmers to-day, of extracting the poison teeth, was introduced later. This is only mentioned in the *paccuppannavatthu*, namely, in the introduction to the Mûlapariyâya Jâtaka, where the monks whose pride Buddha curbs, are compared to snakes whose teeth have been extracted (uddhaṭadâṭhâ viya sappâ II. 259).

trained an ape; when a festival (ussava) is announced, he keeps it in the house of a grain merchant, travels seven days and then lets his snakes play (ahiṃ kîḷâpento). (III. 198).

At such exhibitions and popular festivals in ancient India, music was not wanting: either the dancers themselves made singing and playing on the lute accompany their dances or there came professional musicians to the festivals, in order to practise their art for money. Instruments, mostly very primitive, on which in India even to-day jugglers play as an accompaniment of their dances and skilful performances,[1] were to some extent in existence at that time: besides the lute (vîṇâ), we find the drum (bheri) and the conch (saṅkha) mentioned in our text. A drummer (bherivâdaka I. 283), who, as mentioned in the Bheri Jâtaka, lives in a village, goes with his son to the city, as he hears that in Benares a festival (nakkhatta) is announced, in order to play here on the drum in the circle of those who take part in the festival; he acquires by his play a good deal of money. The same is said in somewhat different words in the Saṅkhadhamana Jâtaka of a conch-blower (saṅkhadhamaka, I. 284).

[1] *Cf.* Schlagintweit, *Indien in Wort und Bild*, 2nd Edn., Vol. II., p. 174.

As there were drummers and conch-blowers in the king's service—edicts of the king, announcements of public sports, execution, etc., were made known in the city by beat of drum or by the blowing of the conch—and others who played on their instruments at popular festivals, so we find, along with the already-mentioned court musicians, also some who were employed by private persons on festive occasions. Tradesmen of Benares who come to Ujjenî on a business tour make an appointment and come to a place of amusement, carrying with them garlands, perfumery, ointment, food and drink. Then they fetch a musician and that the best (jeṭṭha-
[P. 192.] gandhabba) in Ujjenî (te taṃ pakkosâpetvâ attano gandhabbaṃ kâresuṃ II. 249). As the tradesmen, accustomed to the performance of the court musicians of Benares, are not satisfied with his work, he returns the reward paid him and travels with them to Benares. Here he becomes the pupil of the old court musician and meets with a sorry end in the way already described.

That in these artists, as described in the Jâtakas, we have something similar to castelike organisation, is obviously highly improbable. And still these professions in course of time developed into castes: in Manu we find *naṭa* mentioned among the mixed castes, the forerunners of the modern *naṭas* or *naṭakas* who wander in the villages of Hindustan as jugglers, buffoons, actors, acrobats, snakecharmers and exhibit their skill for money or for presents.[1] A tendency towards organisation, towards combination based upon a common profession, as we, I believe, can assume, is present in ancient times even among these classes of Indian people; as proof of this we have the oft-mentioned circumstance that professions were hereditary in artist families: we have already made the acquaintance of a dancer family (naṭakakula), of a drummer or conch-blower family (bherivâdakakula I. 283; saṅkhadhamakakula, I. 284); the son of an elephant-tamer (hatthâcariya, II. 221) practises the art of his father, and the son of an acrobat learns the art of jumping (laṅghanasippaṃ sikkhitvâ I. 430). To this add that these professions were very little respectable and that in consequence, people compelled men who earned their livelihood by the practice of these, probably to live outside the city; thus it is said of a dancer, as well as of a drummer who goes to Benares for a festival, that he lives in a village not far from Benares. Nevertheless, these artists, at any rate, in ancient times, lacked all essential conditions for the formation of a caste: neither the feeling of race-community—a factor

[1] Nesfield, *Caste System* p. 6.

which is of great importance in the formation of the despised castes—nor the need of external organisation could cause them to be formed into a close corporation; rather compelled by their profession to restless wandering, necessity made them seek such other means of earning money as opportunity offered.

[P. 193.]

Often the life of such touring people was spent in the manner, described in the Tittira Jâtaka (III. 541):

"He has (as porter of the tradesmen) wandered in Kâlinga kingdom, he has engaged in trade, stick in hand, he walks over the country road.[1] With dancers he has wandered with hunters; with sticks he has fought with the crowd.

"He has caught birds, he has measured (corn) with the *âlhaka* measure, he has (at a dice-game, with regard to false players) removed the dice, he has transgressed[2] the moral laws, he has staunched the blood of (the punished),[3] his

---

[1] Saṅkupatha? lit., "a path studded with nails."

[2] *Samyamo abbhattto* is explained by the commentator with the words: *jîvikavuttim nissâya pabbajanteṅ'eva sîlasamyamo atikkanto*, "inasmuch as for earning a livelihood he embraced the homeless condition, he transgressed the moral prescriptions."

[3] Abbûhitaṃ pupphakaṃ aḍḍharattaṃ. The commentator adds by way of explanation: "To earn a livelihood he brought criminals whose hands and feet were chopped, to a hall and returning at about

hands are burnt by taking hot food (during begging)."

Here is given us in a brief form the picture of the life of an Indian tramp and of the sphere in which his destiny unfolded itself: dancers, hunters, club-fighters, players—this is the society in which the adventurous period of his life is spent. Finally, after trying all possible occupations he earns his living by begging as a fraudulent ascetic (duṭṭha-tâpasa).

Although more settled than these wandering occupations, the rural professions of [P. 194.] herdsmen, huntsmen, fishermen do not seem in ancient times to have come under the organisation of caste, as, on account of their work, they inclined more towards a solitary life. Only when we see them in great number in the town or united into a village community can we suppose the existence of organisations similar, for example, to those of the artisans. In a sea-port town (paṭṭanagâma. IV. 137) the son of an elder among the fishermen after the death of his father steps into his shoes. He becomes blind, however, later, and takes to the service

---

midnight, he stopped the blood flowing out of the wounds with *kuṇḍaka* (the red powder, which is found in the rice corn under the husk) and smoke."

of the king, as he cannot any more follow the occupation of a fisherman, although he, as mentioned in the passage of the Suppâraka Jâtaka in question, "was the elder among the fishermen."

Noteworthy as an example of the fact that the thorough-going division of work characteristic of the social life of India of to-day is a factor of ancient origin, is the circumstance that the different designations of fishermen appear to coincide with the names of modern fishermen castes and point to this, that even at that time there were special branches in the profession of fishermen whose work was so precisely defined. Thus, the fishermen with nets and baskets (jâlakuminâdini khipitvâ macche gaṇhanti, I. 427) were called *Kevattas*[1] (II. 178, 124); the angling fishermen were called bâlisika (I. 482; III. 52) on account of their fishing pole (balisa).

Also among hunters we find this moment of division of work which surely must have become important in the later development of the castes: the huntsman pursuing the deer is called *migaluddaka* (III. 49, 184) or simply, *luddaka*; a bird-hunter (sakuṇaluddaka, II. 161) we come across in the Kakkara Jâtaka, nay,

---

[1] =Skr. kaivarta, by which, as we saw above, in the Brahmanical system, a certain mixed caste is understood. *Kewat* is even in these days a name of a class of fishermen. *Cf.* Nesfield, *Caste System*, p. 9.

even a quail-catcher (vaṭṭakaluddaka, I. 208) is represented. In the Kuruṅgamiga Jâtaka (I. 173) a *gâmavâsiaṭṭakaluddaka* is mentioned, *i.e.*, a hunter living in the village who prepares an ambush in tall trees under which he has noticed traces of the deer and from there kills the animal.

[P. 195] Much less than in the case of the casteless professions hitherto treated, is mention made of an external co-ordination or any organisation whatever in the case of the serving classes, as they were composed of all possible elements of the population differing in point of race and professional work. He who suffered shipwreck in the struggle with the waves of life and was rendered poor must have been forced even at that time—whatever might be his descent—to win his bread by service. We read of a poor *gahapati* who supports himself and his mother by working as a hired labourer (bhatiṃ katvâ III. 325); he complains that he earns only one or half a *mâsaka* [1] and that his mother can with difficulty be supported. The three Brâhmaṇa daughters of the Suvaṇṇahaṃsa Jâtaka have, as their supporter is dead, to serve in other families and pass their days in trouble (paresaṃ bhatiṃ

---

[1] = Skr. mâshaka, a coin of small value.

katvâ kicchena jîvanti, I. 475). Of course, these members of the aristocratic castes formed a small fragment of the serving classes; the majority was formed by the classes of the population in whom the profession of a hired labourer was as much hereditary as the poverty connected with it. The Bodhisatta, re-born in a poor family (daḷiddakula), as described in the Kummâsapinḍa Jâtaka, works, when he is grown-up, for money at a *setthi's* and maintains his livelihood in this way (III. 409; similarly, III. 444). The payment which falls to the lot of the day-labourers seems, according to the Jâtakas, to be so miserable as to be hardly sufficient to enable them to eke out their livelihood. As the *gahapati* through his paid works earns no more than one or half a *mâsaka*, so also it is said of a *bhataka* who supports himself by carrying water (udakabhatiṃ katvâ III. 446) that he has saved half a *mâsaka*. With such a low pay and owing to the impossibility of gaining access to any higher profession, the possibility seems to be wholly excluded—and in this it has a certain resemblance with a caste—of the Indian hired labourer emerging out of his miserable position: born and bred in poverty, he bore his sad lot as a nature-necessity in order to leave it to his children as a legacy.

[P. 196.]

Those day-labourers enjoyed a comparatively favourable position who were in the service of one and the same employer for a long time or permanently. Every big land-owner, every rich tradesman had, according to the Jâtakas, along with his slaves, a number of day-labourers in his service. One's own people (attano purisâ), the bondsmen, to whom in the Sâlikedâra Jâtaka (IV. 277) the Brâhmaṇa gives a portion of the rice fields for guarding, are contrasted with the *bhataka* who gets a salary (bhati) for watching and who is held responsible for any damage and has to pay a compensation according to the appraisement of the owner (brâhmaṇo sâliṃ agghâpetvâ mayhaṃ iṇaṃ karissati). In the house of the pious Brâhmaṇa Dhammapâla even the slaves and labourers (dâsakammakarâ IV. 50) give alms; they obey the moral prescriptions and observe the fasts. That in the Visayha Jâtaka the slaves and day-labourers (dâsakammakaraporisa) are reckoned among the property of a seṭṭhi has already been mentioned (p. 262). Of another seṭṭhi, it is narrated in the introduction to the Mayhaka Jâtaka, that at the sight of a begging monk whom he sees coming with a full alms pot from his house, he cannot restrain his thoughts: "If my slaves or labourers (dâsâ vâ kammakârâ vâ III. 300) had received this food, they would have done more difficult work; alas, this is really a loss for me."

According to the Gaṅgamâla Jâtaka, these labourers were taken care of in the house of their master; they did not, however, live there but went to their lodgings in the evening (sabbe attano attano vasanaṭṭhânâni gatâ III. 445). Probably these were, like the residences of poor people generally, outside the city. The already-mentioned water-carrier lived with a poor woman who likewise supports herself by carrying water, at the northern gate of Benares. "Living by the side of the gate" signified apparently something like "poor, lowly." "I am the daughter of one living by the side of the gate" (dhîtâ dvâra-

[P. 197.]

vasinô V. 441), says the poor girl in the Kuṇâla Jâtaka to the king in reply to his question whose daughter she is.

If now the position of these hired labourers was in no respect enviable, they still enjoyed a certain freedom, as they in all probability could change their masters when they liked. On the other hand, the slaves (dâsa) had absolutely no freedom; they were, just like the cow, devoid of any rights and were absolutely at the mercy of their masters.

In Mânu (VIII. 415), seven kinds of slaves are enumerated: those who are captured in the field (during war) (dhvajâhṛita), those who serve in return for maintenance (bhaktadâsa) those that are born in the house (gṛihaja), those that are bought (krîta), those that are received as gifts (datrima) those that are inherited from the father (paitrika) and those that are made slaves by way of punishment (daṇḍadâsa). If we exclude the *bhaktadâsa* as not belonging properly to the class of bondsmen and also the *daṇḍadâsa*, there remain four classes which reduce to the three mentioned in the Vinaya Piṭaka (Bhikkhunîvibhaṅga, Saṅghâdisesa I. 2. 1), as we can put "those that are born in the house" and "those inherited from father" on one side and "those acquired by gift or purchase" on the other. Here these classes are distinguished: those that are born in the house, those that are bought with money and those that are captured in a war (dâso nâma antojâto dhanakkito karamarânito). That the *daṇḍadâsa* mentioned by Manu in the last sentence is not mentioned here, must seem strange, as we have in the Jâtakas an example of a slave robbed of his freedom as a punishment. The village superintendent (gâmabhojaka) of the Kulâvaka Jâtaka, who has spoken ill of the inhabitants of the village before the king, is condemned to lose not only his property but also his freedom: the king makes him the slave of the village inhabitants (taṇ ca tesañ ñeva dâsaṃ

katvâ I. 200). We also find "those that are acquired by purchase" and "those that are born in the house" represented in our text. A Brâhmaṇa is sent by his careless wife who pretends to be unable to do household work, to beg money that she may have a female slave (dâsî). The Brâhmaṇa begs 700 *kahâpaṇas*,
[P. 198.] a sum which he considers sufficient for buying a female or male slave (alaṃ me ettakaṃ dhanaṃ dâsidâsamûlâya III. 343). The fraudulent slave Kaṭâhaka who deserts his master and whom we already know (p. 170), is "a slave born in the house"; he is born on the same day as the son of his master, a seṭṭhi of Benares, and is educated along with him. Of slaves captured in war, from which class in the oldest times the slaves were probably exclusively recruited, no mention is made in the Jâtakas; at least in the passages of our source which tell us of wars between neighbouring kings, no mention is made of prisoners of war; only of robbers (paccantavâsino corâ) it is mentioned in the Cullanârada Jâtaka that they plunder a village and capture its inhabitants and make them slaves (karamare gahetvâ IV. 220).

Owing to the complete absence of legal rights of the slaves, their work differed with the individual temperament of their master.

Sometimes in our source the relation in which the slaves stood to their master is represented as a familiar one and their treatment as quite humane. The family of the Brâhmaṇa agriculturist in the Uraga Jâtaka consists of six members; the Brâhmaṇa, his wife, his son, his daughter, his daughter-in-law and the female slave. "They all"—so it is said further (III. 162)—"lived together in harmony and amity." As, however, the son of the Brâhmaṇa dies and is burnt without a tear and without a moan, Sakka, disquieted by such conduct and forced to quit his heavenly seat, asks the slave, "My daughter, in what relation did you stand to this." "He was my master!" "Surely, he has at times molested and oppressed you and therefore you are glad at his death and do not weep." "O lord, don't speak so, never saw anybody like him; patient, loving, sympathetic was the son of my master and loved me as a child reared on the breast." To a similar familiar relationship between the female slave and the master, the Nânacchanda Jâtaka (II. 428) also points; the *purohita* whom the king asks to demand

[P. 199.]

a favour, asks, besides the members of his household, also the slave Puṇṇâ[1] what her desire is. And the

---

[1] Probably, a shortened form of *puṇṇamamanathiâ*, "one whose desire is fulfilled, the contented."

slave desires, humble as she is, a mortar, a pestle and a sieve.[1]

All the same, the examples quoted do not justify our inferring a specially favourable position for the slaves of ancient India; other passages of our text speak clearly of the miserable lot of the bondsmen who frequently had to put up with thrashing, imprisonment and bad food. For this reason, the slave Kaṭâhaka, who has learnt to read and write along with the son of the family and who is otherwise clever and knows the art of speaking, discharges the duties of a store-keeper (bhaṇḍâgârika), but is afraid lest he should lose one day this office. "Not always," he reflects within himself, "will one care to let me have the office of a store-keeper; one good day some defect will be noticed in me and then people will thrash me, lock me up, brand me and give me the food of a slave to eat" (tâḷetvâ bandhitvâ lakkhaṇena aṅketvâ dâsaparibhogena pi paribhuñjissanti I. 451). A female slave, who is sent by her master to work at other people's place for money, is thrown into a corner of the house and struck with a stick, as she cannot bring any money back to the house (I. 402).

---

[1] Udukkhalamusalañ c'eva suppañ ca. II. 428. All the three implements the slave obviously used for crushing and winn wing rice. Also the slave Rohini of the Rohini Jâtaka uses the mortar for pressing rice (vihipaharaṇa, I. 248).

The work which the slaves had to do was naturally extremely manifold and differed with the social position of the master and the intelligence of the slave. Many might be employed, like the slave Kaṭâhaka, in higher employments, like those of the store-keeper, treasurer or private secretary; as a rule, however, the work of the slaves was of a lower nature. The slave Piṅgalâ in the Silâvimaṃsa Jâtaka (III. 101) before she can go to a rendezvous must wash the
[P. 200.] feet of her master; only when he is tranquillised does she sit on the door-sill and await his pleasure. With considerable detail the duties of a slave are described in the Kaṭâhaka Jâtaka. The slave Kaṭâhaka who gives himself out as the son of his master and marries the daughter of a Seṭṭhi friendly to his master, hears that his master has gone to the country and is afraid that he may come to him. He resolves to meet him and propitiate him by doing a slave's work (dâsakammaṃ katvâ I. 452). Everywhere he explains loudly how little respect other young people show to their parents, as they sit at the same table with them, instead of serving them; he himself would, when his elders took their meals, set before them the dishes, place the spitoons in their position, take particular care of their drink and stand behind them with a brush; up to the most common performances

he enumerates all services which a slave must render to his master (yâva sarîravalañjanakâle udakalasaṃ âdâya paṭicchannaṭṭhânagamanâ sabbaṃ dâsehi sâmikânaṃ kattabbakiccaṃ pakâsesi I. 453).

On account of the lowness of such services, the slave himself was considered of little worth by a master who treated him humanely. The female slave Puṇṇâ receives from her master, the *purohita*, who asks her what she wishes, the epithet *jammî* "the low, contemptible." "Son of a slave" (dâsiputtra) was a term of reproach; when in the Nigrodha Jâtaka (IV. 41) the *senâpati* is informed that his friend is there, he comes in angrily and cries, "Who is that friend? He is a despised son of a slave. Throw him out!" "Servant of a slave's son" (dâsiputtaceṭaka I. 225)—so addresses in the Nanda Jâtaka the bold slave his master.

In spite of their low status the slaves occupied in Indiân society a different position from that of the despised castes who will occupy our attention in the next chapter. They could not, like the latter, be regarded as impure, because their work brought them constantly into close contact with their master whom they helped to dress and undress and assisted in the care of their body, whose food they prepared and whom they served at dinner. As they lived together with the families to which they belonged, they lacked the local isolation and external combination of the despised castes; they were, in consequence of this, as little a "caste" as the slaves of the Greeks and Romans, in whom we find the same categories and similar relations, so far as conduct and legal position are concerned. Also the Indian slaves resembled those of the ancient classical ages in this, that under certain circumstances they could obtain freedom. We read of such "freed slaves" in the Sona-Nanda Jâtaka; as the rich Brâhmaṇa renounces the world, he disposes of his property and sets his slaves free (dâsajanaṃ bhujissaṃ katvâ V. 313). It is true, according to Manu (VIII. 414), a Sûdra, even when he is set free by his master, is not released from his condition of slavery: "for who can take away that which is in-born in him?" Still the view expressed here is only a consequence of the Brahmanical system which in practice did not have much importance. In reality, a slave set free—proof of this is not, however, to be got from the Jâtakas—probably either served as a day-labourer or adopted some other profession, for which he possessed the means or the skill.

CHAPTER XII.

The Despised Castes.

We have hitherto repeatedly moved in our accounts within the limits of a province which comprises, according to the Brahmanical theory, the aboriginal population and is enclosed by the barrier of non-Aryan birth and separated by this from the rest of the society. In vain do we look in the bright light which the Jâtakas throw upon the true life of ancient India for a line of demarcation separating the entire Aryan from the entire non-Aryan population ; if we leave out of account the occurrence of the word Śudda (=Skr. Śûdra) in theoretical discussions, [P. 202.] nothing points to the real existence of a fourth caste, the Sûdra. Probably we have to suppose for the first period following the Aryan migration a separation of the dark-coloured aborigines from the bright-coloured conquerors : it is exhibited by the contrast between the *ârya varṇa* and *dâsa varṇa* in the Vedas. But already in very early times—and indeed, the further from the borders of the Aryan culture-sphere, the more pronouncedly—a mixture with the native population took place ; nay, it seems to me in no way certain, in the lands lying farthest east, especially, in the provinces in which Buddhism first made its appearance, in the Kosala and Magadha land, that the distinction between the Aryan conquerors and the conquered who were employed in slavish work was not abolished altogether: many of the non-Aryan stems seem to have preserved their political independence and to have come under the higher Aryan culture by adopting its language and customs. Under the influence of the Brahmanical theory we are extremely accustomed to see in the aborigines of ancient India a great mass, namely, the conquered Śûdras. Surely, this name, applicable in the Brahmanical system to all non-Aryan Indians, is taken from the name of one particular stem out of the innumerable aboriginal stems, which from the ethnical and cultural point of view were no less different from one another than the bearers of the new culture who spread from the north-west to the Gangetic plain.

Among these numerous races some manifestly stood on a specially low culture-stage. Just as the wild hunting races of the Himâlaya must have distinguished themselves by their external appearance, by their undeveloped language, their customs relating to food, from the more advanced population of the plains, so their low position later prevented a mixture with the higher developed Aryans and preserved their racial peculiarity up to this day. Even to-day they have not gone beyond the first beginnings of culture: incapable of lasting work, they lead a wandering life and feed mostly on animals, roots and fruits which Nature [P. 203.] has given them freely[1]; where they set up their residences among the cultivated population, they are compelled to live in isolation outside the city and maintain their livelihood by the meanest kinds of work. These are the races of whom it is said in Manu (X. 50):

"Under well-known trees and in the cremation-ground, on mountains and in the woods should they live, recognised (by fixed marks) and living by work proper to them."

These races were and are even to-day looked upon by the Indians as castes, and indeed, they are classed in the Brahmanical theory with the lowest mixed castes. What gives them in fact in ancient times the appearance of a caste is their local isolation, their living together outside the rest of the society which avoids contact with them, on account of their low position, and their despised profession which is hereditary. From the higher castes they are distinguished by this, that their isolation is not a voluntary one; the

[1] Nesfield, Caste System, p, 6; Peschel, Völkerkunde, 5th Edn., p. 444.

barriers which surround them and which prevent their straying from their narrowly circumscribed profession as well as all mixture through marriage with those standing higher, are not erected by them but are forced upon them by their conquerors.

Of these low races we meet with a number even in the Jâtakas. Above all, we meet with the Caṇḍâla, a race which we come across in great numbers even to-day in north-east India, the scene of our narratives, and in Bengal.[1] In the eyes of the Indians the Caṇḍâla has always been the symbol of lowness and subjection.

"But the residences of the Caṇḍâlas"—so it is said in Manu (X. 51 sq.)—"should be outside the village, their dress should consist of garments of the dead: they must eat their food out of broken pots; black iron should be their ornament and always they must wander from place to place. A man who fulfils a religious duty should not seek intercourse with them; their business they should conduct among themselves and their marriages they must contract with their equals.

[P. 204.]

"Their food must be given them by somebody other than an Aryan in a broken vessel; at

[1] Schlagintweit, *Indien in Wort und Bild*, Vol. 1, p. 216: "Over a million of these people are to the east of Calcutta running up to the borders of Burma."

night they shall not go about in the villages or in the towns.

"In the day-time they may do the work assigned to them by order of the king; the corpse of anybody who has no relations, they must carry out of the house—such is the standing rule.

"Criminals they shall kill, according to the law, by order of the king; the clothes of the criminal, their beds or other ornamental articles they may keep to themselves."

The contempt with which the authors of the lawbooks who were Brâhmaṇas looked upon the lower classes of people, and the attempt to confirm them in their low position by legal prescriptions may have caused them to select purposively dark colours for the sketch they made of the Caṇḍâla, whilst the Jâtakas show that the reality was not far different from the priestly theory.

The Caṇḍâlas of our text live outside the town (bahinagare, IV. 376) in a village (caṇḍâlagâmaka, IV. 200, 390) by themselves.[1] Two Caṇḍâla brothers who know how to blow a Caṇḍâla flute must show their art outside the city gate; the one plays at the northern, the other at the eastern gate.

[1] The Caṇḍâla village placed in the Citta Sambhûta Jâtaka in front of the gate of Ujjain and thus to the west of India, may have probably existed only in the imagination of the narrator who carried the narrow conditions of his home over to the whole of India.

For the despised position of the Caṇḍâla we have already given examples in an earlier chapter (p. 26 sq.); we have seen how the eating of the food left by them (caṇḍâlucchiṭṭhabhatta) had as its consequence, for the members of the Brâhmaṇa caste, exclusion from their caste[1]; we have seen further how the

[P. 205.] wind which had touched the body of a Caṇḍâla was considered impure and how the very look of such a miserable creature sufficed to call up the feeling of impurity in those occupying a higher rank. "Contemptuous as a Caṇḍâla" has become a proverbial expression. Into the mouth of the young lioness to whom a jackal had made a proposal of marriage the words are put: "This jackal is considered low and wretched among the four-footed animals, similar to a Caṇḍâla (hino patikuṭṭho caṇḍâlasadiso. II. 6); we are, however, esteemed members of the highest royal family. This one addresses me indecent and improper words; what shall I do with life after I have listened to such words? I will hold my breath and die." The name Caṇḍâla stands for a word of contempt by which

---

[1] That the food left by a Caṇḍâla is impure, is not a purely Brahmanical view. In the introduction to the Satadhamma Jâtaka (II. 82), Buddha explains to the monks that for the followers of his doctrine the eating of food obtained in an unlawful manner is like eating the table leavings of a Caṇḍâla.

a Brâhmaṇa, for example, designates his adulterous wife (pâpacaṇḍâli IV. 246).

Of the "marks by order of the king" mentioned in Manu, we know nothing from our text. Still even according to the Jâtakas, the Caṇḍâlas appear to be known outwardly as such by their dress: "clad in a bad under-garment of a red colour round which a belt is tied: above this a dirty upper garment, an earthen pot in hand"—so in Mâtaṅga Jâtaka (IV. 379) the exterior of a Caṇḍâla is described.

Also by their speech the Caṇḍâlas apparently were distinguished from the rest of the population. To their isolation, their complete separation, is to be ascribed the fact that in the midst of a population speaking an Aryan dialect they preserved even in linguistic matters their racial individuality. In the Citta-Sambhûta Jâtaka it is narrated how two Caṇḍâlas dressed as Brâhmaṇas go to Takkasilâ and study there; later, however, as one of them, on the occasion of a Brâhmaṇavâcanaka, burns his
[P. 206.] face with a heated lamp, they forget themselves and are detected by their language (caṇḍâlabhâsâ IV. 391).

With the exception of the account of the two flute-players mentioned above, the Jâtakas contain no detailed account of the professional work of the Caṇḍâla. According to the commentary on the Sîlavîmaṃsa Jâtaka, there are people who are engaged in carrying corpses (chavachaḍḍaka III. 195); still it is doubtful whether this work which was also indicated for them in the Brahmanical theory, was in reality their only occupation, although their low stage of culture debarred them from practising any higher profession, even that of an artisan.

Along with the Caṇḍâlas there are mentioned in the Jâtakas, in the enumeration of the castes, the *Pukkusas*, who are the *Pukkasas* or *Pulkasas* of the Brahmanical system where they are called descendants of a Nishâda by a Śûdra wife. These Pukkasas were also most probably a non-Aryan caste occupying a very low position in society. According to the commentary on the Sîlavîmaṃsa Jâtaka, by this are meant men who have for their profession the plucking of flowers (pupphachaḍḍaka III. 195): as, however, in Manu the catching and killing of cave-dwelling animals is given as their work, I don't believe that the Pukkusas were a special professional class but a race that lived generally by hunting and only occasionally by dirty work, like cleaning temples and palaces.[1]

[1] To these Pukkusas belonged manifestly also the elder Sunîta before his adoption of monkhood, who says in the Theragâthâ of himself: "Of low family am I, I was poor and needy. Low was the work which I did, namely, that of removing faded flowers (from temples and palaces). I was despised by men, held in low esteem and reproved." *Cf.* Oldenberg, *Buddha* p. 159, Remark.

Undoubtedly we have to see in the Nesâda, the Nishâda or Naishâda of the Brahmanical caste-theory a non-Aryan race in a barbarous condition. They are regarded in the system as descendants of a Brâhmaṇa by a Sûdrâ; their work consists, according to [P. 207.] Manu (X. 48), in killing fish. As, according to the Jâtakas, the Nesâdas lived by hunting, we can suppose that fishing and hunting formed their exclusive sources of earning. Through this their professional work they fell into contempt, for the occupation of a fisherman or hunter which represents in itself the earliest and lowest stage of evolution of human culture, could not in India come to be held in respect, for this reason, that it necessarily presupposed the killing of a living being. In various ways the despised position of the hunter is indicated in the Jâtakas; it is narrated that a Brâhmaṇa youth adopts the occupation of a hunter when he cannot maintain himself by following any other art (II. 200). Also the words of the king, in which he asks the hunter in the Rohantamiga Jâtaka (IV. 422) to give up his occupation and recommends other means of earning money, such as agriculture, trade, lending money, point to the despised position of the hunter. For the same reason, the son of the seṭṭhi also causes the *luddaka*, whom he keeps with him along with his family and with whom he remains on friendly terms to the end of his life, to give up his profession (luddakakammato apanetvâ III. 51).

We have enumerated above (p. 193 sq.) the occupation of hunters and fishermen among the professions which from their very nature resist a castelike organisation ; if, however, this in-itself despised profession is followed by an entire branch of a low race, then such a group, held together by unity of profession or race and separated from the rest of the population, takes the appearance of a caste and is regarded in all such cases as such by the Indians. This is the case also with the Nesâdas; along with the Caṇḍâlas, Veṇas, Rathakâras and Pukkusas they are introduced in the Assalâyana Sutta[1] as a low caste. Despised and avoided, they must, like the Caṇḍâlas, live outside the town. A Nesâda lives not far from the town of Sakuḷa in the Mahiṃsaka kingdom in a Nesâda village (nagarato avidûre ekasmiṃ nesâdagâmake V.
[P. 208.] 337) ; he sells the birds which he caught with a noose in the city and in this way maintains himself.

The Nesâda of the Mora Jâtaka also who is ordered by the king to catch a golden peacock

---

[1] Ed. Pischel, Chemnitz, 1880, pp. 13, 14. So also in the Suttavibhaṅga Pâcittiya II. 2.1, it is said : hînâ nâma jâti caṇḍâlajâti veṇajâti nesâdajâti rathakârajâti pukkusajâti, esâ hînâ nâma jâti.

practises the profession of a hunter in a Nesâda village lying near Benares (Bârâṇasiyâ avidûre nesâdagâmavâsî nesâdo II. 36). Likewise, in a village inhabited by members of his race and lying not far from Benares, lives the Nesâda of the Rohantamiga Jâtaka; he captures a deer, while he sets up with a stick a sling fitted with leather straps.

Besides these wild peoples whom I might call "ethnical castes," as they were held together by a common race, we meet other groups reckoned likewise by the Indians among the despised castes, in which their mean work seems to have been the separating line which in course of time has stamped them into a caste; they can be characterised, in contrast with the "ethnical castes," as "low professional castes." Originally these despised professional castes were nothing else than non-Aryan races who, although they stood on a higher culture-level than the hunting and fishing races, engaged in branches of profession the practice of which presupposed no acquaintance with metals and their employment and were therefore held in low esteem by the Aryans who worked with iron instruments. To this class belong such occupations as form even to-day the exclusive occupation of people standing on a low level, such as that of making baskets from willows and bamboos, plaiting and weaving, the manufacture of leather and earthen vessels. Not a bias against handicraft in general [1] but against a profession which they found was followed by low races, originally made the Aryans avoid such means of earning a livelihood and leave them to the aboriginal races. Later the stain of impurity was attached to the occupation, even when, owing to the mixture of races, this ceased to be reserved for particular races, and in course of time this stain spread to all possible handicrafts and professions, the more so, as with advancing civilization the higher classes became exempted from manual occupations.

[P. 209.]

Such despised professional castes we have in the Veṇas and Rathakâras who are reckoned

[1] Senart, *Les Castes dans l'Inde*, p. 236: "Nowhere have the Aryans shown any great preference for handicraft. The Greeks and Romans left it to slaves or the middle class, to those that have been set free or the retainers. As the Aryans in India settled in villages where originally agriculture was followed, they were less inclined than in other countries to take to manual work. This must generally have fallen to the lot either of the primitive population or those portions of the population whom their bastard origin or their despised descent placed upon the same level. Opposed to the view stated here, of a disinclination of the Aryans for manual work, stands the fact that the age of Homeric and Hesiodic poetry showed no trace of a contempt of professional work. In Homer a number of occupations which were later followed professionally, fall completely to the share of free men, nay, even the aristocrats were not ashamed of them. *Cf.* K. F. Hermann's *Lehrbuch der griechischen Antiquitäten*, Vol. 4, 3rd Edn., p. 389 sq.

in the already-quoted passages of the Assalâyana Sutta and the Suttavibhaṅga among the low castes (hīnajâti) : these are the castes of the "bamboo-worker" and "carriage-builder." Precisely in the example of the Veṇas we can get, in my opinion, a view of the probable origin of the despised professional castes and a proof of the theory that originally they were nothing else than low races. For when the Aryans pushed to the Gangetic plains and found peoples unacquainted with agriculture or metal work occupied solely with bamboo work or similar things, nothing was more natural than that they should give them names after the material with which they worked. Thus they named those who worked with bamboo (veṇu) bamboo-workers (veṇa or vaiṇa). In a similar manner they must have named another race which possessed special skill in making carriages, carriage builders, after its principal industrial product. [P. 210] That these two branches of profession, the manufacture of bamboo products and the building of carriages, were assigned, even long after Buddha's time, to special races, seems to me to appear from the passage of the Suttavibhaṅga (Pâcittiya II. 2.1) already quoted, where the Veṇas and Rathakâras, along with the Caṇḍâlas, Nesâdas and Pukkusas are called "castes" (jâti) and are not enumerated among the low professions (hīnasippa) which are named as such after these in the following manner: the occupation of the basketmaker, the potter, the weaver, the cobbler, the barber (hînaṃ nâma sippaṃ naḷakârasippaṃ kumbhakârasippaṃ pesakârasippaṃ cammakârasippaṃ nahâpitasippaṃ). This distinction between castes (jâti) and occupations (sippa) has gradually been obliterated and in modern times has been almost wholly abolished.

Individual castes among the low professional ones already mentioned are even represented in the Jâtakas; such, for example, is the Veṇa which in the Kusa Jâtaka (II. 306) is placed on the same level with the Caṇḍâla on account of its low character. The queen reproaches her daughter-in-law with the words: "You are a Veṇî or a Caṇḍâlâ, a disgrace to your family: how can you, born in the house of Madda, bring your husband down to the rank of a slave?" The commentator explains *veṇî* by *tacchikâ*,[1] "widow of a carpenter," and thus explains the despised caste of bamboo-workers by means of another low caste, namely, *tacchika* or "carpenter." All the artisans whose

[1] Skr. *takshakâ*. In the commentary of Mahidhara on the Vâjasaneyi Saṇhitâ (I. 13) the *takshan* is called impure (aśuddha) and of a low caste (nīcajâti).

occupation consists in working with wood, the carriage-builder (rathakâra), the joiner and the carpenter (vaddaki, tacchika), were considered low in the Buddhistic age, so that the guess hazarded above (p. 160), that their living in isolation in a village in front of the city gate is to be ascribed to the lowness of their profession, seems justified. Always, however, as their work is not conceivable without the use of implements, they will have attained even then[1] a higher place in the social scale, than, for instance, the bamboo-workers, who employed their material as they found it without working much upon it.

[P. 211.]

Akin to the *veṇas*, so far as their work is concerned, and treated as contemptuously as these, are the two artisans appearing in the Takkâriya Jâtaka (IV. 251), namely, the basket-maker (naḷakâra) and the flute-maker (veḷukâra); the latter, the *veḷukâra* or *veṇukâra*, is, as we saw above (p. 86, Footnote), reckoned in the Lalita Vistara among the castes in which a Bodhisatta is not re-born.

As the work of the weaver (pesakârasippa) which represents a process similar to the twisting of bamboo and straw, so as to make

---

[1] Now-a-days the caste of joiner or Barhai occupies almost the same social rank as the agricultural caste Kurmi. Nesfield, *Caste System*, p. 28.

mats and baskets,[1] was originally principally carried on by the aborigines, the weaver also occupied a low position in the society of ancient India: in the Bhîmasena Jâtaka, the Brahmanical archer calls the work of a weaver (tantavâya) a miserable, low work (lâmakakamma I. 356).

As the last of the despised professions the occupation of a barber (nahâpitasippa) is mentioned in the Suttavibhaṅga. In this business, we do not look for the reason of its lowness to any ethnical relations: the duties connected with it and which are to some extent dirty show the barber *ipso facto* as occupying a low position and place him almost in the same line with the temple-cleaning Pukkusas.[2]

In the introduction to the Sigâla Jâtaka, it is narrated how the son of a barber living in Vesâli (nahâpitaputta II. 5)
[P. 212.] falls in love with a Licchavi princess and explains to his father that he would die if he did not get her for wife. The father replies to him, "My son, don't fix your desires upon impossible things; you are the

[1] Nesfield, Caste System, p. 22 sq.

[2] The modern barber or *nâpit* occupies a higher position, as he plays a great part in all family events, such as birth, marriage and funeral. He serves as a marriage negotiator among the respectable castes and in the marriage ceremony assists the Brâhmaṇa or takes up himself, probably among the lower castes who cannot pay a Brâhmaṇa, the office of the priest. *Ibid*, p. 42.

son of a barber and of low caste (hînajacca), the Licchavi princess is of high birth (jâtisampanna) as the daughter of a Khattiya and no possible party for you. I will seek another girl for you who will suit you in caste and family."

A further example of the low esteem in which the barber was held is afforded by another instance: the mother of King Brahmadatta calls the ascetic Gaṅgamâla, a former barber, "the son of a filth-cleaning barber born of a low caste" (hînajacco malamajjano nahâpitaputto II. 452) and adds the verse:

"Through asceticism they give up their bad occupation, through asceticism (they give up) their position as barber or potter; conquering through asceticism, you now call my son by his name Brahmadatta."

Conclusion

We have come in the course of our remarks to the lowest rungs of the social ladder. Since the days of Bernardin de St. Pierre people have always complained of the lot of the despised classes of India and thrown the responsibility for their miserable position upon the priests; people speak very often even to-day of a demon which possessed the Indian people in consequence of the caste-organisation and represent the caste as an artificial product of priestly selfishness. European travellers when they first gave us a knowledge of modern India, made the want of freedom and low position of the Parias and the rigid organi-[P. 213.] sation of Indian society an object calling for expressions of pity, and ever since people became acquainted in Brahmanical literature with a one-sided representation of the social relations of ancient India, they believed, as they took the theory for the truth, to have found here the key to the origin and development of caste-life.

The picture which we can draw from our popular sources of the social conditions which ruled in eastern India about Buddha's time, does not give occasion, in my opinion, for a highly sentimental view, nor does it justify the theory that the castes were invented by the priests for establishing and strengthening a hierarchical social organisation. The political influence of the Brâhmaṇas greatly diminished, especially, in the eastern lands, as compared with the position and power of the ruling classes who, leaving out of account special cases, did not allow much scope for any Brahmanical desire for power ; even of an intellectual supremacy of the Brâhmaṇas no trace is to be found in the age and the subject with which we have to do, for even in the spiritual province, other classes, especially, the ruling princely families, challenged the premier position of the worldly Brâhmaṇa caste. As for the position of the lower classes, it was not better, but also not worse, than it would appear to be under similar conditions ; aboriginal races standing at a low culture-stage are oppressed in all ages and times by their more highly cultured conquerors and employed in a slave's work: also similar contrasts between immense wealth on the one side and miserable poverty on the other we meet with wherever a more highly cultured race wants to use its superiority even in economical matters.

The social organisation of ancient India which appears to us very strange, nay, even monstrous, in the form in which we find it in the Brahmanical lawbooks in which it is made into an unalterable system, shows itself in reality as the necessary development of conditions imposed by ethnical and cultural distinctions. Instead of the [P. 214.] four strictly isolated castes of the Brahmanical system and the mixed castes arising from their combination, we notice a number of essentially distinct social groups which in the majority of cases cannot properly be called "castes," in which, however, we see the first germs and beginnings of an organisation of the modern type. A caste in the sense of their own theory only the Brâhmaṇas form; other groups, like the ruling class of Khattiyas, the class of royal officers, the leading middleclass families have particular characteristics in common with the jâti of the Brâhmaṇas; they cannot, however, lay any claim to the designation "caste," because they lack the essential characteristics of this; the same is true of the rest of the *jâtis* which are sharply distinguished from the great mass of the people, such as the guilds of tradesmen and artisans, the lower professions, the despised and shunned races. All these *jâtis*—and in this the Indian society of that time have their own peculiar, specifically Indian stamp—are hereditary and to go out of the circle fixed by birth is impossible, according to the rules.

So far as they are described in the Jâtakas, the social conditions remained probably unchanged even long after Buddha's time. When about two hundred years after Buddha's death the Greek messenger Megasthenes lived in the court of Candragupta in Pâtaliputra, he manifestly found similar conditions. The Greek reports which are traceable to him contain a description of the Indian society of that time which, it is true, does not wholly agree with facts which we can gather from our source, but can be brought much more into agreement with these than with the Brahmanical system. They give the number of *jâtis* or classes (γένη or μέρη) as seven; as the first γένος they mention the σοφισται or φιλοσοφοι who, as we have seen, correspond to the Samaṇas and partly to the Brâhmaṇas of our source; the second γένος, the farmers or γεωργοί, can be placed in the same class with the *gahapati* or *kuṭumbika* of the Pali Texts. By the herdsmen and hunters named in the third place, we have probably to understand the low non-Aryan races of the

[P. 215.]

Jâtakas, whilst the fourth γένος, that of the τεχνίται or the γένος δημιουργιχόν, agrees with the artisans of our text. The remaining three γένη, the γένος of the warriors (πολεμισται), that of the supervisor (ἐπισχοποι or εφοροι) and that of the king's councillor (σύμβολοι or σύνεδροι) belong to the category of râjabhogga, the officers in the king's employ. After the enumeration of the seven γένη the Greek sources point out as their characteristic feature the fact that they did not allow any inter-marriage and that it was not permissible to pass from one γένος to another or to follow the profession of two classes at one and the same time.

Later, in the course of centuries, the *jâtis*, as we know them in the Jâtakas, have experienced continuous changes under the most divers influences: the official theory of the Brâhmaṇas, ethnical and geographical influences, the tendency of the Indians to schematise, the placing of the concepts "profession" and "caste" side by side—all this has worked upon the *jâtis*, transformed them and made them resemble one another more and more, so far as their essence and organisation are concerned, until, finally, they became modern castes. This process of transformation is in no way, as one hears it maintained so often to-day, broken by Buddhism, nay, not even retarded. Buddha's doctrine does not aim at a transformation or improvement of the social conditions: the worldly life and its forms are a matter of indifference to the virtuous Buddhist who renounces the world. He never raises the question whether the worldly life could be different from what it is but accepts it in its incompleteness and badness as something unchangeable. The destiny of man, the external organisation of his earthly life is for the Buddhist a necessary consequence of his *karman*, his former deeds: wealth or poverty, high or low caste, the individual has deserved through his deeds in a former existence. The human social order was for the Indians even of that time a reproduction of natural life and moved, according to their view, like this in eternally identical paths; he who was born a Caṇḍâla must—so long as he did not retire from human society and pass into asceticism—remain a Caṇḍâla during his life-time and bear the lot of such a one, just as everybody who expiates the sins of former existence by re-birth as low beast, has to live through the whole existence of such a beast till death makes him pass into another existence.

The doctrine of *karman* and re-birth and the supposition of an unalterable social order are closely connected with each other and have exercised a mutual influence upon each other in their further development; both dogmas are deeply rooted in the consciousness of the Indian people and rule their thoughts even to the present day Even to-day they influence the organisation of social life and determine its forms: even the modern castes are, as little as the castes of ancient India, an artificial product; on the other hand, they have grown out of the spirit of the Indian people whose stamp they bear.

INDEX OF NAMES AND TOPICS.

C.

PAGE.

G.

H.

N.

PAGE.

O.

P.

Q.

R.

S.

T

U

V

INDEX OF PALI AND SANSKRIT WORKS.

PAGE.

PAGE.

ERRATA.

At p. 121, for *balipîṭitá*, read *balipâḷitá*.
At p. 171, for *uparajja*, read *oparajja*.
At p. 182, footnote, for *Brahmana*, read *brahman*.
At p. 206, footnote, for *Angus*, read *Childers*.
At p. 209, for *arca*, *arcá*.
At p. 213, footnote, for *Sarasicati*, read *Sarávatí*.
At · do. for *udîcca*, read *udîcya*.
At p. 227, for *lakshaṇa*, read *lakkhaṇa*.
At do. , for *lakshaṇakusalá*, re..d *lakkhaṇakusalá*.
At do. , for *l·kshaṇapâṭhaká*, read *lakkhaṇapâṭhaká*
At p. 230, for *lakshaṇáni*, read *lakkhaṇáni*
At p. 249 footnote, for *Gegether*, read *Gazetteer*.
At p. 277, for *kacchapaṭavâṇija*, read *kacchapuṭavâṇija*.
At p. 309, for *puṇṇamanathiá*, read *puṇṇamanorathá*.